GROWING UP IN THE GORBALS

Born to Jewish immigrant parents living in the notorious Gorbals of Glasgow, Ralph Glasser vividly recounts his hardships and childhood troubles. His story is poignantly and intelligently told, avoiding the temptations of bitterness and nostalgia, and reveals an evocative and deeply powerful portrait of life in the Gorbals. Moving from his early years, through a brief education and time working in a barber's shop and a clothes factory, Glasser's tragic tale ends in triumph with his acceptance into Oxford – a lasting testimony to the dedication and commitment of a very talented man.

GROWING UP IN
THE GORBALS

GROWING UP IN
THE GORBALS

by

Ralph Glasser

Magna Large Print Books
Long Preston, North Yorkshire,
BD23 4ND, England.

British Library Cataloguing in Publication Data.

Glasser, Ralph
    Growing up in the Gorbals.

    A catalogue record of this book is
    available from the British Library

    ISBN   0-7505-2059-0

Published in Large Print 2003 by arrangement with
House of Stratus

Magna Large Print is an imprint of Library Magna Books Ltd.

Printed and bound in Great Britain by
T.J. (International) Ltd., Cornwall, PL28 8RW

To my father and mother

CONTENTS

1

CHARLIE DISAPPEARS TO RUSSIA

Charlie Varnett said: 'We're all going back to Russia soon.'

'Going back?' I said, stupidly. 'But you've never been there?'

'I mean, my dad wrote to Russia asking to let us – the family I mean – go back and they've said "yes" and so we're going.'

Charlie's parents were immigrants from the old Russia, or rather from its dominion Lithuania, where the family name had been Varnaitis; they had 'Englified' it, as they put it, into Varnett. Their children had been born here.

We were eight years old.

As Charlie's announcement struck fully home, the cobbled pavement cracked apart at my feet. Charlie had been a solid foundation in my world, my close friend, my *alter ego*. *Had* been – for these words of his, crisply uttered but with an underlying thrill of excitement, had changed everything. That relationship now belonged to another time, already distant, no longer to be reached out for with the ease and simple confidence of other days, but remembered for what it had been, a constant understanding, an unquestioning acceptance, a support that never failed, which I would forever recall as a magical gleam in the dark forest of the past, and wonder at it through my tears.

The words now hung in the air between us, containing an unknowable power that pushed us apart. He was still physically with me, and yet – the most puzzling thing to my childhood heart – part of him was not there, or rather had changed; the emotional linkage between us was now mixed with another, bitter quality. He was not as he had been. He had already begun to move away, and belonged, inexplicably, frighteningly, to a different world. The distance dividing us was a raw wound whose edges, hard as steel, rasped and cut and stung – and could never heal.

So life was taking him away from me for ever. For ever? What was that? It was something people said, meaning, I supposed, a long time. 'She's gone away for ever!' was what they had said when mother died two years ago. The word cancer, which I had also heard at the time, meant nothing. The words 'gone away' suggested a commonplace departure on a journey. So people could just 'go' for ever? *Never* was a thought impossible to grasp. And yet mother had *not* come back from that journey. I *did* know somewhere in my heart, yet feared the knowledge, what 'for ever' meant. And Charlie too would go *for ever*. That was what death meant. Now I knew. Mother and now Charlie. And that was how life would go on, from one death to the next.

Under the grey autumn sky a steely wind had been blowing in from the Clyde, and we had pushed against it with hunched shoulders as we walked, halting sometimes to put cupped hands over our mouths to warm them with our breath. The wind blew straight through me.

Charlie was slightly built, with abnormally high shoulders, the result of some spinal deformity which had also rounded out his chest so that he looked barrel-shaped. Malnutrition was rife in the Gorbals, exacerbating any abnormalities from birth. Rickets was common. Many children had bone and joint deformities, bow legs, knock knees, limbs of unequal length. Some clanked along with a leg enclosed in iron struts from ankle to knee, or thumped the ground with an iron frame attached to the sole of a boot, a device to make a short or bowed leg function as though it were of equal length with the other. These were everyday sights.

Charlie always looked steadily at the world with his wide grey eyes, marching straight ahead, confidently meeting life as it came. Never, for instance, did he get drawn into a fight, an immunity foreign to life in the Gorbals. Not that he did anything especially to avoid a fight. Some rare quality reached out to people like an invisible ray of peace and drained their aggression away.

Fights often had themes, each with its own season. In spring, mysteriously, the constant obsession with Catholic and Protestant feuding erupted in battles between two factions – the Billies and the Dans. The Billies were identified with the Protestant interest, and the Dans with the Catholic. Why Billy? Why Dan? The Billies, I speculated when older, no doubt took their sobriquet from William III and the Battle of the Boyne – echoes of Ireland were strong in Glasgow – but why 'Dan' should mean Catholic remained a mystery. One day in the Abbotsford School playground, a windy expanse of concrete with a rain gutter sloping down the middle of it from the smog-darkened sandstone Victorian buildings, enclosed by high cast-iron railings with a knobbed bar along the top, a gang of boys had rushed at us shouting a challenge:

'Wha' are yese – Billy or a Dan? Billy or a Dan!' Fists up, they were going to beat us to pulp if we gave the wrong answer.

This was the first time either of us had heard of 'Billy' or 'Dan'. And we had no

14

idea which faction *they* belonged to. This was war and no mistake. You had to answer the challenge one way or the other even if you had no means of knowing, as in this case, what the words meant – and *answer quickly*, or you got a beating willy nilly. So we stood a fifty-fifty chance of getting that beating whether we answered 'Billy' or 'Dan'.

Charlie's deeply sunken chin moved up a fraction. Undisturbed, he studied the gang one by one as they crowded round us. Red-faced, their excitement crackling electrically in the air, they hurled the challenge at us over and over again.

In a quiet, enquiring voice, he asked: 'Whit's a Billy? An' whit's a Dan?' They were shocked into silence. Then from their midst came a thin, plaintive cry: 'Och don't yese know then?'

'No.'

The leader, a heavily built, shock-headed boy whose red hair almost matched the high colour of his wind-reddened face, pushed up close to us and seemed about to explain. And then, as if something snapped in the air around us, all the dynamism of the moment faded. To explain to us a cause whose meaning they themselves almost certainly did not understand, was suddenly too heavy a burden. They had never enquired into it, sanctified by battle as it was. Charlie's question came to them as sacrilege, and yet his stillness of the spirit, his solid innocence, left them nothing to oppose, nothing to do battle about. Some primitive sense of justice may have played its part too, which would be violated if they were to fight without a cause to defend. The gang shuffled and muttered, and in a moment streamed away to find some other target, and we were left alone.

When Charlie made his calm announcement about going to Russia, we were passing the gates of Dixon's Blazes, the blast furnace near our school on the southern fringe of the Gorbals. Outside the twenty-foot high gates were clustered a couple of dozen men in cloth caps, fustian jackets and mufflers, heavy black trousers tied with string below the knees. Lantern-jawed, saturnine, faces glazed with cold, collars turned up under their ears and heads bowed, they stood huddled in upon themselves, sheltering within their own bodies, as sheep do on a storm-swept hillside. Now and then they stamped their feet against the cold. A few others trudged back and forth along the pavement under Dixon's high brick boundary wall with its covering of poster hoardings, then returned to their vigil at the gates. Here and there a man would light up a Woodbine from a paper packet of five and take a long slow draw,

16

expanding his chest and holding in the smoke, and blow it out between narrowed lips. A few moments later he would take another; and then, bending over the cigarette with wistful care as he held it with finger and thumb close to the lighted end, flick the red tip cleanly away with his thumb nail, and slide the shortened cigarette back again into the flimsy packet.

Oh that magical tracery of wild honeysuckle on those packets of green and gold! Child of this industrial city I had never set eyes on honeysuckle, and yet this image on the packet wove a powerful spell. I kept a number of these little paper packets and marvelled at the perfect repetition, time after time, of those stylised tendrils and blooms, instigators of dreams.

Woodbines were tuppence for five, fourpence for ten. If a man could afford to buy ten cigarettes at one time, the packet would not be of paper but of stiffish paste board. A twenty-packet was made of even more substantial card, no doubt because it had to last much longer. You did not often see one; a man had to be flush, maybe have backed a winner with the street bookie, or had a birthday, to possess *twenty* Woodbines.

Between puffs the man would hold the cigarette with the lighted tip facing inwards into his cupped hands so as to get the fullest comfort from the little point of warmth.

When, by these restrained instalments, the cigarette was smoked down to a 'dout' too short to hold between fingertips and smoke on its own, the man would store it away in an empty Woodbine packet he kept for the purpose. When he had saved up enough 'douts' he would carefully pick away the remnants of cigarette paper that clung to them, tease out the little balls and shreds of tobacco, darkened from burning and from saliva, and rub them together between the palms to form a cylinder of 'makings'; then, using a leaf of Rizla cigarette paper, roll a cigarette. If he could not afford a packet of those pre-gummed papers he would use a piece of newspaper as a wrapping for the 'new' cigarette and stick the edge down with gummed paper torn from the flap of an old envelope or, failing that, with his own spittle. The result, bulky and irregular in shape, could contain twice – or thrice – smoked tobacco, and gave out such a pungent smell that old soldiers said it reminded them of burning camel dung.

These men waited for a stroke of luck, a call for extra hands. It could come at any moment, or you could wait for weeks; and you had to be there and ready for it. Often enough this good fortune came because ill-luck had befallen someone else, an accident inside the works. A man might stumble too

18

near a flow of molten metal. With luck he might suffer nothing worse than a bad burn. More seriously he could be hit by material falling from an overhead gantry crane. If he were unlucky? We would hear the men outside the gates exchange grim anecdotes, of terrible things – of men crippled for life, or killed outright. The concluding words of one of these tales gave me nightmares for a long time: 'There was nothing left of the poor bugger but his feet!'

When an accident took a man out of a work gang, his absence could jeopardise an entire chain of processes and result in considerable financial loss, and sometimes additional danger to other workers; an immediate replacement had to be found. And so, at the very moment that a victim was being carried away, a call would go to the gates for a man to take his place. As the ambulance drove away with the injured man, those waiting would follow it with narrowed eyes, and turn to each other and mutter 'Aye. Tha' yin had 'is number on it!' – a piece of fatalism brought back from the trenches in France.

To us eight-year-olds the sight of men waiting there day in and day out, in rain and sleet and snow, aroused no special feelings; it was a natural feature of the living world. With the fleeting curiosity of children we did sometimes ask: 'Why are these men not

19

working?' The word unemployment meant little to us, but we did know, again as a familiar phenomenon, that people who were not working went 'on the Broo' – the Unemployment Bureau, a great room crowded with shabbily dressed cloth-capped men standing about in straggly lines. Along one wall were high counters like a defensive barrier, behind which were clerks with card index boxes before them. They took cards out, wrote something on them and put them back in the boxes again. When a man got to the head of his queue he would answer cryptic questions posed by the clerk and sign a card; then he would go to another counter where a clerk would give him a few shillings to jingle in his pocket.

If a man could not go on the Broo, for some reason we did not grasp at the time – usually because he did not have enough stamps on his employment card or had run out of 'benefit' through long unemployment – he went 'on the parish', Public Assistance, to get food, boots and clothing for himself and his family, and blankets and coal in winter. Inexplicably, the grownups thought that being 'on the parish' was shameful.

One thing was certain about the Varnett family's decision to return to Russia; unemployment was not the cause. Charlie's father, an experienced foundryman in Dixon's Blazes, was always in work.

Probably, looking back on it, the Russian authorities had allowed him to return because they needed skilled men for their build-up of heavy industry. Mr Varnett's impulse to go arose from an upsurge of political hope. The Russia he said he was going to was the Utopia he and so many other visionaries had dreamed would one day come to pass. It was a changed land, and not the one he had left; it was a new world in which the workers ruled, not the old despots who had ground the faces of the poor.

The Bolshevik Revolution was only about ten years old. We had heard so much about it and understood so little. The grown-ups talked endlessly about it – exalted, wistful, wondering, eager. In that strongly immigrant milieu the intellectual influence of the Enlightenment was strong, with all its Continental rigour and emotional intensity, Romantic in its belief in the perfectibility of man, and in its high-flown evangelical language. The heady atmosphere would have been familiar and congenial to Herzen and Bakunin.

At the Workers' Circle, over a bakery in Oxford Street near Gorbals Cross, at almost any hour, in clouds of throat-catching cigarette smoke, men sat and reshaped society, as children tirelessly experiment with plasticine or clay. The Circle was a social and political club, union supported, a gathering place for immigrant Jews. It had three rooms and a little kitchen. Two small rooms were for quiet study, committee meetings, English classes, cards; the large room, starkly white-washed, served as a drawing room and open debating chamber, an indoor version of the piazza or village square. It was furnished with a few brown stained tables whose tops had the grain picked out in a lighter shade, long wooden benches against the walls, a scatter of old brown bentwood chairs. In bookshelves fixed to one wall were rows of revered source books – Mill, Spencer, Marx, Engels, Keir Hardie, Lenin, Kropotkin, de Leon, Kautsky. Heaps of socialist and anarchist papers and pamphlets, dog-eared and tea-stained, lay on a table nearby. On the walls, in frames of slender gilt, hung faded sepia pictures of Kropotkin, Marx, and Proudhon, and one of frock-coated men brandishing guns and sabres at a Paris Commune barricade. On a small round table at the rear, near a grimy window that overlooked the baker's yard, a shiny brass samovar bubbled and hissed. In the middle of the room stood a bulbous grey charcoal stove, the wide black flue of which went straight up to the ceiling and then across to an outlet near the window.

Sometimes, drawn to the warmth there, Charlie and I wandered up the reverberating wooden staircase and stood staring in at the doorway, thumb in mouth. Perhaps, with a child's fresh insight, I understood, more profoundly than they did themselves, why these men congregated there: that they found consolation, a spiritual refuge from the struggle with the day-to-day world, a place to recharge their dreams.

They sustained themselves with milkless tea and sometimes with black bread from the bakery. They talked with the certainty and passion of people who saw a bright deliverance within reach, convinced that they were in the van of those who would secure it. Listening to their throaty talk, so often punctuated by tubercular coughs and spitting, voices often raised in impatience with one another, it was possible to believe that at any moment they would compel the world to realise their dreams. Restless exiles, making a hard life in an alien environment, they nourished their souls by fixing their gaze on the far horizon, obstinately proclaiming the innocence of man and his necessary unity with all his kind. Theirs was a desperate optimism. Like storm-lost navigators they fed their hopes with signs and portents. For many of them the Bolshevik coup in Russia was 'the new dawn of human betterment'. Soon the whole of mankind would be delivered from the burdens of poverty, class, despotism, religious prejudice – for Jewish socialists the crucial evil of the old order. Life would be bright and rewarding. Man's nature would become a hundred per cent good once something called capitalism had been everywhere destroyed as it had now been in Russia.

Some of the families in our tenement building pooled resources to give the Varnetts a farewell tea. The Victorian building, in red sandstone blackened by smoke from Dixon's Blazes, was in decay. Splintered and broken floor boards sometimes gave way under your feet. The minimal plumbing hovered on the verge of collapse. Interior walls carried patches of stain from a long succession of burst pipes or ill-mended leaks. Rats and mice moved about freely, seeming to share the accommodation with us grudgingly, as if we were the intruders and they the rightful occupiers. Although every family set traps night after night, and dozens of marauding cats, some half-wild, maintained bloody patrols, the rodent population did not noticeably diminish. On the common staircases, six or eight flats shared two lavatories, each tucked into a tiny intermediate landing between two floors. You had to hold its decrepit door shut with your foot or wedge it with a lump of wood. And when the flush system did not work or the soil pipe was blocked, which was often, the floor was soon awash and the overflow spread freely down the main staircase. Going to the lavatory we had to remember to carry a supply of newspaper, not only for use as toilet paper but also to clean the soles of our boots of excrement and urine before going back into the flat.

For this special day every possible surface on our staircase, inside and outside the flats, had been scrubbed with carbolic soap. Above all, in the festive room itself unfamiliar luxury had been produced. There was a real linen tablecloth of dazzling white, stiff as cardboard, with hard ridges where it had been folded and put away after its use long ago at some other great occasion, a 'briss' – circumcision – perhaps, or a wedding. It may well have lain in the pawnbroker's shop round the corner, been redeemed for this one occasion, and would go back there tomorrow. There were big flowered teapots with wicker handles topped with silver knobs, and best china cups and saucers and plates; and little dishes piled with lumps of sugar, for many of the grown-ups preferred to drink tea in what we understood to be the Russian style, a lump of sugar held between the teeth and the tea sucked through it with a loud indrawing of breath. There were great dishes of sliced pickled herring, and plates heaped with home-baked sponge cake.

All this was set out in the parlour of one of the larger flats, which was crowded elbow tight to the walls; an overflow filled the little hallway. The place seemed to be heaving as people struggled to pass the tea and the plates of food from hand to hand, with everyone shouting across to one another or to catch the ear of Mr Varnett or his wife at their place of honour at the head of the table. It seemed as if the whole street was there, all talking at once.

We children were given especially big helpings of cake as a treat. But my sadness enclosed me totally, and I could eat nothing. My piece of cake was soon drenched with tears.

Mr Varnett gave out an address, a foundry on the Lithuanian border. He would write to us and tell us about the new workers' paradise. The grown-ups talked excitedly about it. Most of the Jews present struggled with bitter memories. Was it true that in this new dispensation, with Jews in positions of power, oppression of Jews was ended? Had the workers in Russia, regardless of race or creed, entered upon their birthright at last? Oh brave new world!

How wistfully they talked – but with a mixed happiness. Certainly some of those present envied the Varnetts as well as being pleased for them. Other faces were shadowed, not so much by the sadness of parting but by something I would understand only when much older: an unidentifiable foreboding.

On a dark December day a large group from the Street walked with the Varnetts to the station to see them off on the train to Leith where the Russian boat would be waiting. A cold mist rose like grey steam from the brown water of the Clyde as we went across the Victoria Bridge from Gorbals Street. My ribs felt frozen and separate from the rest of me, confirming a sense of unreality and isolation. Moisture from half-melted snow on the pavements seeped through the cardboard I had put in my boots to cover the holes in the soles. Some of the children had nothing on their feet at all, so I was lucky. But the cold was really within me. I still could not take hold of the thought that someone so close to me should go so far away, a whole world away.

Charlie wore a heavy grey jacket, made from one of his father's, black trousers of thick cloth, 'polisman's cloth' we called it, and heavy tackety boots. His two sisters also wore their 'other' clothes, as best clothes were called, made of stiff fustian, to which home-knitted scarves of thick rope-like wool added some colour. Charlie held his mother's hand and stared straight in front of him; he held his shoulders higher than

27

usual. We did not accompany them on to the platform: we could not afford the pennies for platform tickets. At the gate Charlie turned and looked at me with his usual steadiness but this time with something added. He seemed to want to transmit to me, as a parting gift, a beam of confidence; and also to draw the moment into his mind and store it carefully away. A gentle smile flickered over his face. He sensed that this parting hurt me more than it did him. Charlie was one of life's accepters. Not in any meek sense; he opened himself fully to what the moment had to offer and then fashioned it into something of his own. Yet he did care about what was happening now, to us, to him and to me, and wanted to show me that he did, so that the thought would give me some comfort. He gripped my hand, and I could see he was trying very hard to think of exactly the right thing to say to me. Later, much later, I would understand how far beyond our eight-year-old emotional understanding and strength the demands of that moment were.

At last he spoke: 'I wonder,' he said gravely, 'when we shall be seeing each other?'

All I wanted to do was to stop him going. I was filled with fury at my helplessness, a new and frightening feeling, at the thought that I was held fast by time and age and the mystifying ways of the grown-up world. A torrent of words rushed through my mind but I choked them all back as useless.

Mr Varnett took his hand and led him away. My eyes were so full of tears that I could see Charlie only dimly through them, and all I properly sensed was the thudding of his tackety boots on the stone platform, growing fainter as the little group trudged away from us.

I stayed pressed against the iron trellis gates, and stared and stared, and poured tears on to the cold metal. I heard the engine whistle. Charlie and his father and mother and sisters, huddled at a carriage window, leaned out and waved, their faces reddened and moist. And then, once more, came the engine's imperious whistle, the last farewell. The couplings clanked rat-a-tat all along the train as the whole long line jerked into motion; and then the chuff-chuffing engine dragged it all away out of sight. I shut my eyes, for I could not bear to watch it go. And then, when all sound of it had died away, I opened my eyes and dully contemplated the empty platform, a still-life of forlorn wheelbarrows and dead leaves of newspaper scattered by the freezing wind that stretched grey into the distance to where, beyond the station canopy, the dark winter sky pressed down upon the world.

A piece of ice was stuck fast within me. I fought against the knowledge that Charlie had walked away out of my life. How could something like that be for ever?

Months went by. No letter came; not from Charlie nor from Mr Varnett nor from any of them. Not a single family heard from them. I wrote to Charlie, many times. Other families wrote to the Varnetts. Whether our letters reached them no one ever found out. In daydreams I saw the train that had taken them away, fixed in that moment, and it seemed to me that perhaps it was still journeying, that it would journey on for ever, out there somewhere in a cold desert of time.

We children, naturally monitoring the conversation of the grown-ups, picked up their perplexity at the fact that no word had come, no sign, not even a rumour. We sensed a nagging disquiet too, and recalled the shadow on the faces of some of the guests at the farewell party.

One evening in the following spring, I was loitering at the street door that gave on to the staircase that led up to the Workers' Circle. A few steps away was the door of Feinstein's bakery, a favourite place to linger. I loved to be near the bakery's sweet and magical warmth that made the air come alive, and the feeling – which I could put into words only much later – that the bakers were working with the living stuff of life, continuing in that hot chamber the life-giving work of the sun and the rain in the fields, and that I shared the magic by being close to them.

On a lucky day one of the men might throw me the burnt end of a loaf, hot from the oven; or even, as an additional treat, let me stand near the ovens and watch them unload the trays and pile the hot bread into deep baskets, my head filled with the powerful yeasty aroma and my heart full of the mystery of it all.

Mottel Bialystoker, a burly man wearing a flat baker's cap and flour-white shirt and trousers, stood at the door taking the air, floury forearms folded, watching people hurrying home from work, greeting acquaintances with a nod, exchanging a word here and there. Pyotr Lavinsky, a cabinet maker who lived in the next tenement on our street, came along. Short and stocky, his hair nearly white, he walked with a stoop, said to be a mark of his trade; but I had also heard that it was due to bad eyesight, worsened by peering at poorly printed political pamphlets through six-penny Woolworth's spectacles. A dirty white apron showed below a ragged jacket. About to enter the adjacent doorway that led to the stairs up to the Workers' Circle, he turned to the baker:

'Motteleh, tell me – have *you* heard anything? From Leibel Varnett yet?'

31

'No, Pyotel, nothing – nothing at all!' Mottel shook his head frowning, 'And no one else has either. I don't know what to think.'

They spoke Yiddish, the common language, as I explain later, of Jews of eastern Europe and large areas of Russia. First heard at his mother's breast, every Jewish child understood it.

The two men stood facing one another in a communion of sad silence. Pyotr rubbed his unshaven chin and expelled his breath in a loud sigh:

'Ech! How can we know what to think, eh? An accident perhaps? But then an accident, God forbid, wouldn't happen to every single one in the family? Somebody would be left to send news to their friends and tell us how they are! It is not much to ask is it? Leib Varnett is not the man to turn his back on his old friends like this!'

'Maybe,' the baker began in a low voice, glancing about him cautiously. Seeing me he hesitated, then shrugged and went on, 'Maybe – who knows – could it be that things have not turned out so well for them? And Leibel is ashamed to write back and tell us? He was always a proud man, no?'

Pyotr became excited. 'No, no, Motteleh! How could that be? Look at the pamphlets from Russia we have up there!' – he gestured up at the windows of the Workers' Circle rooms – 'Look at the marvellous pictures! Happy people! Smiling and healthy children! Everything is good for the workers there! Great new factories! No one goes hungry or without shoes for his children if he is willing to work; and if he cannot work then it is all right also, for it is the dictatorship of the proletariat, remember! The workers are in charge; and they'll look after you! It is all there in black and white! You should come up and see for yourself.'

Mottel shook his head. 'No. All that anarchism and bolshevism's not for me. Live and let live! That's what I say. I don't believe all the things they write down in those revolutionary papers of yours. It's all propaganda – "Come the revolution and everybody is changed into an angel!" No. Everyone's out for himself – and why should it be different over there in Russia? It's human nature! Always has been and always will be.'

Pyotr moved his shoulders impatiently. This was obviously an old, long-continued argument: 'Anyway, Motteleh, we disagree! We agree to disagree – no? But still,' again he sighed, 'it does worry me that no word has come.'

They stood in silence, as if sharing a prayer.

'Maybe,' the baker said meditatively,

'Maybe, after all, the truth is that life there is harder than anybody knows?'

The other seemed about to reject this hotly but thought better of it. Beginning to turn away, he spoke a little over his shoulder:

'No, but one day, you wait! We will know the truth.'

Some time after that I wandered into the Gorbals public library and went up to the counter.

'Please, Miss,' I asked the young woman assistant, 'Could you tell me the address of the high heid yins in Russia?'

She seemed a kindly woman. She had large round spectacles, and wore a floppy grey blouse fastened at the neck, oddly I thought, with a man's black tie. She looked at me in astonishment and then leaned far over towards me, flattening her blouse on the counter.

'And what d'ye mean, my little man?' she asked in a humouring voice.

'I want to write tae the high heid yins of Russia about my friend Charlie Varnett that went there a long time ago. And they said they'd write and nothing's come. And we've written an' written tae them and got nae answer! That's why.'

She looked at me carefully for a time. I stood my ground. Then I thought her eyes became wet, for she took off her glasses and dabbed her eyes with a little lace-trimmed handkerchief. Then she opened a door in the counter and said, 'Come on in here. Ye're a brave little man. You come in and sit here beside me for a minute.'

I went in behind the counter and sat down beside her desk and she gave me a sweet.

I put it in my mouth and then a worrying thought struck me. Was she trying to put me off? I tucked the boiled sweet into a corner of my mouth and said firmly: 'But, Miss, I do want to write to Russia!'

'Aye, I know ye do,' she said seriously, but with a gentle smile, 'And I think I might be able to help you. You just sit there a minute while I go and look up something in a big book. And then we'll see.'

She came back holding a writing pad: 'Now, little man, I have written down here the address of the Russian Embassy in London. An embassy is a kind of big house the governments of other countries have in this country. Now then, have you got the address of your friend in Russia?'

'Aye, I have it here.' I held out the crumpled piece of paper. 'His feyther gave i' oot just before they all went.'

'Wait a minute,' she said.

She sat down and took a sheet of paper and wrote:

To whom it may concern, Embassy of the Soviet Union, London:

I am writing this on behalf of a brave little boy of eight whose close friend, another little boy of eight, went to live in your country some months ago with his parents, Mr and Mrs Varnett, giving the following address for letters... As he has written many times without receiving an answer, it is possible that there has been some mishap in the post or a mistake in writing down the address. Since your government's records will show where the Varnett family are living, I am sure that this little boy would be made very happy, and that he would be very, very grateful, if you could be so kind as to arrange for his letter, enclosed herewith, to be forwarded to his friend? I do hope that this can be done. Thanking you in anticipation...

She took a large envelope, and wrote on it the address of the Russian Embassy.

'Now,' she said to me, 'You run off home and write your letter to your friend, put it in an envelope with his name on it and the address you were given, but don't stick it down. And, mind, don't forget to write your own address very clearly, in block capitals, on the back of the envelope to show who it is from. Bring it back here to me and I'll put it into this big envelope together with this little note that I've written asking them to send your letter on. And maybe they'll be very kind and do that! And then let's hope you get an answer from your friend Charlie.

36

It's worth trying anyway.'

I came back the next day with my letter, and watched her put it with her note into the big envelope.

'Here,' she said, 'I've got a book of stamps in my handbag. Because you're a brave little man I will put a stamp on it for you. And now you take it and post it.'

Before I could say anything to stop her she had licked the stamp and pressed it down on the envelope.

'Oh Miss,' I said, crying a little, 'I've go' a stamp here ready.'

'Never mind. Use it next time. I'm giving it to you as a little present because I like what you've done! Run along then and post it, and come back and tell me when you get an answer.'

A few weeks later my letter came back stamped: 'Communication not permitted.'

Not many years later, with the Moscow show trials, I would see the true face of that world that had swallowed up Charlie Varnett, and which thought it dangerous for him to be in touch with me. Meanwhile, in lingering emotional shock, sadly daydreaming, I threw questions into the silence. *Why* did the great ones in Russia not want Charlie to write to me – or his father or mother or sisters – and tell us what it was like there? What sort of people would stop a letter from Charlie getting through to me?

How could it possibly matter to them? Was this what those people in the Workers' Circle hailed as the glorious new dawn?

2

'LAUGH AS THE WHEEL TURNS'

If there had been anyone at home with whom to talk out my sorrow I might have broken free of the sense of a capricious, implacably evil force always lying in wait, of a world deaf to the pleadings of simple humanity, as a child always sees its logic to be. Home was a lonely place. Father had always been a solitary and distant figure, but after mother's death it seemed – though I could not have put the feeling into words – that his course veered ever further from us. I shall explain that later. More crucially, my two sisters were too distant in age for me to reach them, or for them, it seemed, to want to reach me. Mary was fifteen and beginning to look outwards, and Lilian at twenty-eight was totally absorbed in a hectic, Machiavellian business and private life. Where I craved warmth and certainty their egoism gave me disappointment and perplexity. To have seen my desolation and drawn near me to understand and help was presumably beyond them. And from them too blows would come. In a year or so Lilian would leave home, in a manner that would wound father and me deeply; and Mary would follow a couple of years after that.

We lived in a mid-Victorian tenement of blackened sandstone in Warwick Street, near the Clyde, in the heart of the Gorbals, a bustling district of small workshops and factories, a great many pawnshops and pubs and little shops, grocers, bakers, fish-sellers and butchers and drysalters, tiny 'granny shops' – where at almost any hour of the day or night you could buy two ounces of tea, a needle, *Peg's Paper* and *Answers*, a cake of pipeclay, a hank of mending wool – public baths and a wash-house, many churches and several synagogues. The streets were slippery with refuse and often with drunken vomit. It was a place of grime and poverty, or rather various levels of poverty and, in retrospect, an incongruous clinging to gentility, Dickensian social attitudes and prejudices.

In the late nineties and the early years of the present century the Gorbals was a staging post for the westward surge of emigrants, mainly Jewish, from the Russian and Austrian Empires to the United States. For Jews the motive was escape from oppression, and economic only because of the hope that almost anything found in the west must be better. Poignant anecdotes from 'der heim' – the ghetto of origin –

constantly overheard, seared into the brain: of casual pogroms with their cold, Dantesque brutality, routine rapes, floggings, merciless discrimination, extortion both financial and sexual.

Many of the exiles went no further. Those who prospered moved as soon as they could from the Gorbals to what were considered more refined districts like Langside, Kelvingrove and Hillhead. For the rest the Gorbals was a social and economic sump from which they could hope to escape only vicariously, through sons and daughters.

The older generation read *Die Zeit*, a large format newspaper in Yiddish, printed in Hebrew characters, whose contents, in tone not unlike *The Times* of those days, you would hear chewed over, in the heavy accents of Eastern Europe, by little groups in the street of a summer evening, or at the Workers' Circle on a Sunday morning.

Yiddish, a dialect mixture with a basis in archaic Low German, was spoken by Jews in a wide area of Eastern Europe. The immigrants came to the Gorbals mainly from small towns and villages in their lands of origin – Lithuania, Poland, Hungary, Bohemia – and Yiddish was a life-line on their first landfall, helping them to find their feet in the new place, and to trace relatives or friends; or if destitute – victims of officials or other villains on their journey –

41

to appeal for a crust of black bread and perhaps some barley broth, before being passed on to the Jewish Board of Guardians. Thereafter the 'Mammaloshen', mother tongue, remained an easy means of converse with other exiles, a rest from the struggle with English, a way of retaining links with the more wholesome features of the common past. For many years it was the language of daily life; the younger ones knew it well enough too, for their parents spoke to them in Yiddish and they replied in English. In the synagogue the Rabbi spoke Yiddish from the pulpit.

They wrote in Yiddish to their families left behind, for parents and grandparents – tired, frail, feeling too old to put down new roots – did not often join them.

With its rich written and oral tradition, Yiddish provided a buttress for identity, its colloquial warmth a comfort in retailing memories of ghetto life stripped by time of its unpleasanter associations. A Yiddish Theatre flourished up to the late thirties, not in the Gorbals itself but across the Clyde in Stockwell Street; visits to it from the Gorbals, with sixpences saved over many months, were special treats.

The new arrival was quickly spotted. A man with a week's growth of beard, eyes bleary from wakefulness on his long journey, would shuffle wearily through Gorbals

Street with his *peckel*, his belongings strapped in a misshapen suitcase, listening for the familiar tones of this lingua-Judaica from the East European Marches, and approach such a group with the sureness of a questing bloodhound, He would fumble in the pocket of a shapeless coat and show them a much-thumbed envelope:

'Lansmann! Sogmer, wo treffich dos?' ('Fellow-countryman! Tell me. Where can I find this address/person?'). 'Lansmann', literally, meant someone from the same language area or the same ghetto, but it was often used loosely as 'mate' or 'man', a friendly way of hailing a stranger. From his pronunciation his hearers usually knew his origins instantly. Often, his coming would have been expected, from gossip in workshop or street, or at the Workers' Circle – though far from accurately, for delays in obtaining permits and other document-ation, usually the result of failure to bribe the right official, or by the right amount, might detain him for weeks or even months.

Sometimes the group consisted of men not yet assimilated enough to be able to read the address on the envelope. One of them would call out to a child playing on the pavement near them: 'Shmoolka! Koomaherr! Lezmir dos!' ('Sammy! Come here. Read this for me!').

Father never learnt to write English; he

could sign his name in beautiful copper-plate, no more. However, he taught himself to read English almost perfectly. Mother somehow taught herself enough English to get the gist of the contents of English newspapers. Father, oddly, refused to read the English papers; I fancy he thought more highly of books. I dimly remember evenings, before mother became very ill, when she sat with him at the kitchen table while he ate his dinner, and with obvious delight read an English paper to him. She also of course read *Die Zeit*, and letters in Yiddish from relatives left behind in Lithuania; these came more and more infrequently and finally died away. I suppose she never had time to read anything else; as a rule, especially in her last year or so, when she did sit down in the evening it was to work at her treadle sewing machine in the kitchen.

Often the group did contain a true 'Lansmann', and the stranger was beset with questions about relatives, conditions in 'der heim', their common place of origin – who was married, who else had left, who had died, when is so-and-so coming? Then someone awoke the group to the new-comer's need:

'Genugshen! Sterbter yetzt! Feerten zu.' ('That'll do now! He's all in! Let's get him there.') And one of the group, or the nearest roving child who could be trusted, would show him the way to the tenement address he clutched in his hand.

I pictured father arriving in this fashion, wretched after the days spent huddled with other living cargo in the steerage on a timber ship from Riga. That must have been in about 1902, when he was in his early twenties. Mother, as was the custom, was left behind while father got his bearings, found work, and – as the saying went – made a place for her, and for Lilian their first child, born in mother's birthplace, Liebenyang, near Marienpol in Lithuania, then under the Czar. Father came from the same district.

Lilian never acquired British nationality, which would have been simple, having come to Britain a babe in arms. Asked why, she was evasive – 'Oh I can't be bothered!' I think, being the oldest in the family and therefore closest to father and mother, she had absorbed the well-founded fear of officialdom they had brought with them from the ghetto, and could never shake it off.

Mother was small in build, with broad brow, wide eyes, fine straight nose, small mouth, and jet black hair. She dressed neatly in black skirt and black blouse fastened high under the chin, and a white apron that always seemed freshly ironed.

The small tight mouth and the drawn features, recalled from early memory, must have already shown the work of the cancer that would shortly kill her; as well as the pain of protecting the family from the effects of father's struggles with himself.

Father was the son of a rabbi. In Yiddish, as in the demotic tongues of other cultures, there are plenty of sardonic jokes and pithy comments about traditional figures. In this vast oral stock, the rabbi of course is a convenient target. One, about the rabbi's son, goes like this: 'If you go to the farthest and most uncivilised place in the world and pick up the roughest stone, you will find that it is the rabbi's son!' Father must often have brooded on it. Paradoxically, great as were his deviations and conflicts, in his heart he kept a core of faith inviolate. There, perhaps, lay his tragedy – the unavailing, self-punishing, and in its way naive struggle to marry purity with worldly compromise, and the stubborn postponement of movement until it should succeed.

He was of medium height, strongly built, with ginger hair and moustache, and grey-blue eyes whose liquid appearance could give his stare a frightening ambiguity. Essentially solitary, laconic in speech, he veered unpredictably between aloofness and tenderness; he could be brilliantly wide-ranging, imaginative in story-telling and in

46

anecdotes of life in the ghetto, tireless in applying himself to a child's small interests. Once, in the season for spinning tops in the street, he used his early training in wood turning to make me a whip with a beautifully finished handle and a leather thong magically inlaid into the wood, the envy of all the other children. These times were rare. For the rest he would try to show interest and then I would feel a chill, a tiredness spreading out from his soul. Perhaps I had arrived in the world too late for him to give me of his best.

One terrible event he recounted stuck in my mind. Later I would wonder whether it had contributed the tincture of poison that tortured his heart. He had a cousin, Aaron, to whom he was closely attached. One night Aaron's wife, heavily pregnant, longed for fish. It was winter and fish was scarce. Aaron lovingly told her he would go out and bring her fish. And so on a bitter Baltic night he went alone on to a frozen lake and knocked a hole in the ice; a freak gust of wind, it was said, made him overbalance, and he fell through and was drowned. 'It was said!' Father uttered the words again in ironic dismissal. 'So somebody did see him fall down – maybe pushed him, who knows? It wouldn't have been the first time that happened to a Jew! But in any case it was only a Jew on the ice – who cared what happened to him!'

He told me the story not long after mother died; I was about six or seven, and we were walking back from the synagogue in South Portland Street on a Friday evening. After a long silence he said, 'The wrong people die.'

Then he added, trying to pull himself up: 'Basherrt! [It was fated!] Your mother always said: *"Lach zum draydl"* [Laugh as the wheel turns]. That's hard to do – but you've got to try.'

The flow of Jewish immigrants, stopped by the Great War, became a trickle after it, and in the early twenties, with tighter Bolshevik controls, stopped altogether. By that time, too, the Gorbals itself was in flux, as earlier immigrants moved away, or onwards to the Golden Land. The word community, often used to describe these collections of exiles, would not have been appropriate. Perhaps the strongest bond was created by loneliness and poverty, and anti-semitism's poisonous proximity. Despite the roseate vignettes often painted, the Jewish religion, far from being a wholesome unifying influence, was identified with the oppression from which they had fled. The bitter-sweet picture of the semi-rural ghetto left behind, the subject of sickly sentiment many decades later – in *Fiddler on the Roof* for example – would have been angrily rejected. For many exiles, and even more so for their children, the best solution for the Jewish problem was to cease to be Jews. The Balfour Declaration of recent memory, that flight of British *realpolitik* in 1917, the crucial year of the Great War, pledging Britain to work for the establishment of a Jewish National Home, was often talked about at the Workers' Circle, but with fading hope, as pointing the way to ultimate escape, not to preserve the religion, but to close the door firmly on the past.

Few tenements were occupied solely by Jews – a situation that was probably avoided for good protective reasons, since a mixed tenement was less likely to attract the impulsive anti-semitic attack. Where the immigrants lived, Jewish or Irish, was determined by their level of poverty. To be fair, until the advent of Mosley's Black-shirts, there was little organised molestation of Jews in the Gorbals; there is reason to attribute some of this moderation to the quiet influence of Christian clergy.

At school, however, persecution was relentless, though patchy. When I was about nine, I challenged a boy who was kicking me in class; we would fight in the play-ground after school. I was short-sighted and wore glasses, and soon, in the gathering gloom of the winter afternoon, with the tight circle of boys – none of them Jews –

around us, I was getting steadily beaten up. I went on slugging it out, or tried to, for my opponent was stronger and a much better boxer. After a time my glasses fell off and my nose bled.

'Are ye gointae gie' up?' he shouted.

Something made me shout back: 'Not till ye say ye're sorry!'

He stopped in amazement: 'Whit for?'

'For callin' me a Sheeny.'

'But ye *are* a Sheeny, aren't ye?'

We started fighting again. A few moments later, when I thought I could not stand up much longer, an older boy shouted from the crowd: 'Hey, it's no' fair, he's gettin' beat. Come on. Stop it.'

The crowd filtered away. Someone had picked up my glasses and now gave them to me and wandered off.

I was never attacked again. That perhaps proves nothing. But it must be remembered that part of the prejudice of that time was that the Jew triumphed over the guileless Christian by art and subterfuge, that he was somehow slippery, hard to pin down, a coward. I had stood and fought, and though I had lost the battle, I had done something to weaken the myth.

When I got home, father spoke more in sadness than to chide me: 'Don't get into trouble again. Always remember, if a Jew gets into trouble he's always blamed more than the Goy. It's the way the world is.'

Keep your head down. Don't be noticed. He handed down to me the lesson of the Pale.

Another exile population with a special identity were of Irish origin, almost exclusively Roman Catholic; they held themselves distinct, in some ways defiantly so, partly for religious but perhaps more for political reasons. Although when drunk – and often when sober – many were as ready as Protestants to shout 'Sheeny' and 'Ikey-mo' or 'fuckin' Jesus killer' and worse at Jews on their way to synagogue on Friday nights, their relationship with the Jewish exiles seemed slightly easier than with the 'Prods', the indigenous Protestants. One reason may have been that their perception of the Jew, a blind expression of lurid emotional prejudice, was uncomplicated by any political animus, such as that which was directed against the Protestant ascendancy in Ireland and transferred to the local Prods – and seen at its most savage in the bloodletting between Prods and Papists on the annual Orange Walk. Another reason may have been economic. Most Jewish families put aside a few pence each week to enable them to employ a Christian neigh-bour – more often than not, as it happened, a Catholic – as a 'Shabbos Goy' to light the gas or the fire on the Sabbath or do some other task that the strict Hallachah, the Jewish ritual code, forbade.

Even at that early age the practice mystified me, and shocked me too. If certain deeds on the Sabbath constituted offences against the Almighty, surely He would *know* that you were getting someone else to do them for you and be just as angry as if you did them yourself! The Torah said that the preservation of your life took precedence over ritual; ergo, if to preserve your life and that of your family you needed to light a fire for warmth or the gas to cook food, why did it make you feel holier to get a Shabbos Goy to do the lighting for you? And the same had to be said for all other actions, classified as 'work', that were forbidden on the Sabbath. Surely it was monstrously sinful to try to deceive God?

I must have managed to express these thoughts to father, for I remember him trying to answer them somewhat as follows: 'You see, the rules were made many hundreds of years ago for rough and simple people, to protect them from their own ignorance! If you told one of them it's all right to light a fire to cook food with, he might say to himself, well a fire is a fire! I am a baker, I will make the fire a little bigger and bake bread with it for the whole village! Or if you said to him, you must not do work but it is all right to carry a little flour for your family – well, he might say to himself, I am strong, what is the difference between carrying a small sack and a big sack? I will carry a big sack so that I can bring back a whole load of flour from the mill! And if to carry one sack is all right, why not another – and then another one, and another, and so on, and soon he will be *working* as hard as on a normal day! So to prevent that the Rabbis said: you must carry nothing – not a single thing. You must light not even a small fire! That is the reason.'

'But father, why is it better to get a Shabbos Goy to light the fire for you than to do it yourself? Surely he's got a soul just as well as we have?'

He nodded as if to say he had often asked himself that question. He looked away and tugged at his moustache: 'When you grow up, please God, you may have the wisdom to answer that for yourself. I don't know the answer.'

George Gideon's father tried to be a latter-day exemplar, in theory at least, of the total observance demanded of those primitive People of the Book all those centuries ago. He would spend a year or so doing no work at all while his family worked hard to support him, and devote his entire time to prayer and total obedience to the Hallachah. Every day was fully taken up; he devoted the early morning to 'lay tefillin' –

binding leather straps, with little leather boxes at intervals along them containing sacred scrolls, on forehead, elbow and wrist and finger, saying prescribed prayers the while – and set aside the rest of the day to attending synagogue for four devotional sessions each of about two hours, and to 'learning', the study of the Torah and the Commentaries. For him, observance of every jot and tittle of the Hallachah was a 'Mitzvah' – an absolute good, a holy deed – and earned blessedness not only for himself but for all in contact with him. To this end he solved the Sabbath problem of 'carrying' a handkerchief by binding it round his waist and pretending it was a belt to keep his trousers up, though like most men in those days he wore braces. When he unwound the handkerchief to blow his nose he gripped the waistband of his trousers and pretended to be holding them up till he could replace the handkerchief.

This conduct frightened me. I must be missing an important truth. God could not be deceived! Surely He must be furious? Were we not told at our religion school, the Talmud Torah in Turriff Street, that the heart of the Jewish faith, its very core and basis, was right behaviour – summed up by the sage Hillel as 'Do not do unto others what is hateful to you'. What had tying your handkerchief round your waist got to do with that?

Hillel, challenged by the proselyte Shamai to condense the Jewish faith into a few words, stood on one foot and did so: 'Do not do unto others...' He added, significantly, 'The rest is commentary' – meaning, 'Go and learn what adherence to the Hallachah is intended to do to you as a person!'

Disappointed as I was that father had not given me a ready answer I must have seen, with a child's clarity and wonder, that he had searched for one over the years and, failing, some sense of rightness had made him reject the unthinking observance and self-deception of the Mr Gideons of the world. I respected him for that, but I would not understand my feelings about it till I was much older.

On Saturday mornings the dimly-lit synagogue with its rows of battered wooden benches was packed, the men on the ground floor in blue serge suits and skull caps, the more prosperous in homburg hats; the women, many of them wearing the *sheitel*, the ritual wig of the married woman, were segregated, as orthodoxy demanded, in the gallery that ran round three sides of the chamber. Many of the smaller Jewish businesses and workshops closed on Saturdays but were open, braving intermittent Christian objections, on Sundays. The rabbi, his long white beard brushing the outer edge of the lectern, stretched his arms wide under the faded, parchment-hued Talus – prayer shawl – and thundered at the congregation, as I imagined Moses did when he came down from the mountain. With detailed examples he examined their misdeeds: neglect of the spiritual, leading to inconsiderate conduct between husband and wife, children and parents, brothers and sisters, neighbours, friends, and fellow-workers; sins of the market place; and, I assume in retrospect – for I was too young to catch all the inferences – sins of the flesh as well. And he warned them of the retribution they had earned, *now*, in this life: 'Gott will ihr stroffen!' – 'God will punish you! There is no escape from His wrath.'

His words frightened me, but when I looked round they appeared to frighten no one else. In later years I would realise that such occasions, this outwardly dutiful assembly, that minatory voice, were ghosts of a once effective past, when thunder from the pulpit did have some restraining hold. Or perhaps that was wrong too? Perhaps that lonely, sad, despairing rabbi up there did have some effect on the baser instincts? Without his lamentations and homilies and exhortations would life have been infinitely worse?

Even so, in later years I would wonder how

different my life might have been if a few people, those closest to me, *had* been frightened – just a little.

3

BARBER'S SOAP BOY

We lived on the top, third floor of our tenement. At night, when everyone was asleep, I often crept to the window and stared out and saw visions.

To the right the sky was tinged orange by the perpetual flame above Dixon's Blazes. But to the east and north on clear nights I could see the stars hanging like distant snowflakes on a vast curtain of dark blue velvet stretched across the world, and I imagined that I pushed my way through the window and stood on the ledge outside and floated away into the sky and journeyed through it deeper and deeper, through limitless space and time. And in that silent flight I would sometimes turn and look back at the earth and see it as a ball bounced by some all-encompassing hand long long ago, and still continuing to soar through stars that fell around it like white blossom scattered before the wind. And so it would soar and sail on and on. Where, when, would its flight end?

In dreams I wrestled with the question of

how to encompass the mystery of the heavens, and how to draw them into a pattern; that, and so much more. What pattern? That I did not know. Why a pattern at all? Some search for order, in a world where my infant mind could observe none but longed for it, must have driven me. Perhaps the stars and the heavens stood for many other things.

One day, when I was about seven, I woke up and I knew that I had found something apocalyptic. I was so sure of it that I had to tell it to someone who would understand. I would tell my sister Mary. She was then about fifteen, slim, mercurial, a darting sprite whose long brown hair, stretching to below her waist and done in two pigtails, flew behind her, She, surely, would understand me.

'Listen. Just imagine you could travel through the sky, on and on and on, and suppose you came tae a sort o' finish tae it, like a wall, yes?'

She looked fearful, impatient, wanting to move away: 'Oh ah wish ye would-nae talk nonsense! It makes me frightened to hear ye talk like tha'. Ge' along wi' ye now.'

'No, wait!' I had to tell her. It was desperately important. 'Wait, listen a minute. Jist try an' imagine i'? So, you'd get to a wall or something like tha' – wid ye no' think?'

'Ye-es. I suppose so.'

'Well' – I was triumphant – 'Wid ye no' say tae yoursel': "There must be somethin' on the *other* side o' tha' wall," wouldn't ye? Come on now, wouldn't ye?'

'Oh leave me alone. Anyway, ye shouldnae worry yer little head aboot such things. I'm goin'...'

'No!' I caught her hand, my excitement barely overcoming my tears. 'Please, oh please listen. Just this once. Now wouldn't ye say tha'? Wouldn't ye say: "Whit's behind tha' wall?"'

'All right then. Yes.'

'Right ye are then! And just think. Ye'd climb over tha' wall and ye'd travel on and on again, an' ye'd come tae another wall. An' ye'd say the same thing: "Whit's on the other side o' it?" And another, and another?'

'Ye-es.'

'There ye are! We say tha' because oor minds cannae think o' something that just *ends* – wi' nothing comin' after i'. There must be something the ither side o' the wall! An' tha's got tae go on and on and on, forever. Tha's called infinity! It means there cannae *be* an end to the universe, a wall wi' *nothing the other side of it.* That's proof of the existence of infinity, don't ye see? But because oor minds cannae imagine infinity, that proves tha' God really does exist! Because only He could have created infinity. What d'ye think o' tha'? Isn't tha' wonderful?'

Her dark brown eyes opened wide and she stared into me, and she held out her arms and took me close to her and hugged me and rocked back and forth, and I leaned into her, glad that she was pleased with me. And then I felt her cheeks were wet against mine and I was afraid, not knowing how my wonderful thought could have made her unhappy.

'Oh ye mustnae think these things,' she moaned, 'Ye'll have such nightmares. D'ye hear? Now yew run along down tae the back court an' play an' forget all aboot i'. Go on then.'

Who else could I talk to? Father showed a passing interest, and I did feel, for one glorious instant, that he understood and was pleased with me. He picked me up in his strong arms and put me on his knee and said softly: 'These are thoughts too big for a little boy. Keep them for when you grow up, please God.'

He sat in shirt sleeves in our cold kitchen, dirty dishes beside him on the oil cloth table cover. His calloused hand felt rough on my knee. The liquid blue green eyes were fixed somewhere far away. The fire in the grate had gone out. My skin felt cold, but that was nothing out of the ordinary; this time, however, I knew that it was for a different reason, not then understood. A signal from the waiting future.

He added: 'I do not need proof that God's there. I know He is. Only too well sometimes.'

That too meant nothing to me then, Later I would understand his sense of being punished for mother's death, and for his gambling. But now all I wanted was someone to see what I had seen. The symmetry I had found was joy in itself. The music of the spheres rang in my head.

Alas, such visions, fitting into no language, a poetry of the soundless ether, I could communicate to no one.

Indirectly, that private play with ideas and relationships, a euphoric marshalling of thoughts whose amplitude I would understand only much later, brought suffering. At school, in one of the annual examinations, I was the only pupil ever to get a hundred per cent in mathematics. For weeks afterwards, everyone else in school seemed united in hatred and envy of me, wreaking vengeance. I was not only frightened but innocently amazed. Why should I be hated for getting good marks? I had done nobody any harm!

Looking back, it is plain that the teachers were either too indifferent or too overworked – we had classes of over forty children – to think of coming to me to offer comfort, much less advice on how to conduct myself in the face of all this venom; nor did they intervene and stop it. And no one at home bothered about such things. So, desperately, I must have decided on my own self-wounding method; at every subsequent examination I got low marks in mathematics.

Privately I still listened to the music of the spheres, contemplated the heavens, wondered and dreamed. At what age I first heard of Einstein I cannot recall, but increasingly over the years the name rang in my head like a golden bell. I spent hours, days, in the great Reading Room of the Mitchell Library. Young as I was, in my ragged shorts, frayed jersey and ill-fitting jacket, incongruous among the sleek, well-nourished university students, I became so familiar to the staff that they dubbed me, in kindly fashion, 'the young professor'. One day, perhaps as a piece of sympathetic magic, I looked up Einstein's massive entry in *Who's Who* and copied it out word for word, his universities, degrees, honorary doctorates, publications. I kept that transcript pasted into an exercise book, a talisman.

By the age of about thirteen I had some grasp, or thought I did, of the theory of relativity. A few weeks before my fourteenth birthday I read that Einstein was coming to Glasgow to address the university, and made up my mind to go and listen to him. How I gained admittance to the great hall at

Gilmorehill I have no idea. I sat on one of the back benches. All around me were people arrayed in what to me was the majesty of full academic dress, with draperies of crimson, gold, purple, vermilion, green.

On the raised platform far away at the other end of the hall, it seemed to me the length of a football pitch away, a figure in brocaded long sleeved robe and silver trimmed and tasselled mortar board ushered in the great man – small, stooped, brown faced, with a little walrus moustache. How could such a giant be so insignificant? He read his address in a soft, clipped voice, slurring certain passages in a casual, dismissive manner: '...as I explained in my special theory of relativity,' as if these immense strides in thought were to him mere tip-toes.

I thought I understood a good deal of what he said, and with that I was exalted – a feeling I can only liken to the glory, years later, when I breasted the last ridge of a mountain in the Haute Savoie and breathed the needle-sharp air, and saw in the tumbled masses of sun-glinting snow and ice far off the outline of Mont Blanc, dubbed locally 'tête de Napoleon'. But another euphoria, over-stepping this, was the sense of being near him, in some way part of that world where, one day, I dreamed of joining him. As he sat down, my mood of communion was shattered when two men in the row in front of me, gowned with crimson hoods, turned to each other. One said, in comic despair: 'Well, I suppose you understood all of that, eh?' And the other replied with a grin:

'As much as you did I imagine!'

Well, I thought, if these great people had not understood much, there was hope for me.

When I got home that day, ecstatic, full of power and confidence, I told father where I had been; and foolishly blurted out that I meant to study hard and go to university and be a physicist like Einstein.

Father was standing in his shirt sleeves washing dishes at the long shallow sink. Without turning, he said: 'You'll be fourteen in two weeks time and that means you can leave school. I can't keep you at school. You'll have to go to work. You've got to have a trade in your hands.'

I turned away so that he should not see the tears that flooded down my face. But he had seen them.

In later years I would understand that his rages were fuelled by guilt. I may even have sensed as much at that moment. From as far back as I could remember I had known that gambling had him by the throat, but the wider significance of that knowledge, if dimly seen, had been shrugged off. And even now, it was hard to relate it to his decision. He had always been a giant to me, clever, resourceful; he could do anything if he made up his mind. If he did not, it was because he did not really want to. In my black and white logic at that moment there was no sympathy to lessen my misery. Whatever else father was, he was neither stupid nor insensitive, even though he often behaved as if he were both. He knew what my dreams meant to me. To pretend he did not was his way of making his actions tolerable to himself.

He repeated, parrot fashion, a piece of conventional wisdom of the slums: 'You must have a trade in your hands. With a trade you can go anywhere!'

A trade lifted you above the common labourer.

Two weeks later, on my last day at school, the headmaster said to me: 'Pity. You should go to university. You would do well there, but still... I understand.'

He knew there was no chance, and probably knew why too. Not that the specific reason mattered. Of the boys I knew, none remained at school after fourteen.

And then my father took me to a barber shop in Gorbals Street, and I started being a soap boy. The ritual was simple but strict. You ushered the customer to the wooden armchair, clicked its ratchet-held neck rest to the correct height, spread a white sheet over him and tucked its top edge into his shirt collar, and then spread a small towel like a bib under his chin. Then you applied shaving soap to his face with a bushy bristle brush, spread the soap and lathered it into the skin with a massaging action of the fingers and hand. The barber then stropped his cut-throat razor with brisk back and forth strokes on a length of leather that hung from the back of the chair and, to the accompaniment of breezy chatter, shaved the customer. 'Soap boy!' he would call, 'Ready now!'

You applied hot towels and cleaned up all the flakes of soap round the edge of the shaved area of the face, combed the man's hair, smartly whipped away the bib towel and the sheet, and turned and called the next customer.

I felt miserable having to touch these beery, bristly faces, but I tried to be stoical. One day, somehow, I would escape.

Perhaps father sensed my feelings. Perhaps he wanted to test me further. One evening, after only a few days at the barber shop, he said: 'An intelligent boy like you should learn the trade in no time. Come, I'll sit here and you can practise shaving me.'

He pulled one of the battered wooden chairs away from the kitchen table and sat in it and put a towel round his neck and I soaped his face. Then he stropped his open razor and handed it to me, the concave hollow ground blade shining like bright silver. I took the razor, held it as I had seen the barber do so, between thumb and forefinger on the haft of the blade, the other fingers steadying it by resting on the little curved tail that projected behind the guard, and drew back the loose skin under his chin to make the first, grazing, upward stroke. I hesitated.

'Come on!' he barked. 'Don't just stand there like that. It's easy!'

Tears came again, and I could hardly see. Quickly I put the razor down on the kitchen table. 'I can't do it, father. I – I am afraid I – I'll cut you!'

I could not bring myself to say why I had to put the razor down quickly. But I could see that *he* knew. I was afraid I would cut his throat.

I knew I could not do that. I also knew that with that scalpel-sharp blade in my shaking hand the risk was there, and I dare not take it. Forces worked within me, shaking me with their battle against filial discipline and moral restraint, in furious rebellion against what he had done to me. Knowing that he had fought in vain against his destiny, I felt an enervating fear that I too might fail, indeed that he was bequeathing a similar destiny to me, insisting that I too should not rise above it.

He did not meet my eyes. Without saying a word he took the towel from under his chin, stood up, turned the chair round and tucked it once again under the flap of the kitchen table, took the razor, a fine German one and a prized possession, and carefully cleaned it in his own special fashion. He spread a handkerchief across his left hand and held it taut across the cushion of flesh at the base of the thumb, held the rounded butt edge of the hollow blade on it and slid the blade over it from butt side to the hair-thin edge, then swivelled it over on to its other face and slid it back again across the fabric; back and forth, back and forth, in a smooth, rhythmic, hypnotic motion, intent, absorbed, almost tender, as if he caressed a loved one. Then he held it up to the light and twisted it back and forth, inspecting it for specks of dust on the fine edge, and the blade glittered with a vibrant mirrorlike sheen, as if it answered him in a private communion, as the magic sword Durendal might silently have spoken to its heroic master. Then he folded the blade into its ivory guard and placed it gently in the shaped blue velvet cushion in its slender leather case and closed it.

At last he turned to me, the jaws tight, and spoke with a softness that I knew meant suppressed anger: 'All right. You won't go back to that barber's tomorrow. You'll come with me and learn to be a presser. You won't have to be afraid you'll cut someone's throat *that* way.'

The next day I started as an under-presser at Bompert's garment factory in Stockwell Street. The work was simple. Soon I could stand all day in a hermetic kingdom of my own, while I pressed seams open, edges and stitched canvas fronts and collars into shape, working fast and pushing the work pieces through to keep pace with the other workers. The hard part was to swing and manoeuvre the iron, an eighteen-pound block of metal with a high twisted bar as a handle, I got used to that and soon forgot the strains, but they must have taken their toll on my still-growing body, and led to the agonies of back trouble that would hit me years later.

I counted my blessings. I was free to dream, to think, to wonder, the long day through – sixteen hours in the busy time – and wait for the blessed moment in the evening when I could bang the iron down for the last time that day, and walk across town and sit at my accustomed desk at the Mitchell Library, my only true home,

In the years before I was taken from school – from about eleven – I think I read to fuel dreams as well as from curiosity; I dreamt of a magic stairway to a kind of Olympus where the great ones held a rarefied converse in which I might one day join. At about that time I started to write a book about a group of people setting out to cross a wilderness; but the further I got into the story the more discouraged I became at my lack of knowledge about the world and about the way people thought, their passions, the triggers of action. I decided that I must put it aside till I knew more. Years later I looked for those two red-covered exercise books with their close lines of copperplate writing. In the course of many flittings they had been lost. Perhaps I have been trying to complete that book ever since.

After I left school, the Olympian dream shattered, the Mitchell became if possible even more important. I read widely, indiscriminately: the lives of the great philosophers and scientists, history and ideas, particularly of the Renaissance and the Enlightenment, logic. It was a halting progress, for at every step I had to make up for lack of background, of facts, of definitions of words, and buried my nose in dictionaries and the *Encyclopaedia Britannica*, which led of course to more and more sideways reading. At about sixteen, timidly, I started going to Extension Courses at the University, in Logic, English Literature, Philosophy.

Father was well read in politics and in the nineteenth-century novelists, Dickens and Trollope being his favourites. But his reading nourished the sour scepticism that deeply possessed him. One day, when I was about fifteen, he said to me sharply, a shade enviously I afterwards thought, 'Why d'you waste your time with all this reading? It won't get you anywhere!'

'I don't know,' I answered. 'I can't help it.'

4

MESSIAH AT GORBALS CROSS

While still in his teens, first in the Gorbals, then in all Clydeside, Bernard had been acclaimed as a demagogue, Messianic revolutionary, coming man in the forces of radical change. At Gorbals Cross of an evening, among the vociferous groups on the pavements, people spoke of him almost in the same breath with Harry McShane and Willie Gallacher, living legends of Red Clydeside.

Bernard was a cutter's assistant in our factory, about five years older than me. His friendship had in some ways filled the void Charlie had left. Perhaps because he was older, the relationship had a sense of proper separateness, being based more on a sharing of curiosity about the world than of emotional attitudes. Stocky, deep chested, he had the brilliantly ruddy complexion of some dark haired people, sparkling dark eyes and full lips. He was a mercurial character: striding forcefully along, in a brown tweed jacket the pockets of which bulged with pamphlets, and baggy fustian trousers, he radiated electricity, the force of his chosen role as saviour of the people.

Gorbals Cross was a large open space, roughly circular, a little way along Gorbals Street to the south of the River Clyde, where Norfolk Street came in at right angles from the west and became Ballater Street to the east of the crossing. Gorbals Street stretched about a third of a mile, from within sight of Dixon's Blazes at its southern end up to the Clyde at the Victoria Bridge. Gorbals Cross was also the name of the square granite monument in the middle of the open space. At each corner of its central block a plinth jutted out, supporting a Doric column from the capital of which a scrolled buttress curved inwards to where, high on one face of the main block, were the city's arms; above was a clock with a white dial on each of the tower's four sides, the whole topped by a little four-sided stepped pyramid with a decorated cross of wrought iron at its peak. The embrasures between the plinths had stone ledges or benches, little open air drawing rooms where in fine weather men in cloth caps and mufflers smoked and talked. In one of them, stone steps led up to a bronze drinking fountain with two iron beakers hanging on heavy chains on either side of its basin.

The space occupied by the monument and the broad pavement surrounding it was some twenty-five feet in diameter. At the outer perimeter of the crossing, like an enclosing wall, rose black tenement buildings in the handsome classical style favoured in their epoch, the middle years of the nineteenth century.

Tram rails set into the smooth grey cobbles took a wide curve round the monument. As the tall glass-sided vehicles moved sedately in their circuit their wheels grated on the metal with a sonorous, brassy note that reverberated from the walls of the close ring of tenements, and rang in the mind like the sustained call of a horn in a far valley. In the quiet hours late at night and in the early morning you could imagine that the call came from a lonely oracle sending a message to the world. As it faded, taken up perhaps in another valley, and another, you felt its continuing power even in the ensuing silence. One day its meaning would come plainly through the mists. Long years afterwards, wherever you were in the world, you had only to think back to that time, and the poignant and questioning call vibrated in your head once again.

The day would come when the trams stopped. The rails would be dug up from the cobbles. But the horn note in the far valley would still sound in one's heart.

As long as motor vehicles shared the streets with many horse drawn carts and vans, till about 1930, traffic was not heavy, and moved with convenient slowness. People walked unhurriedly over to the Cross from the periphery, took a drink of water from the fountain, stood and stared, passed the time of day with friends. They took one of the large iron beakers, pitted and dented from years of rough use, and pressed its rim against a button under the spout to release a jet of sparkling water, crisply refreshing, that came from Loch Katrine in the Trossachs, some forty miles to the north of Glasgow.

I had never seen Loch Katrine, but the name had magical power. It conjured up steel engravings of *The Lady of the Lake*, remembered from English lessons at school, gothic scenes of wild crags and dark groves full of mystery, and figures on the Silver Strand moving in their romantic destinies – thoughts of the earth spirits. In dour contrast was the inscription, in gold letters beneath the coat of arms, that met your eye as you drank from the beaker: 'Let Glasgow flourish', a shortened version of the City's motto: 'Lord let Glasgow flourish through the preaching of thy Word and praising thy Name'.

Did they want us to believe that religion was good for business? Did they themselves believe it? They. Them. The people who had mastery over the likes of us.

Children played on the uneven paving surrounding the monument. Grown-ups lingered there and talked and watched the passing scene, or called to friends on the far perimeter; and the latter might thread their way through the traffic to join them. As the years went by and motor traffic filled the streets more and more, there were demands to have the Cross removed – from business interests arguing for faster transport, and do-gooders, mainly from the better-off parts of the city, who felt that the Gorbals should be shorn of its old ways and appearance. In 1932 the City Fathers did have it taken away – not for any of these reasons, it was said, but because it led to accidents by tempting people to wander over to it across the path of the now faster-moving vehicles.

For a long time Gorbals folk behaved as if this had not happened. They returned again and again, halted at the periphery of the crossing and stared with unbelief at the empty place in the centre; turned and paced about restlessly, deprived of a mysterious comfort, vital but indefinable. The monument had been the focus of many emotions and many associations of ideas, a source of answers to myriad unspoken questions; it had drawn them close, the hub of a moving wheel, its magic acknowledged, or rather felt, only in retrospect, after it had gone.

No one could put the loss fittingly into

words. Few were inclined to dwell on it. It strengthened the conviction that the world, 'they', cared not a scrap for the feelings of people without power.

When I first saw the patch of concrete where the monument had been, I was transported back to the moment when Charlie Varnett went away. I saw the empty station platform again, cold and wounding as on the day itself long ago. 'Is this what life will always do to you? Are there no enduring links?'

For Bernard it was simply the fault of the System. Under the dictatorship of the proletariat, 'they' *would* care.

The time would come, in the decades after the last war, when a new generation of City Fathers went vastly further. The whole of the Gorbals was wiped off the map, all the tenements for nearly a mile around the spot where the old Cross had stood, the little workshops and family businesses that had given the Gorbals bread and work and life, the ancient street plan obliterated entirely, leaving a desert that stretched from the Clyde to where Dixon's Blazes used to be. In it they erected a few twenty-four storey tower blocks, sombre monoliths presiding over windswept vistas of sparse, muddy, littered turf, all the old landmarks gone.

One day, years after I had left, I walked through that desert and could not decide where Gorbals Cross had been. Here and there in the devastation stood a bit of broken masonry, a jagged piece of railway arch, a gable with only the sky behind it. What had it belonged to? What street had it been in? Pacing the emptiness between the Cyclopean monoliths, memory was not enough. At the Mitchell Library, hardly changed from when it had been my special home, I found an old street plan in the Glasgow Room. Even with its help the new wilderness defied efforts to place Warwick Street, where my first-remembered home had been and where mother had died, or where Oxford Street and the Workers' Circle rooms had stood, and Mottel Bialystoker's bakery, or Norfolk Street where Aunt Rachel and Uncle Salman had lived and worked and died. I wandered to the south, to where Dixon's Blazes had flown its yellow plume of flame and sent out its angry furnace roar, where I had stood with Charlie Varnett when he had made the shocking announcement of his going. The site was silent; the great chimney no more. Near it, all points of reference gone, I threaded my way among great piles of fallen stone, builders' debris, isolated lumps of blackened masonry.

Why had they erased the old Gorbals? Class guilt about its sordid slums, its poverty? A fear of folk memories, in the new days of discontent, if its identity was encouraged to survive?

Something in this dismal wreckage prodded my memory. I stood before a broken railway arch whose black rusticated blocks framed high curved double doors, only emptiness behind, a rusty padlock still joining the two arms of a retaining bar. I stepped closer. On the door, in lettering nearly washed away by time and weather, I read 'A G Emet – Master Upholsterer and Cabinet Maker.' A ghost walked over my grave. Cold sweat made me shiver. Phil Emet, one of our group at the swimming baths long ago, had taken over this workshop from his father! Phil, clever and fiercely worldly, careless architect of tragedy for Annie Dalrymple, fallen star of my adolescence – of whom more presently. After the war, when he had left this place behind on his way to bigger things, no one had bothered to erase the name.

There was not a soul about, and I went over to the archway and stood in it. I touched the rotting wood of the doors, a physical link across time, the only one I had found, and thought of Annie's fight with the new life in her and with death; and Phil's indifference, and his brilliance, the dark and the light; and of Meyer Melek, crushed when he opposed the debt-collectors' terror in our street. The perplexities of us all.

I trudged on among the misshapen

standing stones, disdained when the bulldozers passed by. I emerged into another cleared space, rounded another fragment of a broken gable, and there before me, unbelievably, stood a piece of the past completely intact, the first school I had ever been to, Abbotsford Primary School, named after the then adjacent Abbotsford Place, now erased. With the eyes of a child of four or five I had never seen it in its wholeness, or so I thought, but I must have done so for I recognised it instantly – a beautiful building, strongly classical, the upper windows grouped and recessed within moulded frames and divided by Doric pilasters. Above the rusticated main entrance, where I had first climbed what seemed at the age of four to be high stone steps, and been given a whole penny to calm my fears and tears, were stone heads of John Knox and David Livingstone, appropriate attendant spirits when it was opened in 1879. It had survived, pristine it seemed, as a listed building, still carrying out its original function. I went in, and there was the wide central double stairway divided down the middle by an iron railing; little boys and girls must not mix while ascending or descending. Outside, near the entrance, was the stone for sharpening our slate pencils.

Here at last was a piece of my past still living, comforting if poignant, for the rest now crowded in upon me. This desert was peopled again: all the tenements sprang up once more, and the past reasserted its hold upon the present.

On Sunday mornings on Glasgow Green, the park on the northern bank of the Clyde opposite the Gorbals, at the speakers' pitch on the park's edge facing the High Court, Bernard set up his wooden rostrum in the crescent-shaped space in front of the gates, helped by a group of the faithful from the party rooms in Hospital Street across the river. They had carried the rostrum for him, and a stock of literature to sell during his meeting, including the *Daily Worker* – renamed *The Morning Star* a generation later – and party pamphlets.

The speakers' pitch was bounded by a line of poplars, between whose slender sentinel trunks the eye was drawn past the Doric portico of the High Court to a structure in the middle distance that dominated the scene not so much by its bulk as by the attitudes it proclaimed. A massive; red sandstone railway bridge was planted in the river like a great squat gate, with bulging rusticated piers and crenellated towers, disclaiming refinement. It blasted forth a forceful counterpoint to the political discussions taking place, lustily affirming the heroic materialism of the later Victorian age. Here was a historic dialogue, two attitudes to life irreconcilably apart but in some fundamentals at one; a belief in material values, for example, was basic to both.

Bernard claimed to take his stand on Reason alone, but his message reeked of faith, not logic; faith, especially, in the instinctual sureness and purity of Man in the mass. Destroy capitalism, and Man will regain the innocence, the clear and certain vision he had possessed in the state of Nature.

The bridge held to faith too, in the glory and enrichment to be found in Man's exercise of power and free-ranging creativity. Certainly compassion for the weak and the unfortunate was often lacking, but this dark side of life would always be with us, needing constant vigilance and charity. Any other view of human affairs was a delusion.

Cynically one thought of the stock image of the bloated capitalist, silk-hatted, perched on the back of the honest son of toil. Even so, some instinct told me that its rough approach was more firmly rooted in life's realities than Bernard's, with his gospel of root and branch destruction and starting Man's pilgrimage afresh. How many old and warm and valued things would he willingly destroy in saving Mankind?

The party shared the speakers' pitch with other evangelistic groups – the Anti-Parliamentarian Workers' Republican Party, the Independent Labour Party, the Social Democratic Federation, and a few individuals who spoke for themselves alone, each with a recipe for saving the world. One, nicknamed the Clincher – no one seemed to remember his name – tall and cadaverous with a voice like a bass drum, whose long steel-grey hair furled itself round his head in the keen river breeze like a worn battle flag, was fond of brandishing a piece of paper, evidently his discharge from a mental hospital, as a telling piece of theatre:

'There ye are ma friends,' he boomed, 'they gave it tae me in black and white! And now ah'm askin' yese – ah'm givin' yese this challenge! Is there anybody here that can hold up black and white proof that *he's* in his right mind?'

From beneath tufted grey brows he glared at his semi-circle of listeners, poised to discredit a rival claim. They acknowledged the familiar gambit with friendly sympathy, smiling and nodding to each other, knowing what would follow.

'Aye, ah thocht as much!' he roared in triumph, 'No' a soul among yese can match the proof ah have here.' He waved the paper again. 'So now yese can listen tae me! Ah'm goin' tae tell yese how tae make this wurrld a better place.'

An eclectic prescription, compounded of theism, Rabbie Burns' individualism and tolerance, and goodwill towards human diversity. Where did it stand with Bernard's destruction and rebirth? Or the bridge's reliance on Man's free-ranging assertiveness – get on with what you want to do and the Devil take the hindmost? And the faith Bernard and the bridge shared, that people would always behave well to each other given a completely free choice; completely free meaning a choice that did not conflict with self-interest! The Clincher was more honest, or more clear-sighted; selfishness was the great evil. 'Live and let live!' The key was to give free rein to Man's 'better nature', another name for his primordial purity.

Could it be true, I wondered, that each of us came into the world with a lodestone that would guide us truly if we allowed it to? If so, why was it so hard to know what course to follow? Why did life contain so much conflict, selfishness, deceit, hatred, domination, cruelty?

Like most radicals of the day, Bernard at this time was under the spell of the naive behaviourism that marked the New Enlightenment of the early years of the century. With the right conditioning everyone could be, *would be*, benevolent. Ethics were simple commonsense, requiring no state power, and no religion either, to instil and maintain. Even with its reluctant curbs on its own savagery, and the enlistment of charity – itself an insult to Man's dignity – to heal the wounds it inflicted, Capitalism red in tooth and claw was so rotten as to be beyond redemption. To destroy it was the prerequisite for curing the ills of men and women. *Anything* you put in its place must be an improvement. Oh the childhood dream of destruction and renewal, the world reborn fresh and clean! Power of the thought and the word:

'To make, then break,
the springtime fancy...'

5

ZEITGEIST AT THE BATHS

One blustery winter evening when I was about eighteen, Bernard and I were making our way to a meeting at the Workers' Circle. Walking in Bedford Street, which ran west to east, in the lee of buildings on its northern side, we were sheltered a little from the cold rain sheeting across the Clyde on the hard north wind. At the corner when we turned left into Gorbals Street and went towards the river, we lowered our heads to shield our faces and pulled our coat collars higher. Rain bounced off the flagstoned pavement. Trouser legs were soon soaked. My boots let the wet straight in, as if I walked in bare feet. Never mind, in the Workers' Circle rooms it would be warm, steamy in fact. We would go to the big stove in the middle of the main room and drape our socks on the hot casing to dry. Their smell would soon be lost in the fug of tobacco, coal smoke, and the accumulated expiration of sweat in the crowded room.

The Lipchinskys lived round the corner

from us in Bedford Street, in a tenement that backed on to the Gorbals Baths. The Baths was an important building, as magnetic and significant, though less obviously spiritual, as Gorbals Cross. Its Victorian façade was encrusted with corbels and scrolls; its interior walls were clad with coloured and moulded tiling, and wherever stained glass could be used, in doors, windows, transoms, skylights, were panels depicting flowers, foliage, urns and garlands, scenes of Arcadia. In its display of romantic sentiment, classical culture, condescending commitment to the uplift and care of the lower orders, and above all its display of industrial virtuosity, it spoke for its epoch.

One of its departments was a wash-house, aptly known as the Steamy, a long barn-like room kept in perpetual twilight by clouds of steam rising from washing boiled in rows of coppers, a miasma in whose crepuscular depths one dimly saw figures in kerchiefs, long fustian skirts and dark cotton blouses, sleeves rolled up above the elbows, hauling and lifting, scrubbing and banging and carrying, moving with the heavy measure of fatigue, enchained in punishing ritual. In a clangour of boiler doors, iron buckets and chains, rumble of slack gears in the mangles, scrape and clatter of metal-lined scrubbing boards, and counterpoint of shrill voices calling, they heaved bundles of clothing and bed linen and blankets about, banged press irons, turned the drive wheel of a mangle with rhythmic push of straight arm and shoulder on the handle projecting from the rim, and then a pull back with the whole upper body, while the other hand fed layers of wet washing, like lumpy slabs of glistening clay, between the thick wooden rollers.

Now and then one of the vaguely seen figures became distinct as she emerged from the grey cloud and hastened over to a bench against a wall at the entrance, beneath high begrimed windows that supplied the only natural light; a number of babies lay there in a row, wrapped in stained and tattered blanket, sucking on dummies, with here and there a barefoot child of three or four standing in patient attendance. She snatched up her baby, comforted it with a cuddle and a rock in her arms or sat down and, unbuttoning her blouse with flying fingers, impatiently gave it the breast, then laid it down again and moved heavily back into the rank half-light.

In the streets their leaning outlines were familiar as they trudged to the Steamy or homewards from it, backs bent under sagging bundles of washing, often 'taken in' to earn a few shillings – staring down at the pavement, lustreless hair drawn tightly away from the face in a bun or a thick plait, the washing wrapped in a sheet with its four corners knotted together and held under strain with a two-handed grip at the shoulder, long skirt swaying at thickened ankles, grey stockings wrinkled over battered black shoes. Here and there one of them also carried a living bundle in front. The baby lay diagonally across her bosom with its head resting on her free shoulder, cocooned in a shawl wrapped tightly round her upper body and secured at her waist with a long safety pin.

Another department of the Baths had the genteel title 'Slipper Baths for Ladies and Gentlemen' – rows of narrow cells each with a glazed stoneware tub, a duckboard on the cement floor, and a wooden stool. The bath's timber casing was a pale tan streaked with silver from years of scrubbing, its broad-headed brass screws burnished to shine like old gold. Such signs of elbow grease, and a strong smell of carbolic, reminded ex-servicemen of barrack room days, as did the smell of bodies and sweat and old, worn clothes. A burly attendant, arms covered with tattoos of mermaids and anchors and flowers, showed you into a cell, with rough courtesy if you had tipped him, brusquely if you had not. Tuppence, one-third of the entrance fee, was an adequate tip.

Having cleaned the tub after the previous occupant, at least in theory, he ran a bath for you. On the tiled wall at the head of the bath, instead of handles marked Hot and Cold, were two bolt heads needing the attendant's spanner to turn them. Presumably the idea was to prevent you dispensing free baths to members of your family or friends smuggled into your cell. Implied, too, were Poor Law attitudes to the lower orders. Your use of these baths proved you belonged to the lower orders and were therefore not to be trusted to make prudent use of the amenities here 'given' you.

On brass chains bolted to the wall hung a long-handled back brush and a hand brush, bristles almost as hard as the tufted wire of horse brushes, with 'Corporation of Glasgow' burned into their wooden backs. Most clients brought their own soap and towel. If you were flush you could hire these, but we never heard of anyone who did. Twenty minutes' occupancy cost sixpence, expensive for the likes of us. So the clients were mainly our parents' generation. People of our age sometimes went there in preparation for an important function, a wedding or Bar Mitzvah, that warranted the expense of a long soak in hot water.

The swimming pool cost only threepence. Bernard and I went two or three times a week after work, less often when the factory was slack, before Christmas and in the spring, when we were on the Broo drawing fifteen shillings a week dole money. Among the pool's attractions, apart from physical uplift as we entered into full possession of ourselves after ten or twelve hours' heavy work, was the luxury of standing and talking under the hot showers. Unlike the slipper bath, you could stay virtually as long as you liked for your money.

Under the showers a group of us debated the world – or thought we did, for it was more of a debate each one with himself. How should you confront the world? What should you try to do with life? We shouted to be heard above the noise of pumps and the hiss of water and the cries of the swimmers, thrown back thunderously from hard surfaces of tiles and stained glass. We shouted to quell the tumult within us.

For Bernard's family, living more or less on top of the Baths was a blessing in winter. The boiler room, which heated water for the pool and its showers, the slipper baths, and the Steamy, was below their windows; its hot flue ran up the wall of their tenement and heated their flat so well that they hardly ever had to light a fire, and the coal cooking range in the kitchen was damped down for most of each day, whereas most other people kept theirs going all day for warmth.

But in summer the money saved by using fewer sacks of coal was paid for in extreme discomfort, for the boiler flue made the heat in their flat almost tropical; and even with many sticky fly-papers hanging from the ceiling, there was no escape from the swarms of great black flies that bred in the open rubbish dump – the ash-pit – in the unpaved yard below.

I lived only a hundred yards away in Warwick Street, which ran for most of its length parallel to Gorbals Street, from the Clyde southwards to Cumberland Street where it was crossed by a railway bridge; and where Pollokshaws Road, a continuation of Gorbals Street, veered west to meet it. Arches under the bridge housed little workshops – furniture makers and repairers, carpenters, jobbing engineers, repair shops of various kinds, many of them serving the large engineering works, factories and shipyards along the Clyde.

Our street was a backwater, mainly of three-storey tenements, of red sandstone blackened by smoke, interspersed with older buildings, one storey stable blocks and sheds, and a fine building by Charles O'Neill in the Italian Renaissance style, St John's Catholic School. A few stables still housed horses, great Clydesdales used for general cartage and coal lorries. Often at evening, passing the tall wooden gates, one heard a stamping of hooves muffled by straw; one of these strong and patient and beautiful animals heard our step and banged down a great fringed hoof in greeting. A blacksmith, one of the last in the locality, worked in one of the sheds; as well as shoeing horses he repaired broken ironwork on carts and vans or made new parts. He also did household jobs like making brackets to keep a broken table or chair in service, mending an iron bedstead or welding a new hinge plate on the door of a cooking range. Other sheds were work-shops. A few had been divided; the front part made into a small shop, and the back a combined living room, bedroom and kitchen for the family running it. In this style our street had a cobbler, draper and dressmaker, grocer, dairy, tailor.

The tailor earned his living mainly from 'altering and making-over', making second-hand garments fit the new owner; or altering clothes handed down to growing children so that they could go about 'respectably'. This work usually came from the better-off Gorbals family, for in most Gorbals homes the mother did it. If prevented by illness or disability, and if she had no daughter at home able to do so, whenever she could she put a penny in a special tea caddy on the high shelf above the kitchen cooking range against the day when she would ask the tailor, or a skilled neighbour – for that was cheaper – to make over a pair of trousers or a jacket for a child. It must not be too obvious that her family wore reach-me-downs, for that was not respectable.

'Respectable' was an important word. Certain ways of behaving, using bad language, a girl wearing a blouse or dress too close-fitting or in other ways too revealing or suggestive, staying out after ten at night, were not respectable. When a mother was getting children off to school of a morning, she would make sure that each had some pieces of newspaper stuffed into a pocket for nose blowing, because to do so on your sleeve was not respectable.

For your underwear to be respectable could be more important than life and limb, especially for a woman. Seeing a teenage or grown-up daughter putting on a torn under-garment, or one that too obviously needed washing, the mother would cry out in alarm: 'What if you met with an accident in the street and had to be taken to hospital, and they saw your underclothes in that state! What are they going to *think?*' That was usually enough to bring a lazy or forgetful girl to heel.

One of the neighbourhood's many pawn shops was at the corner of Warwick Street where it crossed Bedford Street. The three

95

golden balls hung from a wrought iron bracket, with a motif of slender leaves like willow fronds, that jutted out from the angle of the building and could be seen from either street, a life saving beacon, a reminder of failed hope washed up on a barren shore. In the window a notice said 'Unredeemed Pledges for Sale', adding, with unconscious irony, 'Good Quality!' Eternity rings, wedding rings, gold watches engraved with twenty-first birthday wishes, used blankets and bed-linen, carefully laundered shirts, china teapots, dinner plates, soup tureens, cutlery, a linen tablecloth embroidered with the words: 'To our beloved daughter Bunty on her wedding day. May The Good Lord bless and keep her.'

As I relate later on, mother knew it well. When father came home skint from gambling on pay day, there she would hurry, a prized silk blouse or linen tablecloth wrapped in newspaper tucked under her shawl, and bring back a few paper bags of food.

After our swim and the talk under the hot showers, we dashed home to hang up swimming briefs and towels to dry above the coal range in the kitchen, swallow a 'tea' of bread and margarine or fried bread, and then sally out to meet again at the corner ten minutes later. The Workers' Circle was about three hundred yards to the north, past the Cross towards the river.

Bernard had always seemed to march ahead with total confidence, fully armed with maturity, values, a comprehensive world view, a certainty I envied, though I knew that his road was not for me – the only certainty I had.

There was a thrill in sharing, in the shower room group, the mood of the time – unfocussed discontent, resentment at having been cozened into believing in the solidity of a world that consisted of facades, stage sets sustained by, and sustaining, make-believe. People said the Great War had destroyed them, but they still stood. The make-believe was weaker, that was all.

We hungered for a world whose values were true and dependable, though how we would know it when we found it we had no idea. How could we know that we never would? And that in the world we were entering we would find even less solid ground than in the one we knew?

We longed to reject the world view that the preceding generation seemed to be passing on to us, attitudes of submission, of 'make do', of finding comfort in old saws and signs and portents, in thrift, prudence, automatic religious observance with little faith, in survival one day at a time.

Examples were dinned in our ears: 'Life is

a see-saw. So smile when you're up, and smile when you're down!' or: 'Expect nothing and you will never be disappointed!' Such profound resignation, pitiful and frightening to young sensibilities, repelled us. Did they want us to abandon hope before we had even started? Yet theirs were the only values we knew. Reject them and we faced an icy wilderness, with no signposts, no goals, no belief in anything or anybody. We swung between revulsion at received values and fear of living without them.

Perplexity was worsened by the suspicion that the world view of our elders did have fixity and pattern and certainty, of a sort. Deeply hidden beneath the phlegmatic humour and resignation we sensed an obstinate faith in the ultimate triumph of good over evil. The world was not as bad as it seemed, or as it might be. Beneath the appearance of confusion a striving for order and decency did somehow sustain itself. We must help it to hold its own. But we must not expect too much from it.

Some of us were aware that the elders' code was beginning to be attacked in literature and the theatre, and timidly in the press, as at best self-deception, at worst an elaborate hypocrisy generated by an arrogant and opportunist elite. Faith and trust and honour and integrity were the corner stones of society. Hard work, and pride in work, were worthy ends in themselves. Respectful and courteous behaviour would always be reciprocated. Life conducted on those principles acquired a fulfilling grace. As a world view it had certainly had its charm. But it had been pounded into the mud at Passchendaele and the Somme.

Of that we were reminded many times a day. Survivors dragged themselves about in tenement and street, some on crutches with an empty trouser leg, or a sleeve crudely sewn up and swinging in the wind. Seeing them we felt guilty that our bodies were still whole. With a cold shiver we marvelled that the glorious image of God could be shattered like this – and being so, could live. In rags they confronted us at the factory door on pay day, begging for pennies. Young men, or rather young in years, theirs was a world beyond all time. Not our world. From within the prison of their broken bodies they stared at us with eyes frozen in disbelief, silently crying out to God: 'Why? What for?' We echoed that, but not in their presence, for we had not suffered as they had.

Sometimes the thoughts boiled over. One Armistice Day morning the signal sounded for the eleven o'clock silence, and in the streets people stopped in their tracks in living stillness like the arrested figures of Delvaux or Magritte. A group of youths at the Broo violated the silence by stamping back and forth along the pavement, filling the air with the ugly staccato of tackety boots slamming down; saying nothing. People in the street all round them, held fast in the silence, glared in shock and fury. Then came the long eerie moan of the siren terminating the two minutes of reverence. The stilled figures exploded in roars of indignation and abuse: 'You fuckin' traitors!' 'Cowardly scum!' 'Insultin' the men who laid down their lives for yese!' 'Have ye no' go' any feelings at a'?' 'Have ye nae pity?' 'Rats like you don't deserve such a sacrifice. Ye should be pu' up against a wall and shot!'

The youths stared back in confusion, vainly blustering. They had meant no disrespect for the dead or their sacrifice. They knew no other way of saying that the outpouring of a generation's goodness of spirit had achieved no sensible purpose. They thought they expressed a general revulsion at the influences that had made it happen, or failed to prevent it, or stop it when it had begun.

No one asked a different question: what 'gain' could ever justify putting millions of people through a titanic slaughter machine? Doubtless many who abused the youths secretly shared their anger and sorrow and frustration. The young fellows' mistake had been to force these emotions into the open.

In their innocence – most of them were about the age of the men who had marched away to that slaughter – they had expected their gesture of rejection and disquiet to be received at least with understanding if not sympathy. How, they asked, could that past continue to be honoured by the generation that had lived through it? Too young perhaps, they could spare no sympathy for that generation, nor see that it must cling to what remained of its faith, including belief in the sacrifice, or be left with nothing. Instead, they felt resentment, and disgust for its seeming weakness of vision and of will. It had brought its sorrows upon itself. It had no right to pass them on, much less to expect sympathy. They refused to accept the elders' pain as the inheritance that each generation had to accept from the one that had gone before.

A moody despair gripped the mind. Or was it divine discontent? Virtuous, in a sense, it certainly was, or rather virginal. Some of us tried, for a time, to reject all action as tainted. We knew this position to be untenable, for apart from anything else it made us feel inadequate. Action flowed from certainty, and lack of certainty showed lack of manhood. Guilt accumulated as we waited for certainty, like Grace, to flood over us. We drew uncashable cheques on the bank of experience. We hoped for hope.

Most of these questions were screens for other, deeper perplexities, about relationships and the movement of the personality. Delicate materials – how did you *work* them? Most of us were not deeply self-regarding. To formulate one's concerns clearly, let alone decide what would cure them, was beyond us. Instead we dealt in images. In our group under the hot showers someone mentioned a folk hero – Benny Lynch the boxer, Johnny Weissmuller, Olympic swimming champion and screen Tarzan, Ronald Colman. 'Don't you think he was great when he...?' – mentioning an attribute he wanted to copy, hoping for the others' approval so that he would have the confidence to attempt it. There would follow a discussion in minute detail, on whether the hero's behaviour had been admirable or not, which facets of his personality it expressed, and what we each would have done in his place. At the same time, secretly, we chewed over our private doubts.

Bernard put himself above all this shadow boxing, and insisted on bringing us back to 'objective reality', a favourite bit of party jargon. He would move away from the showers, dart to the line of hooks on the one dry wall, take his towel and drape it over one shoulder, Roman toga fashion, assume a declamatory pose, gasping from the steam in the air, and shout out loud to silence us:

'Hey! You're wasting your time! It doesn't matter how much you try to change yourself. You're in the hands of the System. It will frustrate any plans you make. The *basics* – that's what you should worry about! The fact that the control of the means of production and exchange is concentrated in too few hands. That's what we have to change...'

The rest listened politely for a minute or two, then someone would say with a tolerant chuckle: 'Och Bernard, come off yer platform! Ye can't expect us to talk politics all the time!'

And then, brushing the hot water from faces and eyes, they resumed the talk about Jack Dempsey or Gene Tunney, or whoever had been the heroes focussed on that day – golden images of maturity.

I asked him one day, 'Why d'you always turn away from discussing life, people, how they should behave to each other, what sort of people we should try to be? It's as if you thought all those things weren't important?'

'Life? Did you say life!' A teasing smile spread over the ruddy cheeks. 'Who says this is life we're living!'

'Come off it!'

'All right, then,' he sighed. 'But we've been through all this many times. No, of course I see what you mean. But we shouldn't be wasting time on all that introspective stuff. It's no good pretending we can escape from the immediate task, which is to achieve the Revolution. That's the only goal. Nothing must distract us from it – nothing! – if we really want people to have a better life. That's all there is to it!'

I said, 'That's just running away from life! It has to be lived *now*, at this minute. You can't wait till you've made your "System" exactly as you want it! Life doesn't wait for you! You can see so much else, so why can't you see that?'

'First things first!' he said irascibly. 'This self-questioning, yours and the others', is escapism! I'm doing something *about* things. You're marking time.'

We were all living on borrowed time as it turned out, but not in the sense he meant. Perhaps he was right but for a different reason altogether. Maybe most people did not question life as we did, lived for the moment as best they could? How lucky they were! That evening as we butted against the drenching north wind, I voiced the thought.

'There must be plenty of people who accept without question whatever life sends them, who go on working, eating, sleeping – day after day! It must be fine to be like that?'

104

'I don't think it's fine at all! They don't understand what they're doing. They're nothing but' – his lip curled – 'lumpen proletarians! The slave mentality!' He halted and seemed to ponder what he had said, looked at me warily, and added with a faint smile, 'I'd never say that in public of course. But I get fucking well fed up with such people. If only they would wake up and help us a bit! The Revolution would be that much nearer.'

'I won't tell on you!' I said.

He disapproved of me as one of life's dreamers. 'Be practical!' he pleaded. Practical and objective were favourite words of his then. To dream was an excuse for staying out of the 'objective' world, the world of action, meaning action of the only kind that mattered, aimed at destroying the System. Life, the party line said, had no other terms of reference.

Most of us were dreamers to some degree. Visions of escape, like mirages indistinct yet irresistible, turned the energy inwards in day dreams, leaving just enough free to do the day's work and push the day itself away. Dreams of power, acclaim, virginal conquest. Above all release from the treadmill of thrift. How wonderful not to have to scheme and calculate about pennies and ha'pennies!

A few in the shower room group, in some

matters as rebellious as the rest, followed the old standards in their own way.

George Gideon, bull-necked physical culture devotee with an arcane language of calories, proteins, muscle balance and muscle tone, wanted to be a professional racing cyclist, and reach out for fame and money that way. Meyer Melek, dark and sleek and heavy-shouldered, with the boxer's measuring eye and poised step, had already won a few professional bouts as a lightweight. He was going to join the army when the next slack season came round.

'Join the army and see the world!' said the recruiting posters outside the Baths and at the Broo.

'No sense in hanging around here,' he said in his clipped, careful way. 'They give you plenty of facilities for training in the army. And that is worth a lot. I will serve out my time and save hard; and with that and the gratuity, whichever way my fights go in the meantime, I'll start something when I get out, maybe a gym and sports equipment business.'

Meyer was careful of his diction. He wanted to be accepted into 'refayned' society. In the determined way that he prepared for his fights he was in strict training to lose the Gorbals twang. On his early morning run, when only a few carts rattled over the cobble stones in the empty streets, he would repeat to himself, in rhythm with his pace, his 'words of the day': I, I, I – for 'ah'; or my, my, my for 'mah', 'matter' and 'bottle' without the glottal stop – 'ma'er', 'bo'lle'. Sometimes his diction slipped back: 'When ah was oo' on ma run this mornin' ah saw a lo' o' bo'lles fallin' aff the back o' a larry, an'...' He endured our good-humoured laughter calmly. Like most serious minded fighters he reserved his aggression for the ring.

Phil Emet cared nothing for diction. He would use worldly power to compel refayned society to accept him, Gorbals twang or no. A powerful back and shoulders attested to his hard work in the upholstery workshop, pulling tight the jute and sisal belting and the covering fabrics, and manhandling finished pieces of furniture. Black wavy hair grew low on his forehead; his dark eyes were watchful and darting. A long nose, slightly aquiline, gave his sallow features a narrow, pointed appearance, almost timid, at variance with the strength radiating from him. Fast-talking, nimble-witted, we called him a 'chancer', local slang for a schemer you should deal with carefully – not unkindly, but in the way members of a family tolerantly refer to one of their number.

Phil prepared himself in his own way for an attack on the world. He worked long hours at his upholstery apprenticeship and in helping in his father's small furniture-making and repair workshop under the Cumberland Street railway bridge. Wherever he went he carried an old school satchel containing a dozen red-covered exercise books, his detailed dossier on the furniture business, one book for each topic. With the black triangular-shaped marking pencil he used at work, he filled the pages in the rounded copperplate handwriting we were taught at school, with figures, diagrams, cuttings from trade journals, about production methods, materials, costings, suppliers, design trends, and changes in market demand such as the furniture and equipment needs of the new housing schemes rising up in the suburbs.

'When ma apprenticeship's oo' o' the way,' he said, 'ah'm goin' tae take over ma feyther's workshop. Ah'll ge' tha' wurrkin' a damn sight be'er! An' then ah'll move intae mass production.'

He went on: 'That's the way furrniture's got tae go, mass production for the mass market! The day o' the craftsman like ma feyther's over an' done wi'. You just wait and see! Ah'll have ma hoose up at Newton Mearns, wi' a big garden an' a car, afore ah'm thurrty!'

Newton Mearns, on high ground about ten miles south of Glasgow, showed crucially how the world was moving from patterns that had seemed set for all time. When I first went up to the Mearns I saw a tranquil rural world of fields and cows and hayricks, copses and burns and flowering hedgerows, with here and there a little hamlet and a church: a secret, ancient design. On a hot summer day some of us would make a foray up there, to a foreign land, the country. Timidly we looked at a life we had known of only in the abstract, from hearsay, from old people speaking of childhood in the country, from fairy tales or the scant Nature instruction at school, or the penny matinee at the cinema on Saturday afternoon. We saw the people of the Mearns as a different race, purposeful, endowed with quiet certainty, unhurried, at ease in their mystery, their dealings with the earth and with beasts, plants, wind and rain and the great sky, who walked erect in the world. They looked at us as if *we* were the foreigners.

We got up there by tram and then by bus, or on bikes. You could hire a bike for sixpence a day: to buy one cost four or five pounds. Buying for cash was beyond any of us. George Gideon and one or two others were buying bikes on the never-never at sevenpence-ha'penny a week.

We carried bread and hard-boiled eggs in our pockets and picnicked on the bank of a burn. We lay prone and leaned out over the shallow stream where it sprang over broad flat stones streaked with reds and yellows and slate greys, to catch the cold, tangy water, flashing with rainbow light, in mid-air between our lips. Then we turned on to our backs and gazed up through waving traceries of leaves at the great openness of the sky, listened to blackbird and lark and the gentle murmurings of the earth and the multitude of creatures sensed moving on it. And life floated on the scent of freshly-cut hay and the mingled smells of many growing things. It was hard to take it all in, and we knew in our bones, sadly, resentfully, that we never could, because our roots were not there. We were exhilarated and disquieted, strangers in Arcady.

That first vision was only a year or two earlier. Perhaps, knowing so little of rural life, we had not noticed the changes already begun. Now they were plain. Fields and boscage and hedgerows were being eaten away. The mysterious race of country folk was in retreat. Villas had sprung up, others were building, red and raw, in discord with the gentle greys and browns and greens of the old settlements, Prosperous Glasgow people moved out to live in the Mearns, in the country but not of it, proud of this step up in life.

Why was living in the country a step up? It

had not always been. Many Gorbals dwellers were no more than a generation or so away from it. Their forebears had seen 'the country', whether in the Highlands and Islands, Ireland, Italy or Eastern Europe, as a place like any other where you worked hard for a living. To go and live there from choice, or to visit it for pleasure or for one's health – the latter often a Calvinistic cloak for the former – was an urban invention filtering down to us from the lower middle class. Moving to the country following material success often amounted to ostentatious expenditure, as in later years would be an expensive car or a winter suntan, which other people blindly strove to copy.

Helping to form this new attitude to the country among the lower orders was the propaganda put out by groups of do-gooders promoting schemes to take poor city children on country or seaside holidays at subsidised prices or, in 'deserving' cases, gratis. 'Fresh Air Fortnights', one of them was called. Intentionally or not, their message implied that country air was a cure for deprivation.

Bernard and the party detested the charity element in such schemes. The aim, they thundered, was to gull the workers into believing that charity was the proper answer to social ills and injustice, and to deflect them from insisting that the System itself should be replaced with a better one. Such 'benefits' should be available as of right. Acceptance of charity blunted the lower orders' discontent and quenched their militancy.

Shrewdly, the party stopped short of advocating boycott, for that might alienate support, especially among women. In this they implicitly acknowledged that among the poor it was the women, more than the men, who carried the burden of life, in unceasing toil in the home and the Steamy, and in heartache for their families when money was more than usually short for food, fuel, clothing, blankets, medicine. For many women in the tenements, charity could be in truth a life saver. And in these Fresh Air Holiday schemes they saw a heaven-sent way of getting children off their hands for a while and giving themselves a spell of lessened work and worry, a holiday for them too. If children benefited, as the propaganda said, so much the better! Competition for places was intense, short of money as most of the schemes were. Some mothers had to be content to go on a waiting list for possible cancellations later in the year or, failing that, for places the following year.

Up there in Newton Mearns the new immigrants from the city could boast of having fresh air all the time.

In the villa settlements, lanes and landmarks kept their rural names – Rick Lane, Smiddy Crossing, Lang Byre Brig – but the ways of life they signalled were gone, leaving only echoes and symbols, a few oases of greenery, glimpses of distant fields; enough, however, to charm the new arrivals. But a decade or so later most of these residues would disappear under a further wave of building and transformation, in effect the creation of new *urbs* – shops, garages, workshops, offices. The true 'country' gone for ever.

For the present, however, Newton Mearns was the Shangri-la on which many Gorbalian focussed their hopes, and some would one day attain. And to own a car! No one we knew owned one. On top of your achievement in moving to Newton Mearns, the sight of you in your car would proclaim to the world day in and day out, especially to the Gorbals slum-dwellers you had left behind, that you really were on your way up.

'Traitors to their class!' Bernard said angrily, 'Using their abilities to perpetuate the System. They don't see that. *Will* not is more to the point! But they will one day. By God they will!'

There was menace in his words, sad to hear from this warm-hearted soul. There was bitterness too. Phil and the others were determined on joining the ranks of the class

113

enemy, the capitalists. When the day of confrontation came, they would be on the wrong side of the barricades.

Part of him, I suspected, saw his political dedication as self-denial on their behalf. He too could have chosen the golden road. He must often have asked himself whether his sacrifice was no more than masochism. So Moses raged at those who knelt before the Golden Calf.

Of late I had sensed a less secure note in his affirmation of faith, and attributed it to the compassion central to his character. Did he say to himself sometimes: 'Let them enjoy worldly achievement while they may. Why must it be jam tomorrow and never today? Alas, how sure am I that it *will* be jam?'

The hounds of doubt paced close behind.

No wonder the menace in his words sounded overdone. If you fear that you have not enough cold commitment to see you through, you fall back on passion.

'You talk,' I said, 'as if the Revolution will answer all life's questions. That's impossible. Life is about *the individual*, the sort of person you want to be, not people in the mass as when you speak about the System, this system or that system.'

'How can you be anything but a wage slave when the System keeps you chained in that position?'

'Come on!' I said, 'The word "slave" makes it sound worse but it doesn't change anything. We'll still have to work for wages whatever the system! You can still be a person of a special kind, with feelings about life special to you, even if you *are* earning wages. You talk about people as if they had no faces, as if they all had exactly the same feelings, or none at all – the people this, and the people that! The individual does matter, what he is and what he wants to be.'

He gritted his teeth: 'For Christ's sake it doesn't matter a damn what you or anyone else *wants* to be! The System doesn't allow you to be anything else than a cog in a machine making profits for the capitalists. Only after the Revolution, when everyone will have equal rights to the fruits of production, will people be able to develop their talents the way they want to. "From each according to his abilities, to each according to his needs." That's the only possible way to look at it.'

Stock repetition of the creed was his way of turning a deaf ear. I wanted to share with him the thought I was wrestling with: the person you are, or are trying to be, is your own work of art to refine and change through life, a burden no one escapes. Substitute another System for this one and that burden will still be yours alone. Even Bernard, tougher-minded than the rest,

115

resisted ideas that came too close for comfort.

I was learning a depressing lesson – the truer the insight the greater the peril in revealing it, what Mephistopheles had in mind when advising Faust:

'Das beste, was du wissen kannst,
Darfst du den Buben doch nicht sagen.'

('The most precious knowledge you can attain, you must not tell to boys.')

I said: 'It's something hard to explain. I'm trying to talk about the questions life puts to you as a person, *inside yourself*. They must be the same whether you're living in comfort in a house with hot and cold running water and a bathroom and wearing a bespoke suit, or in a Rose Street tenement and getting free clothes off the parish!' Rose Street was a byword for the lowest of the low in slums, even by Gorbals standards.

He shook the rain off his head like a dog, and seemed to chew over what I said. This was new too. His mercurial mind was always so quick to answer.

I went on: 'And another thing. You talk as if revolutions are made by angels! It's all about people hungry for power! They'll murder and torture to get it and hold on to it. Look what the 'high heid yins' in Russia are doing to people, even to their own old comrades who risked their lives for the Revolution! When it comes to villainy there doesn't seem much to choose between the new bosses there and the old ones they got rid of!'

On the public platform, Bernard dutifully echoed the self-righteous Russian communiqués on the Moscow trials and purges: the great new socialist state, in self-defence, was meting out well-deserved retribution to its enemies.

Honest soul, the party line had to be the truth or he could not live with it. But the revelations coming out of Russia worried him, the partiality of its legal procedures, the cruelty to those of inconvenient opinions, the Machiavellian misuse of words like democracy, the treatment of people as units of conformity. More crucially he was troubled by the cynical and manipulative elements in the Comintern's *realpolitik*.

Tough-minded politician though he had become, the sensitivity that had drawn him to the cause ruled him still. Suffering moved him even if the creed condemned the victims. Later I would understand why his anger boiled over now. He had made up his mind to join the International Brigade in Spain, and in a few weeks he would go.

These were days of strange faiths and nostrums, of innocence still hungry for causes to follow. The day of the heroic and exemplary act was not past. Belief and action could gloriously coincide. The Spanish War was a holy war for liberty and democracy, for good against evil. But Bernard, surely, was not fitted to the Quixotic role! Dapper speech-maker with the intellectual's stoop, what was he thinking of, going off to shoulder a rifle in Spain?

How wrong I was. He was to prove himself as tough as the rest. Tougher in fact, luckily for him. But he would not find the cause he had gone to fight for.

Was he going to Spain to put himself through a test of suffering and danger, as some ascetics scourged themselves to strengthen their faith, fleeing the hounds of doubt? My questioning of his creed that day, innocent then as it had always been, must have given him particular pain. His anger came as a shock:

'It's *you* that's closing your eyes to the truth!' He spat the words from the side of his mouth, blowing the rain away. 'These are the growing pains of the Revolution. Only fifteen years ago this country, and other imperialists, had troops in Russia fighting a war of intervention. They financed the White armies of Denikin and Kolchak and the rest, trying to kill the Revolution and restore the Czarist oppression! And they still dream of doing it.

118

They'll use any means, including getting discontented comrades to sabotage the Revolution,'

'I will give you this much,' he went on, 'I suppose it is just possible some comrades in Russia disagreed with the party line on how to build socialism, disobeyed the rule that the Central Committee's decisions must not be opposed, and fell foul of the authorities from honest conviction. I admit that's worrying. But this is too dangerous a time to be soft with such people.'

He wiped the rain from his face with the back of his hand and said quietly, 'It's hard to judge what's going on in Russia from where we are standing.' Frowning, he fell silent again.

A few months ago the hint of weakened belief would not have slipped out. He hurried on as if to blot it out: 'What I mean is, you can't afford to go on giving deviationists the benefit of the doubt. Whether you call them traitors or misguided people is not to the point. If you're convinced that what they're doing is endangering the Revolution then they've got to be stopped.' Awesome words spoken with tight lips and a dying fall.

The echoes of his doubt continued in the air between us: 'It's hard to judge...'

Press reports from Russia had an unreal quality, suggesting that observers did not

119

dare believe the horror thinly concealed in what they saw. Enough filtered through. The Old Bolsheviks at their show trials moving and talking like sleep walkers, the standard wording of their confessions, and other signs, pointed to the truth, or rather a minute degree of the full horror. We shrank from believing that such things could happen in a civilised country in the enlightened twentieth century. Soon, equally unbelievable truths of Nazi barbarism would be revealed. In both cases the most chilling characteristic was that such things were done by 'ordinary' people, the sort you would pass in the street or in a bus queue without a second glance.

After Hitler's War I met an aristocratic German ex-officer in Italy, and Eichmann's name cropped up. Count M had come across him during the war, in circumstances left unclear. 'That little Scrooge!', he exclaimed with contempt, meaning an insignificant, ordinary little man. But his laugh as he said it told me that he dismissed as of no importance, also, what Eichmann and his like had done.

Count M, too, was in his way ordinary, a man of his class and time. Observing this hardened but well cared-for middle-aged gentleman with the ramrod back, bearer of one of the most distinguished names in the Almanach de Gotha, one saw what he once had been, the athletic and debonair young nobleman much like many another, of easy cosmopolitan manner, not given to deep thought but shrewd enough, pursuing the patterned life of his landed class in the inter-war days, schooled to hold the reins, heading smoothly towards hierarchical and business influence.

His mind was serene. Nothing that anyone had done in Germany, during the war or before it, was worth a second thought. Spilt milk, errors of judgement, that was all: 'My dear chap, politics! What can you expect? All I know about politics, which isn't much, is that it's about power, and the power game is a kind of war! It's tough. Oh yes! People make mistakes and behave badly, stupidly.' He grimaced, putting aside the thought. 'All part of the tough game of life one might say!' He laughed again, 'Preferably tougher for the other fellow than for me, of course! It's the way the cards fall. What else can one say?'

An understandable attitude, remembering that the very existence of the old aristocracy exemplified the principle of 'Anything goes and Devil take the hindmost.'

Those were the words, too, of that bridge across the Clyde.

6

THE FRIGHTENERS

I said that Meyer Melek confined his aggression to the ring. Only once did I see him break that rule – a traumatic experience for him, both in itself and in its denouement. For me, sorrowing for him and for all of us, it was an awesome visitation of demonic powers.

We grew up with violence. It simmered and bubbled and boiled over in street and close, outside the pubs, at the dance halls in Bedford Street and Ballater Street and Crown Street, sometimes in gang raids from adjacent slum areas, Kinning Park, Hutchesontown, Govanhill, Kingston. Seldom did such attacks find the defenders unprepared. Like the raiders they would be armed, with bicycle chains, knuckle-dusters, chisels, open razors, or the fearsome Razor Cap – razor blades embedded in the peak of a cloth cap with their cutting edges projecting, and swung in a scything motion across an enemy's face and neck.

More often, violence settled private

accounts, transgression of codes, the spilling over of grievance or spleen. It was so closely intertwined with everyday life, its inescapable rough edge, logical, cathartic, that its occurrence, like rain and cold and frequent shortage of food, was recognised with equal fatalism. That it could also be an instrument of cool business calculation never occurred to me, until one day in the slack summer season a ruthless enactment in our street brought a harsh awakening. I saw that the smooth face of successful business could conceal a use of violence and terror as merciless, as detached and as passionless as anything in the annals of the Borgia or the Medici. I shared Meyer's misery, the hurt to his sense of manliness, his pride, his simple view of right and wrong. It darkened the sun more cruelly than anything since Charlie went away. It was a reminder from the Furies.

With two older brothers Meyer worked in his father's joinery workshop, part of old stables in a lane behind Warwick Street, a few minutes from our tenement. With its cobbled floor and high blackened rafters, it was a place of saturnine gloom, in which a half-light was provided by three gas mantles on long thin pipes projecting from high up on the dun-coloured walls; ankle deep in sawdust and curly shavings, one could barely move for planks leaning tall against the walls, workbenches, partly assembled shelving and shop counters and wall fixtures. The business was probably too small for four adults to earn a living from it, and in better times one of the brothers, probably Meyer as the youngest, would have gone to work somewhere else. As it was they worked hard for what they did wring out of it. I often saw Mrs Melek – small, stooped, plaited black hair wound in a tight roll on top of her head, sallow features deeply lined at the mouth – hurrying towards the workshop carrying an earthenware jug of soup covered with a towel to keep its contents warm, and half a loaf of black bread wrapped in a handkerchief. Though their house was so near, they dared not spare the time to go home to eat.

Early one evening I went there to collect Meyer on my way to the Baths. As we rounded the corner into our Street we heard shouting from a little group on the pavement outside Meyer's close a few doors away from mine.

'Fuckin' hell!' Meyer ran ahead. Two heavily built young men were scuffling with an older man in shirt sleeves who, as we came near, fell to his knees on the wet pavement. Blood from his nose and lips had made dark streaks on his collarless shirt. Like a penitent before inquisitors he held up his hands in supplication. It was Mr

Fredericks – middle-aged (old to us), white hair thinning, narrow-chested, afflicted with the almost universal bronchial cough. With his wife and consumptive daughter he lived on Meyer's staircase. Like many of us in the garment trade, he was out of work in this off-season.

'It's the fuckin' menodge men,' Meyer muttered.

The street was unnaturally quiet. Here and there a face peeped out from shop doorway or close mouth. This was a time, the code said, when it was safer to see nothing. To be known to have watched could be interpreted as participation, support for one of the contestants, and retribution might follow. It was a time not to be involved.

The words 'menodge men' carried terror for the tenements – more than 'the factor' or rent collector, and perhaps comparable to the black shadow that hovered round the sheriff's men who came to distrain on property for non-payment of rent or, since there was seldom anything worth distraining, to put you out on to the street.

A menodge – a local word, probably from the French 'menage' – was in its origins a thrift system. It became for a great many people the only way to buy clothes, bedding, household equipment, furniture, on credit. You began by making payments, usually through a neighbourhood collector working on commission, of perhaps sixpence a week to a 'warehouse', in effect a retailer selling at a high mark-up to people lacking the ready money to buy at a normal shop. When your 'menodge book' showed a stipulated credit balance you went to the warehouse and chose goods to that value. In the interim the money held in your name was of course at the interest-free disposal of the warehouse. If you undertook to continue weekly payments of a stated figure you could become a credit customer and take away goods up to a certain 'loan' value. Concealed in the price of the goods was a high interest rate on that loan. From then on, as in the 'loan shark' system exploited by the Mafia in America, you were encouraged to be in debt for evermore.

Since you would not be in the menodge at all if you could afford to buy elsewhere for cash, you were a captive customer in every sense. One-and-three-ha'pence a week was a common loan repayment figure, high for most people even when in work, impossibly so when they were on the dole and bringing home fifteen shillings a week.

Almost by definition menodge customers had no reserves, so when life hit them hard, through illness or unemployment, and the one-and-three-ha'pence could not be found, they could do nothing but hope, miserably, that the menodge men, 'the frighteners', would not come to their door and make a public example of them.

There was a dreadful irony in that. People became menodge customers from a desire to remain respectable, to pay their way and avoid the great indignity, 'going on the parish', the pauper's way. And so the others, those who *were* on the parish, showed little sympathy for them when the frighteners did come. They stood back and watched, not with satisfaction but allowing themselves a breath of comfort, as if they said to themselves: 'There but for the grace of God – or our better judgement – go we! They shouldn't have been so stuck up – they should've gone on the parish like the rest of us.'

The label Rachmanism had not been invented then but the form of customer discipline was familiar and, from a narrow point of view, effective. For the menodge or credit warehouse the purpose was twofold – so to terrorise the defaulter that he would put his debt before every other need, even food and coal, and to send a terrible warning to everyone else. For the latter reason the defaulter must be attacked and humiliated publicly.

These frighteners, we would hear, were acting for Great Universal Stores in Cathedral Street, a forbidding factory-like building of blackened sandstone with broad, flat-arched windows, beside the railway lines at the back of Queen Street Station. Seeing it I always thought of 'the dark Satanic mills'.

As we ran up, Mrs Fredericks was standing at the close mouth, shaking with distress, wiping away her tears with a soiled black apron. Then she too held out her hands in appeal. The men stood over her husband's crumpled form, dour messengers from the Inferno, seemingly pondering what further suffering to inflict.

'For God's sake have pity on us! We're at our wits end! Please give us time – till he's in work again. It's not our fault. We *want* to pay but we can't!'

One of the men kicked Mr Fredericks in the ribs and he howled in pain and toppled on his left side and lay groaning and gasping for breath. With a cry she tried to push past, reaching out to him. The other man put out a foot and she fell heavily to the ground.

I had seen Meyer in the ring, a figure of poised, scientific intensity, showing no emotion. In these few seconds it seemed that his whole frame shook as with a fever. His face had gone dead white. I was afraid for him.

'Fuckin' bastards!' He leapt between them and with a shoulder lunge and a trip kick, toppled the one on his left. The other,

128

turning, slow to react, accustomed perhaps to meek submission, had time only for a few snarled words, the beginnings of an automatic response: 'Fuck off! This is none o' yewr...'

Meyer, swivelling like a dancer, chin tucked in, shot out a left to the solar plexus and, as the man grunted and bent forwards hurled his weight behind a straight right to the jaw that toppled him like a falling log. The back of his head hit the pavement with a sullen, bony thud and he lay still.

Turning as the first one got to his feet, Meyer ducked a wild swing and delivered a straight left to the jaw; and as the other rocked back, followed with a lightning right hook to the head and another straight left to the chin, his whole frame lunging behind it like a battering ram. The man's knees sagged and he subsided vertically like a collapsing building and lay inert.

I glanced round. Every furtive face had disappeared. We stood in an icy desert.

We helped the couple to their feet and led them to their house.

'It's no good,' Mrs Fredericks muttered through sobs, 'They'll come back. They never give up.'

'I don't understand,' Meyer said. 'They can't get money out of you if you haven't got it.'

We both knew that that was not the point.

The supreme purpose of sending in the frighteners was *pour encourager les autres.*

In our simplicity we felt their hurt as our own. We raged for them within, all the more because we felt so powerless to help them. In truth we could do nothing. We went downstairs.

We feared, primitively, the contagion of their defeat. We raged again, this time for ourselves. If we could have raised swords and struck hard at the world and made it weep too, how golden that moment would have been. But where was that world? Who? What? And in what gruesome way were we ourselves accomplices in it?

We lingered in the close mouth. Where the frighteners had lain the pavement was empty. Meyer contemplated the blood on his cut knuckles.

We had crossed a dangerous frontier.

I think we knew that the hardest lessons of this episode were still to come, added to other tremors in the ground beneath our feet. And that the chain of effect would be understood only much later – perhaps too late.

'It's no good,' Mrs Fredericks had wailed. 'They'll be back.'

We were too full of it to say much as we walked the hundred yards or so to the Baths. Meyer, I knew, would suffer most, at least immediately. He had attacked the menodge's front line troops. Who could tell what would happen now? Perhaps *all* the menodges would close ranks and bear down on us, a massive show of strength to snuff out any thought of further challenge? Who could prevent them? We knew nothing about the law, how to appeal to the mighty in the land to protect us. For us the menodges *were* the mighty – part of the big battalions of the boss class. Who could challenge them on level terms? Who, for that matter, would care?

We reached the Baths about twenty minutes after the fight, but plainly news of it had flown ahead. The shower room group showed muted sympathy, ashamedly uncomfortable that, in self-protection, they could do no more. Few families felt immune. In any case, what had happened to the Fredericks, and what was almost certainly in store for Meyer, were simply variations in the common round of life's hard knocks. A fear of a quite different kind was that the menodges might blacklist any family seen to be linked with Meyer's revolt – a penalty far worse, in most people's short-term reasoning, than the chance of a visit from the frighteners in the future.

No one paused to think that the menodges needed all of us just as much as we might need them. The immediate truth was that the menodge struck hard when and where it chose, and with impunity. It was wise to stand clear.

Two evenings later I again went to collect Meyer at the workshop. As we walked along Bedford Street towards the Baths a large black car drove slowly past us and stopped at the kerb a few yards ahead. Private cars were a rare sight in the Gorbals then, especially large and expensive-looking ones. We looked at it with interest. There were five men in it, two in front and three in the back; the one in the front passenger seat was expensively dressed – it must have been the first time I had ever seen cuff-links worn – and that might have been enough to give him an air of authority. In his eyes there was an expectation of obedience, but above all a cold, implacable will. He beckoned to us. As we came up to the car the other four, in a well-drilled movement, got out and surrounded us – large, silent, menacing. At a signal from the leader, two of them pinioned my arms and lifted me like a sack and set me down again a few feet away. Then the four of them closed in on Meyer and pushed him close to the open passenger window so that he stood before the leader like a prisoner awaiting sentence.

The hard eyes held him fast. Fingers drummed on the car window frame. At last he spoke in a flat, soft, menacing voice: 'You were a bit rough with my lads the other evening. You're interfering in business and we don't allow that. You'd better get that into your head before you get hurt. Understand?'

Meyer had obviously tried to prepare himself for something like this. Strong as he was, finely tuned physically, he was young in the world, and could hardly have foreseen the pitiless force he would face.

He said as through clenched teeth: 'How can you go around knocking harmless old people about like that? It's a crying disgrace. Why don't you go and make a living some other way?'

The man tapped his fingers again, studied Meyer stonily: 'You've got spirit, I'll say that for you. But there's a lot you don't understand. One thing's for sure. I can't afford to have any more of this.' He stared hard again. 'Tell you what I'll do. I could use a lad like you who can look after himself. I'll give you a tenner a week plus expenses. You do what I tell you and ask no questions, that's all. And don't worry, I look after my lads when there's any trouble.'

'You mean dirty work like the other night?'

There was a snort of impatience: 'I said I look after my lads didn't I? What do *you* care? You've only got to ask yourself one question; could you pull in that sort of money anywhere else?'

He pointed to Meyer's cut knuckles: 'You

133

ought to look after those hands. You could get them hurt bad. That's right lads, isn't it?' He looked up at his cohorts, who by a slight movement of the heavy shoulders signified agreement. 'You could get your fingers jammed in a car door maybe, or someone might accidentally smash your knuckles with a sledgehammer. A great pity. Happened to one or two promising young boxers, I seem to remember.'

As if in reflex action, Meyer stuffed his hands in his trouser pockets. Reddening, he removed them.

'That's right,' said the man. 'I advise you to be careful of those hands.'

Meyer's features paled and flushed, and paled again. In the smooth face before him he saw the savage world for the first time. He could find no answer.

The other said: 'Listen, I'm a busy man; I've no time to waste. I'm a man of my word and that means I don't make idle promises, and I don't make idle threats either. You've got till tomorrow to make up *your* mind.'

He signed to the driver, who stepped quickly round the front of the car, got in and started the engine.

Turning back to Meyer he said: 'Tell you what. I'll make it fifteen there you are! We'll be back tomorrow. Don't get any more foolish ideas. It's my last word. You just think about those hands!'

He signalled to the others. They piled into the car and it moved softly away.

As on that other evening, we stood in an apparently deserted street. Not a single face looked out. Of course everyone had seen, and understood.

The car turned the corner and was gone. As if on cue the street was full again. Shop door bells tinkled. People came and went. Children were let out of closes to play. No one looked us in the face. There must be no connexion with us till our fate was decided.

Meyer was taking the brunt of it and I was sad for him. One generous impulse, one quixotic moment, and what cataclysmic forces he had summoned up?

Yet I too had felt the chill of that basilisk stare. I too had been warned.

For him nothing could be undone. They would never let him be. They dared not, or their power would be at an end.

He might have been echoing my thoughts, for he half-turned as if to retrace his steps to the workshop, then faced me again. No, his look said, there's no way back.

The street swirled about us. Did any of these hurrying people guess the revelation that had come to us, that we saw this world, at last, in all its invincible savagery? Perhaps some of them did, reflecting that this initiation had better come to us now than later? The wound would grow its protective

135

scar. It always did.

Slowly, in silence, we continued on to the Baths. There, at least, we were in our own world. No, that was wrong: there was no such place, not any more.

Once again the news had preceded us. Amazingly, they even knew about the offer of employment. Perhaps, with the threat of retribution, it had been deliberately put about, for if Meyer accepted he would be diminished, and if he did not, the lesson would still be driven home: opposition was futile.

No one spoke of it till we had done our stint of lengths and were in the shower room.

Phil said: 'Ye could do wurrse. It's no' yewr fault if people buy stuff they cannae pay for. Business is business efter a'!'

Meyer shrugged, tight-lipped.

Bernard, unusually, remained silent till we were about to leave: 'You can't do that!'

'But there's the money!' Meyer muttered unhappily. 'We don't make that in a month! Anyway, father could do with taking it easier now. And what chance have I got if I don't?'

'You couldn't do it. I know you couldn't.'

'I wish I could. God help me if only I could!'

'Listen, you were going to go into the army? Your father's going to have to manage without you sooner or later. Maybe this'll turn out for the best. Your slack time's coming on. Now's your chance.'

'I have been thinking about that.'

Meyer's eyes were moist. This was not the way he had wanted it to be.

Early next morning he went out to Maryhill Barracks.

7

ANNIE

For me the hints and rumours coming out of Russia were evidence enough. The later flood of anecdote and reportage would simply add detail.

Not everyone had been troubled. The Gorbals was not a place of political sophistication. Few people, apart from soldiers and sailors and merchant seamen, knew other countries. Not many had travelled more than fifty miles from Glasgow. When, later, Chamberlain would speak of Czechoslovakia as 'a little country far away that we know little of', it would be true for everyone we knew.

Ruled by folk lore and simple stereotypes, how innocent and prejudiced we were. Italians were dagoes or wops. Germans all had duelling scars on their faces. The French? Incomprehensible and wicked: had they not invented the French letter, the French kiss, French knickers?

Soldiers' tales. Black and white visions brought back from the mud. Tommy Atkins' fugitive pleasures:

'Mademoiselle from Armentieres,
Parlez-vous?'

And who were we? Some of those from exile
families sought certainty in stock images of
the host culture. We belong to a great
country! Nobody tries anything with us or
we give them what for! We send in the Navy
and that's that. The Empire on which the
sun never sets, that's us and we're proud of
it. And Glasgow's its Second City. And
we're the workshop of the world!

Seafaring men confirmed them: 'Aye, ye
go ashore a' any place ye like tae name,
Rangoon or Shanghai, Valparaiso or Fiji,
anywhere, an' walk over tae a crane on the
dockside, or look a' a generator or a boiler
or a pump or some other bit o' machinery,
an' there's the plate on it with the name of a
British company – Carron, or Braby's or
Babcox and so on – frae Clydeside,
Birmingham, Manchester, some place in
this country. The same on the pilot boat or
some other craft. An' the locals there'll tell
ye: "If it comes frae Britain we know it's the
best!"

Sunset visions. How could we know the
sunset had begun some fifty years before?
With unexplained foreboding some of us
wondered if these stereotypes did belong to
the past, as the light of the stars we could

see was not of the present but of a time far off in the past. If they did belong to today, why did the great leaders in London put up with the hooligan behaviour of Hitler and Mussolini?

What rights and wrongs; from long ago, what unpaid debts, now clamoured for settlement?

Had people always walked in shadow, oppressed by uncertain identity, belief, direction? We knew we needed loyalties, though we couldn't have said why. Where should ours be?

With the workers, was Bernard's answer. 'The workers owe loyalty to no country, only to each other! That's why we must be loyal to the Spanish workers. Their cause is ours too.'

'When Joey Morris' father went bankrupt,' I said, 'and had to close his factory and go and work for somebody else, did he stop being evil because he wasn't an employer any more? Did he become a good person overnight because he was working for somebody else for wages?'

He disdained to reply. Talk was over, and the time for action had come. Though neither of us could know it, this particular difference between us would soon be over for ever. Spain was about to write *finis* to a page of his life.

Some of us were sure that Spain was a

curtain-raiser for another Great War. Would that war – could it – be any different, less horrible, less disillusioning?

We sensed in the older men around us – old to us, but some only turned forty or so – a continuing shock from the Great War. They remained in the grip of a timeless ordeal for which nothing had prepared them, continuing to struggle with an enigma to which there was no key: how to fit the cataclysmic scale of the slaughter, and especially its impersonal character, to the world of human warmth and meaning they had grown up to believe in. The individual had been overwhelmed in man's first production line war, in which millions of able-bodied men were executed as a terminal stage in the manufacture of killing machines and their delivery to an appointed place. It was not merely organised slaughter; in a sense it was *mutually agreed slaughter*, a shocking negation of a tradition, instinct with honour and nobility, they could not bear to see pass away, in which war was *personal*, the enemy an identifiable individual, whose cause you could at least understand if not accept, whose aggression you could respond to with passion of your own, muscle with muscle, skill with skill, steel with steel.

The survivors had brought back only fragments of the picture. It was an unbelievable one, but believed it had to be. Many could not bear to speak of it at all. Others told what they knew again and again, possessed by a grim wonder, of remote machines raising higher and higher the mounds of dead in front of the trench fire step, and still knew no face to fix their fury upon. Even the word enemy had lost its old meaning. Death, like life, had to have an aim, a purpose. In these dunes of putrefying flesh there was none. From life too a needed rationale had gone. The old one, for all its faults, had served them and their forebears well enough. Who could read the broken message of life in these piled-up fragments?

We also sensed among them a feeling that what they had given, an affirmation for which all life had prepared them, had failed of its purpose. They had given everything but not enough.

Would *anything* more, even if they had had it to give, have led to anything worthwhile? What, after all this, did worthwhile mean?

It could mean righting wrongs, one supposed. Old men remembered 'wrongs' that politicians, as proxies for the people, had fulminated about: the Kaiser and the Ems telegram. The Fashoda incident, the murder at Sarajevo. Were *we* in the Gorbals today better off because these wrongs had been 'righted' – and who could say they had been? And now, though causes had different labels, Danzig, the Sudetenland, as abstract to us as earlier ones must have been to the common folk, it seemed that a profound essence of feeling, the springs of passion and action, remained unchanged. Was the 'cause' irrelevant?

How could the Spanish War be different?

Not long ago we had been to an anti-war exhibition – horrifying photographs of mutilation, death, destruction in the Great War. It had been mounted by the party, in the interests of the current Comintern strategy active in the disarmament and anti-war movement, to project its desired image as the only genuine worker for peace.

One photograph imprinted itself especially on my mind – a huge enlargement in grainy black and white, more than six feet high, of a man's face with one side blown off by a shell. In place of half his mouth and one cheek was a yawning cave of flesh kept open with metal struts so that food and breath could pass. There were others.

Disturbing in a different fashion was a section devoted to the arms industry, telling of a factory on the border between France and Germany that during the Great War had supplied munitions to both sides.

Bernard snorted: 'That only happens in a capitalist war! Spain is a working-class war. The first one!'

We would soon learn that worse things

were happening in the Spanish War.

The tidal wave of anti-war and disarmament movements, the first of our time, displayed an innocence now hard to understand, until we think of the Flower Children of the Sixties – an appeal to the softer side of human nature, faith in the power of gentleness and the will to peace. 'If only people and nations would let themselves be swayed by kindness! If only "they", the people who fear us and insist on arming against us, would believe we are innocent and that we only wish for good to prevail – and not attack us first!'

One was the Peace Pledge Union, its name a naive throwback to the campaign in the early years of the century for 'signing the pledge' against the demon drink, instinct with the belief that if you but had the *will*, everything was possible. So the will to peace, the mind suppressing the brutish passions, was all that was needed to 'outlaw' war. Many peace propagandists declared, and some still do, that for a nation to be armed at all was to provoke aggression. If only *one* nation would disarm it would exert an irresistible moral pressure on all the others to do the same.

Many of the disarmament and peace groups were party front organisations; in others, party underground members formed cells, and by their dynamism and through

144

constitutional manoeuvres moved into positions of control. The party steered money into them, and boosted their efforts with opportunist propaganda. In these ways it created a Fifth Column to fulfil Russia's designs, one of which was the military weakness of its 'host' country.

In spite of our inexperience, or perhaps because of it, our sympathy made us feel the trauma of the Great War survivors as our own, so that the peace movements' plea spoke to us powerfully. It joined together two fears: that the Western powers' war plans would steer us into mass slaughter again and another lost generation, and that in the process a ray of hope for a humaner society, the image of Russia that so many people wanted to believe in, would be extinguished. War plans? How could we know that Britain and France were militarily at their weakest for twenty years! Party branches were ordered to monitor the movements of trains and ships carrying munitions and chemicals and military units, and send the information to King Street, whence of course it went to Moscow. Some of it, one must assume from later events was filtered by Moscow onwards to German Intelligence.

Groping for some sense, a clear view, trying to provoke Bernard out of his stonewalling, something made me say: 'All right, about this worker solidarity you talk about, if I go and fight in Spain, will the workers here make up my dole money to more than fifteen shillings a week when I get back? Better still, will the union fight to get me a decent job all the year round?'

I was ashamed the moment I had spoken. It was a silly way of expressing futility.

His forbearance snapped. Angrily he halted, tugged at my sleeve to stop me in my tracks, and pointed past me at something:

'Just you look at that!' He was hoarse with fury. 'For Christ's sake stop bellyaching and take first things first! Do you want to live like *that* all your life – you and everybody else round here? Do you! Look, man! Look!'

I turned to see what he was pointing at. We were at the mouth of a close, the narrow slit in a tenement façade entered directly from the street, giving on to a stone-paved corridor barely wide enough for two people abreast, about five yards long, leading to stone stairs up to flats on three storeys above. At the foot of the stairs the corridor angled itself sharply past them and continued, narrower still, in darkness untouched by the feeble yellow light of the gas mantle projecting from a slender pipe on the wall above the stairfoot, to a little unpaved back yard with its ash-pits – rubbish dumps – and posts for clothes lines.

I took a few steps into the close and he

followed. At first glance it could have been any one of hundreds in the Gorbals, sights and smells so familiar that I had long ago ceased to be aware of them. Looked at carefully as we stood between the nudging walls in the dim light, this one was worse than most, the one where I lived in Warwick Street for instance, but it required an effort to remember and compare. Nearly all the stone steps in the first flight up to the half-landing were broken, with jagged edges where bits of tread had fallen away. Some had almost no tread left. Plaster had come away from the walls from ceiling to floor, and along the lower part the bared cement, originally grey, was stained yellow and smelt of urine. On a patch where the rough surface of brickwork was exposed, someone had vomited, probably a passing drunk whose sense of propriety, demanding privacy, had deterred him from being sick in the street; or a returning resident who could not wait to climb the few steps to the communal toilet on the first half-landing. The detritus had stuck to the pitted surface in a wide streaky band as it slid lumpily from chest height to the floor. Judging by the strength of its smell, a mixture of beer and fish and chips, the vomit was recent. Another powerful smell, of decaying rubbish, came mainly from the ash-pits at the far end of the corridor, but also from a deposit scattered over the floor. Despite the cold wet wind blowing in hard from the street, the cloud of mephitic vapours lingered stupefyingly about our heads.

No one could afford to throw away food leavings that had any good left in them. They used up what they could in broths and soups and pies. But a final residue, potato peelings, fish heads or meat bones from which repeated boiling had extracted all nourishment, or food that had gone off – refrigerators were for the rich – was thrown on the ash-pits, whence it was scavenged by rats and stray cats. At dead of night, sometimes even in daytime, one heard their furious scrabblings there, resulting in a scatter of rubbish all over the close, so that one picked one's way among little heaps so far gone in putrefaction as to be rejected by even these ravening beasts. Here at our feet, great holes among the broken flagstones overflowed with such rotting material, foul bits of paper, excrement, mud, broken glass.

I realised I was looking at a close, really looking, for the first time. Perhaps the sickly yellow gloom, all the light the tiny gas mantle produced, worsened the impact. A revulsion hit me like a heavy punch to the head. In the fleeting dizziness I had a nightmare vision. I stood among gigantic glistening boils that had burst and the pus spattered on me and oozed down, like the

148

vomit on the wall, in a foul stream to the floor.

How could I not have seen all this before, surrounding me as it did everywhere I went? Of course I had seen it. I had shut it out, tolerated it, accepted it as the given. We all had. Except Phil and his like. Traitors to their class!

Yes, it could be any close.

Bernard stood at my side, silently insisting on an answer. It was now his turn to blow the flame of inner crisis within me, as I had done to him. He wanted me to come away from the sidelines, stop my inner war of uncertain aims, resentments and thwarted will, and harness the wasted energy at last. And become, presumably, as committed as he?

Why should I be so disturbed? What external spark had I been awaiting? I knew only one thing for certain, Not only Bernard would shift: I would too. How, and in what direction, I had no idea.

In provoking him I had sapped at my own position too. Nothing made any sense – though what did 'sense' mean?

I told myself that my dismay and sadness and self-accusation were simply the shock of looking upon these lower depths and seeing them truly at last, that I recoiled not from these visible truths alone but from all the questions in life they stood for, and from what its recognition would demand of me. I had tried, amazingly, to forget that I myself was part of this horror.

And yet I made excuses. This was only part of life after all. You didn't look at life layer by layer, like Peer Gynt with the onion. You looked at the whole. At relationships as they were and as they could be. Yes, that was the heart of the matter. How could you make 'sense' out of fine gradations between one face of suffering and another?

I heard myself say, and wondered afterwards at how inadequate the words were: 'It could do with a bit of titivating, couldn't it, like a lot of other things?'

'A bit!' he shouted. 'My God! Are you blind! Look at the shite flowing out of that lavatory, and that broken tap up there with all the water pouring away and taking the shite down the stairs with it...' This close, like a great many others, had a shared water tap, as well as a shared lavatory, on a little half-landing at the turn of the stairs between floors. '...and the ash-pits stinking out the whole street! And the shite and the piss and the vomit and God knows what else! We're *standing* in it! And how do you like *this?* No wonder there's disease everywhere!'

He pointed down to fresh rat droppings on the flagstones.

A shout startled us. It came from the far end of the corridor at the opening to the

150

back yard, in the dark angle of wall beneath the stairs that the weak gas light could not reach:

'Aw, fuck aff an' gie us a bi' o' peace wull ye!' – a young man's voice, breathless, grumpy.

There was a rustling sound in the darkness and a girl's loud whisper: 'Wheesht, dear, wheesht!'

The man growled: 'Aw, hen, ah hadnae time tae ge' intae ye!'

The girl giggled and whispered audibly again: 'Maybe that's just as well dear! Ah teilt ye ah never minded when tha' happened!'

'Bu' ah *do!*' came the furious reply.

In her throaty whisper she said soothingly: 'Anyway, dear, ah'll ge' ma monthlies all right this way, won't ah?'

The man grunted non-committally. Her thoughts of pregnancy – calculation or fear? – were evidently of no interest to him.

'Wait now,' he muttered. 'Ah'll be ready again soon enough.'

More whisperings, now subdued.

The natural vigour in the venial sin,
Is the way in which our lives begin...

Oh Venus of the ash-pits! How many virgins have you bled here? How many seeds of life implanted?

151

A private place, in effect the only one, where lovers expected to be left undisturbed, where exploration began, love's fruit set.

Parental approval of 'walking out' seldom extended to canoodling, petting, at home. In theory, canoodling did not take place. Apart from moral prohibitions, most houses, as tenement flats were called, were full to bursting, and privacy was out of the question. A spare room was a rare luxury, possessed by a few better-off families, better off by Gorbals standards – clergymen, skilled artisans – who might live behind Renaissance facades in the tenements in Abbotsford Place on the southern edge of the Gorbals near Eglinton Toll, where Victoria Road and Pollokshaws Road took you to the lower middle class districts of Langside, Shawlands, and on to Newton Mearns.

In most of the houses we knew every foot of space was taken up by beds, mattresses on the floor, a few bare wooden chairs, a battered kitchen table. One or even two of the younger children commonly shared the parental bed, usually a mattress on planks resting on trestles in a curtained alcove in the kitchen.

To enable a coupling to take place in a semblance of privacy behind the curtain, the woman would step out in her shift, snatch a blanket off the bed and wrap the child in it and lay him on the floor boards near enough to the cooking range for him to get some radiated warmth from its banked-up fire. Afterwards she parted the curtains and came out naked to lift the unsleeping, finely aware child back into bed, to lie between her and the man lying open mouthed in post-coital sleep. And then mother and child might lie awake for a while, locked in unique perplexities. She, her body prompting her still, with no finality in her, turned her world over and over again in her mind's restless fingers. The child, possessed by wonder and nameless haunt-ings, tried to join together the heavings and creakings and groans and gasps and little cries he had heard as he lay on the floor, his mother's disturbed concentration now, his father's stillness as if felled, and the sticky warmth in which he lay between them, something more than the sweat that was there before, a substance he divined as elemental, mysterious, newly decanted, that touched his flesh and his senses with profound, unattainable meaning.

If there had been two children in the bed, the other, a toddler, also put out on the floor, might well have slept through it all. His turn for nocturnal wonderment would come.

For an unmarried girl to live away from

home on her own was unthinkable. Even if special circumstances, such as the death of parents, led to her living under someone else's roof as a lodger, she would not be allowed men visitors in her room. As for the few unmarried men who could afford to live on their own in single ends, one-room tenement flats, no respectable girl, or married woman for that matter, would want to be seen visiting one of them unchaperoned.

That corner of a close beside the ash-pits was a place outside time. Because the celebration did not take place under anyone's roof, moral responsibility could be kept at a distance if need be.

The place of that shrine of Venus in the life of the locality was understood by everyone. Fathers knew where to look for daughters out too late.

A girl impatient to escape from home might go there with her 'feller' and let him 'stamp her card' – get her with child. And then, with luck, persuade him to accept paternity and marry her: a common enough route to matrimony.

No one approved. Few openly disapproved. Fatalistically, all connived.

Residents making their way through the close to the ash-pits or the clothes lines in the back yard, sensing a couple's presence, retreated discreetly and returned later. Lovers seeking a vacant shrine wandered on to the next close, and the next. Some, driven and impatient, gave up the search and stood together in a lavatory on one of the half-landings. But that infringed the code and nearly always led to trouble. In theory each lavatory was shared by people from two floors, about six flats, but in practice by many more. Almost invariably the other lavatory in the close, or some in closes nearby, would be out of action because of blocked pipes or damaged cisterns or flush mechanisms, so there was seldom a moment during the day and well into the night when every functioning lavatory in a tenement was not in heavy demand, often with a queue stamping their feet waiting to get in. If a couple were making love in one, the anxious souls waiting on the cold stone steps made their feelings plain, firmly but usually not unkindly: 'Och come on! Go an' find yersels a place o' yer ain doon the stairs tae do yer canoodlin' in! Ah'm tellin' ye, if ah don't ge' in there in a minute ah'm gonnae shi' ma troosers!'

Most people entering a close, especially in the evening, would have half-expected that dark corner by the ash-pits to be occupied, and not lingered talking. Forgetfully, we had infringed the code, and being shouted at was only to be expected, and nothing to be disturbed about. But I had recognised the girl's voice, and a ghost had walked over

155

my grave.

I had a surreal feeling of being outside everything, the present moment cancelled, the future already joined to the past.

Annie! That voice, that whisper. Annie, Annie!

Annie was a sewing machinist in the garment factory where Bernard and I worked. That was where it had begun, nearly two years ago.

Our sewing machines were in three double banks of twelve, each of two lines of six facing one another, the whole powered by a master motor from which transmission belting ran on pass wheels slung from the ceiling, with a transfer wheel and a separate belt taking power down to each bank. Separating the facing lines of machines in a bank was a smooth wooden trough; when a machinist finished seaming up a section of garment she tossed it into the trough and pushed it towards her neighbour in the line to do the next operation. At the end of the trough a passer – inspector – quickly checked the work, and if satisfactory threw it into a bin to which the pressers came to replenish their supply of work at the long pressing table, about thirty feet long and six wide, a few paces away. All of us, on piece work, depended for the level of our wages on the speed of those in the previous work stage, as well as on our own of course. With everyone increasing the pressure on everyone else, stress was high. The sewing machinists in particular showed it, with their heads down and their hands frenziedly pushing the work under the drumming sewing heads as if to urge the power needles, moving so fast as to be blurred, to sew faster still. And all the while the throaty hum and thump of power, the slap-slap-slap of drive belts, the bang and hammer of the press irons and the hiss of steam, the clang of metal as the irons were slung through narrow slots in the cast-iron chambers behind each presser where gas jets re-heated them, filled the head to bursting, drove out all sense. The only escape was to numb the mind.

And accidents happened.

The commonest injury at the sewing machines was a needle through a fingertip. The trade joke was that you were not a proper machinist till that had happened to you. But it was far from a joke when it did. In the immediate agony the victim instinctively pulled her impaled finger away and the needle broke, leaving part of itself embedded under the nail. Blood-poisoning, and sometimes amputation, could follow.

One day Annie's hair caught in the sewing foot of her machine. Some was actually drawn down to the shuttle and sewn into the seam she was working on, and her head was pulled down and banged hard against the fast moving vertical piston of the sewing head. No great injury was done, but she sustained a nasty bruising on the forehead and some blood was shed. Her cry was heard, as might the high-pitched mew of a kitten, through the general clamour and roar. Her bank of machines was the nearest to where I stood at the pressers' table and I got to her first, seized a pair of shears and cut her hair free, and then ran and got the first aid box from the boss' office and dabbed iodine on the cuts on her forehead. She wept a little but set her lips together and tried to push me away so that she could turn back to her work. Fearfully she glanced round at the other machine hands pushing pieces of garments along the wooden trough towards her work place and then at the passer who was getting worried because of the blockage of work beginning to grow at this point. For when an accident happened, unless it was a serious one, as when Jack Nimms dropped a press iron and burnt and tore the flesh all down his leg and broke the shin bone and some bones in his foot, never to walk properly again, the pace of work did not slacken. So now the machinists to Annie's right continued to push their completed pieces along the trough to her, and the two on her left were sitting waiting for work, losing working time, and money.

Until she did *her* seaming up on these pieces, they could not do their part on them. If the hold up lasted much longer we would all be losing money. Even as I put a bandage round her forehead she reached under the sewing machine to remove the shuttle and began to clear it of shreds of her hair preparatory to re-threading.

Her voice shaky with the pain she said: 'Ye'd be'er le' me go! Thanks all the same. Ah've got tae ge' on wi' ma pieces now!'

'Can ye that?' I asked, for she was white as chalk.

'Ah'll have tae!' She gave me a quick taut smile and bent her head to re-thread the needle.

And so we drew close.

Annie had fiery red hair, greenish eyes, dimpled, laughing features, creamy skin, and a lovely, taut, sinuous figure. She did not walk so much as strut, swinging her body on flexed muscles in a way that shocked some of the older folk.

'There's that Annie Dalrymple flaunting herself! The brazen girl!'

I did not think the word brazen fitted her. With me she was innocent. She had, however, a hungry awareness, an impatience for experience, that might have been misunderstood. Or perhaps it was I who misunderstood?

She seemed to look far into me, eyes wide

159

in wonder, face aglow; and her body sweat, a hot vapour sweeping up from the depths of her, overwhelmed me like a potent drug. That first experience of mingling chemistry was like a magical discovery long imagined, and claimed at last.

We sought to know everything about one another at one breath, one glance. Miraculously that did seem to happen as we walked the pavements at night hand in hand, or stood on the Suspension Bridge over the Clyde, feeling it vibrate with passing footsteps, and watched the lights along the river bank reflected in the dark oily waters; or sat in silence in the front seat of the upper deck of a tram and let our dream worlds flow together. We played the game of telepathic sympathy, comparing what we had each thought at a certain hour when we had been apart and taking delight in finding that we had been closely in tune.

Sometimes we bought a tuppenny bag of chips to eat together as we walked, and after a time would be amazed to find that we had forgotten to eat them, and that the greasy chips were stone cold.

One day, some weeks after we had first gone out together, we wandered in silence to some long grass in the Park, and lay down and looked up at the sky, and after a while timidly turned to each other. Innocents, we learnt from each other intuitively, slowly.

After a few months we went for the first of many hiking weekends to the Socialist Camp at Carbeth, a few miles north of Glasgow.

Before we set off she whispered shyly: 'Will ye put somethin' on yersel' when – when we're taegither?'

'Aye, ah've bought some.'

Our sublime unity continued for about a year. Then one evening I waited for her as usual at the factory door. I heard her step clicking down the stone stairs, and she was close beside me, speaking fast, in an unfamiliar monotone: 'Ah'm no' goin' oot wi' ye again. Ah cannae explain. An' don't try to come after me.' She walked briskly away.

Pride prevented me following. In shock I stumbled away to the refuge of the Mitchell Library. A light had died.

That was centuries ago. And the 'I' that had become entwined with her, body and soul I had thought, was lost in the past. No, not lost, not entirely. That was what the savage resurgence of sadness and hurt now told me. Why, after being dormant so long, should these feelings hit me so hard now?

The full meaning of her presence here in the back close struck home.

I had hardly spoken to her for a year. When girls and fellows stopped going out they treated one another with a remoteness

161

we did not think of as unfriendly, rather as a decent correctness.

For a time Annie was one of the few politically conscious girls of the neighbourhood. 'Politically conscious' was a fine new jargon term, meaning that you were one of an elite who knew what was wrong with the world and would devote a few days or months to curing its ills before you sorted out your own life. They were far more impatient for *change*, far less tolerant than most of us fellows. Any action would do, so long as it upset the conventions that restrained them.

Apart from the common discontents, they were fired by resentments special to them, puzzling to the rest of us; long battened down beneath a pretence of conformity, now coming into the open. Unread as most of them were, they had somehow picked up the mutterings of the female soul, like unheard voices in the air, part of the *Zeitgeist*.

They seldom attempted to express these feelings, perhaps could not; understood later, they are obvious enough. Women, in so many ways treated as less eligible both privately and publicly – paid lower wages than men, for instance – were owed a heavy debt by society for past and present injustice, and the time had come to set the account to rights. And so they strove to tear themselves away from their roots, reach out for freedoms only dimly perceived. Many were drawn to the party, beguiled by its pretence that all the unfairness in thought and deed was the fault of the System and only awaited the Revolution to be put right.

Meanwhile they snatched at ways of acting unconventionally, sympathetic magic to conjure that indistinct identity they hungered for, 'turn the wheel on which you turn.'

Innocently they transmitted their confusion to the fellows they went with, who, blindly following the masculine convention that girls should be treated as 'good for only one thing', at first refused to believe in their unfeminine rejection of submissiveness and dismissed them as prickteasers. Or, pretending to meet the girl on her own terms but unwilling – or unable – to resonate with her questing spirit, retreated in ill-tempered perplexity.

For each of these girls a time of private reckoning would come. Rebellious behaviour had failed to move their world. Time was passing. Resignedly they resorted to precisely that 'only one thing', a valuation of themselves previously dismissed as soulless, the base metal and not the gold. They too, in their turn, would assume the conventional strategy for fitting themselves into the world as it was.

The New Woman dream was not abandoned: it had to be put aside as a luxury.

In going composedly to the shrine at the ash-pits to get their card stamped, they were content – or so they pretended – to confirm the masculine prejudices.

And soon the exultantly physical girl ripened into the burdened mater-familias, reddened arms folded beneath sagging bosom, worriedly gossiping on stair landing or in close mouth, or trudging along the street with an infant cocooned in a shawl and another on the way, withdrawn in a frowsty female freemasonry, tired drudges of the Steamy.

Whether a girl was the conventional sort, or rebellious and politically conscious, if she was well into her twenties and still unmarried, time became the whipper-in. She must move fast if she was not to drift away into isolation, lose links hitherto dismissed as old-fashioned and valueless, now seen to have worth, retain the warmth of a shared outlook with mothers and grandmothers, and friends already settled.

And now, shockingly, Annie too was following the same ritual.

Annie was about nineteen now, surely too young to be driven by that fear. How could I know what other conflicts drove her now? Regret about *us?* Hardly. She had never once given me the slightest sign of that. If only she had! Or simply impatience to be free of home? That and something else perhaps, much worse, a shift of the spirit altogether. The ripening seed in the belly freed a girl simply by leaving her no time to remake the world – to remake anything, herself least of all.

In a delayed reaction, it struck me that I knew the man's voice too. Phil Emet. And that, to my surprise when I later thought about it, did not immediately make me jealous, or any more unhappy for *myself* but rather for her. It explained her behaviour in a completely different way – money and status, a seemingly clear escape from all this.

On the face of it, Phil was a sensible choice for an ambitious girl. He was marked out to make money. He would reach the Shangri-la of Newton -Mearns.

But if she thought he would take her with him she was vastly mistaken.

If she followed the usual pattern, once she knew her card was stamped, she would noise it about that he was the father of the child she carried. And he, if he behaved with conventional masculine arrogance, would already have abetted her plan by boasting of the conquest.

The form modern, the sense ancient.

I entered the sacred wood;
I made her heave in joy!

165

I thought of the ritualistic scene enacted many a time in our shower room group.

The girl's name would be mentioned by one of the group with pretended casualness. Of course they all knew! They were feeding lines to the proud conqueror: 'Aw, man!' he would respond, voice guttural and compressed, right fist clenched as the forearm rose up perpendicular under the impact of the left fist in the crook of the right elbow. 'Aw that was a marvellous lumber!' Dreamily, eyes half-closed, a soft smile on the lips, his voice stretched out the remembered ecstasy and the triumph: 'An' ag-ain and ag-ain and ag-ain!'

'An' ye're no' carin' if ye've stamped her caird or no'?'

'Widdy ah care? Them hairies know whit tae do don't they?'

Perhaps a shadow of a care did flit across the face. And then a shrug, as if to say: 'Well, if ye're goin' tae be caught – ye're caught! It's got tae happen sooner or later?'

Social pressure, tradition, tribal force of habit, or more respectably convention, usually fulfilled the girl's plan.

This must be a recent conquest for Phil, or we would have heard of it. Who was going out with whom was quickly known. But Phil would not be caught that way. He would defy the tribe and turn his back on a stamped card. He would follow his own star no matter who he left by the wayside. That was Phil.

Who could tell Annie this with any hope of her believing it?

Filled with these thoughts, lacerated by bitterness at what she was doing a few yards away, I retreated to the close mouth. Bernard joined me and we stood there in silence. I stamped my feet to get the circulation going again, and wriggled frozen toes in the soaked cardboard padding in my boots. The pain of numbed feet returning to life brought me sharply back.

To my surprise I saw intense disapproval on Bernard's face. The shrine at the ash-pits was as familiar an institution to him as it was to all of us. But then, I recalled, the thought of it always had disturbed him much more than any other feature of Gorbals life, an odd puritanism when one thought of the party's inclusion of free love in its revolutionary ethic. In practice, however, its support for sexual freedom, and other personal emancipations like that of women from the kitchen stove, were minor themes, stated conditionally, with care, so as not to upset too many sensibilities. Privately, the party mandarins were strait-laced. They explained away this inconsistency by arguing that promiscuity's consequences – unwanted pregnancies, illegitimacies, forced and sordid marriages, venereal disease – like other over-indulgences such as drunkenness, only more so, deflected comrades' energies from the basics. Apostles must not waste their energies in wild living. Remaining pure they were better fighters for the cause.

He looked up at the sky. The rain had stopped. A watery moon, waning, appeared fitfully between banks of black cloud, gale-driven across a steel grey sky. A bleak night on which to look for renewal of hope, or faith. Reverting to the Spanish War he sighed:

'It's part of a bigger war – a war to destroy the System. The symptoms of its evils are all around us.'

He gestured behind us, in a manner that succeeded in including not only the squalor of the close but the now silent lovers: 'What a place to start your life together, the stinking ash-pits! Isn't that enough to poison life for evermore? So this war in Spain is vital whichever way you look at it. We had to start somewhere.'

'Tell me,' I said, 'what's Russia doing to help in this holy war?'

He frowned. 'They've sent a few military experts and technical advisers and so on, and some food and arms.' He shook his head. 'They're fully stretched building up on the Revolution. We can't expect them to do any more, like sending troops, to weaken themselves to the extent that the imperialists can go in and destroy the revolution! After all, their revolution is really *ours*, and we must help them to keep it strong.'

He turned to face me. His shoulders drooped, an exhausted runner. Quietly he said: 'Let's leave all this for now?'

Let me be! I must keep going the way I am or I'm lost.

In all the years we had been friends I had never seen him so unhappy. And I was unhappy for his sake now.

A thought struck me that I knew was important but understood fully only much later. Being unhappy for other people's sakes was a way of holding the world at arm's length. Bernard had been doing that too. How much longer could he continue? Should I hope, for his sake, that he could do so forever? That would be cruel. Self-denial dried up the soul.

I saw too that being sorry for others was a kind of condescension, in the end self-wounding. Some time, somehow, I would find a way of striking a blow for myself.

In silence we stepped out of the close and went on to the Workers' Circle.

8

A TASTE OF FREEDOM

'Annie Dalrymple came here, 21st June 1936.'

Incised on a block of ironstone in the remnant of Roman wall, her proclamation, in the stealthy dawn of a summer day long ago, her dawn, and mine. Through the long slow measures of the constellations, forgotten but preserved, waiting in the shadows to be rediscovered, as Destiny had preserved that flint axe-head in the earth, debris of a skirmish at a Roman outpost, for her to snatch it up, as from the banks of Phlegethon, and set her exultation in stone.

Moment of light and fusion.

Beginning and end of youth.

I think, as she did so, as in a warning intuition I foresaw that I would return and find it again, long after she herself had become a ghost. I saw that future day in something very like its eventual detail. Both visions have their place here.

What Destiny ordained, wandering near that place probing for the past, that I turn a corner in a street of peeling bungalows and discover these words, her shout of joy and triumph, poignant as a distant cry at evening, fixed here in shadow as it had waited deep in memory, in this forgotten patch of rank undergrowth, all that remained of the wilderness of stunted oak and wild blackberries and acrid bracken that we had ranged in freedom, Carbeth Muir?

Her memorial to herself. Skull beneath the skin.

Her moment had outlived her. So it would continue through time and chance, as had the embrasure in the wall long before.

Carbeth Muir, a great stretch of moorland north of Glasgow that had separated the city from a region of arable and dairy farmland beyond Milngavie, now lay buried beneath a scabby dormitory sprawl in decline, suburban twilight.

On the far edge of the Muir had been the Socialist Camp. Tuppence ha'penny on the tram to the terminus at Milngavie, and then a tramp across the hummocky wasteland on a Friday night after work – if we were not wanted in the factory on the Saturday – tired but drunk with freedom. Dreams could soar. With every step we were renewed. The track across it led *out* in every sense.

On it you met habitués of the Socialist Camp, or hikers aiming further afield, sometimes singly, meditatively whistling or playing a mouth organ while striding along, or in little voluble groups whose voices came to you long before as a murmur on the wind. Or you came upon them in the shelter of an embrasure in an old wall or beside a massive oak felled by lightning, having a 'drum-up' – a halt to fill a gap with tea and bread and jam, and perhaps a fry-up of bacon and bread – at a fire of fallen branches. You saw the red glow as a spark in the far darkness well in advance of the scent of wood smoke wafting to you. You could count on a welcome at a fire, even from strangers. Hikers were still few, the enlightened who were joined in a mystic affinity. There would be a shout from the little group seated on boulders round it:

'Come on an' have a drum-up.'

You stopped and unshouldered your pack and dumped it on the ground and unhooked your enamelled tin mug from one of its buckles. A space was made for you, and someone with spare tea in a billy can would pour you some, to refresh you while you brewed up your own, to be shared in its turn, and you moved into the flow of talk as if you had been there all the time.

Talk was of politics, of jobs and apprenticeships and what to do next with one's life, of sex and conquest, except when there were girls in the party, when there

172

would be a strong admixture of gossip and mild sexual banter. There would be talk of the outdoors and its freedoms and what it did for you, 'the road', of good places to sleep out and drum up – urban dwellers picking up scraps of intelligence about the country, learning from each other as guerrillas learn how to survive in alien territory; except that with us the mystic affinity made us protective towards it. An enlightened self-interest, a shared ceremony of thanksgiving for what we breathed and dreamed on the road, for the expansion of the soul we found there.

And then the people who had called out to you to join them might stretch and look up at the sky. Thoughts of the waning hours, the moments of freedom drifting by. Time to stow food and plates in packs, hang mugs on buckles, stand up and shrug the shoulders snugly into the broad webbing straps. Time to move on. Turning away to rejoin the track, they called out the customary parting:

'See you on the road then!'

A benediction.

And you gave an equal reply: 'Aye. See you on the road!'

Staying and tending the fire while you finished your own drum-up, you might hear other footfalls approach, and you in turn would hail a pack-laden figure or little group to join you at the fire. When they did, the flow of talk continued as if there had been no interruption. And then, moving on yourself, you handed over the fire to their care. If no one else came along by the time you wanted to move, you would follow the rule of the mystic affinity. You stamped out the fire and piled stones over the embers, after burning combustible left-overs, and buried empty cans or bottles.

Encountering someone at a crossing of paths on the Muir, you might be told: 'There's a fire about a mile back there.'

So pilgrims long ago, meeting in the wilderness, passed on news of comfort to be found along the ways they had come.

Sometimes, when hailed by people sitting at a fire, you might not be in the mood to join a group, or in a hurry to catch up with someone further along the track. You shouted back: 'Och, no' the noo, thanks. See yese on the road!'

'Aye, see ye on the road then,' came the answering murmur, and they turned again to the comfort of the flames and the talk.

Most of us carried old army webbing packs, some brought back home by survivors of the trenches and handed down within families, but mostly bought for a shilling at the government surplus stores. Some of the 'surplus' packs had never been used, to judge from the stiffness of the heavy cotton, nearly as thick as the belting that powered the sewing machines in the factory. Others showed signs of many treatments of army blanco. Here and there a dark stain would send a shiver down the spine. Thoughts of shot and shell, of blood.

These square packs were just big enough to hold a spare shirt – often army surplus khaki – and pants and socks, towel and soap, a loaf of bread, a few small tins of baked beans, slices of sausage loaf wrapped in greased paper, tin plate, knife and fork and spoon, old tobacco tins for tea and sugar, salt and pepper in little twists of paper. The pack fitted so closely on the back that, even with this light load, after half-an-hour of walking your jacket and shirt and vest were soaked in sweat; and sometimes the skin got painfully blistered. We looked with envy at the superior equipment of some of the people we met, from the better-off parts of Glasgow like Kelvinside or Hillhead, near the University – the Bergen rucksack for example, one of the first with a frame to keep an air space between your back and the pack, preventing painful friction and the accumulation of sweat; and breeches and long stockings or puttees, and boots with tricouni nails round the edges of the soles. Our boots were the single pair we possessed, perhaps with an extra sole hammered on at home. To buy special hiking clothes was totally beyond us.

The Socialist Camp, high on a stony hillside, was approached by an old farm track that meandered a mile or so up from the road that went north to Drymen and the Trossachs. Large ridge tents, pitched to form a square, stood on wooden platforms, some with two or three broad plank steps at the entrance to offset the slope. It was a place of traditional socialist earnestness and uplift. The grassy space within the square was used for community singing in the evenings round a log fire, and lectures and Socialist Sunday School meetings.

As you turned off the road, and just before you began the stiff pull up a cart track lined with blackberry bushes leading to the Camp, you passed an old single-decker bus body standing alone beneath the spreading branches of a venerable oak. Crammed with shelving, fitted with a sliding window in its side like that in a railway booking office, with a corrugated iron canopy over it to shelter customers in rainy weather, it had been ingeniously converted into a rural general store. In a tiny compartment at one end of it were sleeping quarters; and a lean-to at the back, made from old doors and tarred felt, contained a primitive kitchen and chemical toilet. Here, running a business with many mysterious ramifications, Jimmy Robinson dreamed and preached.

176

It was hard to tell his age, for his tall and lean figure looked strong and he moved lightly and with vigour, but the close cropped hair was silvery, the leathery face deeply lined. He could have been in his late fifties or older. He went about in a frayed khaki shirt, perhaps the same one, and old khaki trousers with flat brass buttons on the waistband, anchorages for elasticated red and white striped braces, heavily stained.

He studied you from between narrowed lids, seeming to stare through you to some distant horizon and place you in context with it: the hard, measuring gaze of the wanderer. We envied what we saw in him, the free spirit *par excellence*, new in our experience, who had been to the far places of the world and brought back a cargo of wisdom. It had come, he proclaimed, from privation, from wounds inflicted by the harsh edges of the world, the forces of nature and of man, in coal mines and timber camps, in the ruthless tempo of New World factories, the Dantesque realities of the Chicago stock yards. We did not pause to think that the people around us in the Gorbals had suffered as much, if differently, and if that were the sole test were as fitted as he to pass on to us the lessons of living. The magic of far places, the sound and scent of battles under strange banners, gave him a stronger claim. We sat at his feet.

Those summer nights at his door were not really endless and totally wonderful but they seemed to be. Dark outlines of hedgerows and trees, and tall bracken dimly seen and merging. Prussian blue velvet sky spangled with silver. Whispers of the earth. Life itself whispering, nudging us. Wonders waiting in the wings.

We drank strong tea from mugs dipped into the blackened skilly can never absent from a brazier made out of a holed oil drum, that stood under a sheet of corrugated iron he had rigged as a canopy under an over-hanging branch at his back door; in its shelter we sat round him on empty packing cases or logs stood on end. We listened to his memories of bumming across America, of working with the Wobblies, the International Workers of the World, and groups of anarcho-syndicalists – 'the Movement' of O'Neill's *The Iceman Cometh* – who would destroy the System with bomb and gun and bring purity to the world. Preachers of beneficial death, curative killing; early urban guerrillas.

Shades of Sacco and Vanzetti. Fighters under the black flag. Honoured martyrs. Purity of vision excuses any act. They must not have died in vain.

It was never clear whether he had been an active member of the Movement or a fellow-traveller, literally and metaphorically, experimenting with its underground life while riding the rails across America and sleeping in the 'jungles', shanty camps to be found at railroad junctions on the way. If he had been a member, he was certainly among the more successful of those it left behind as the dream of world dominion by a brotherhood of the horny-handed sons of toil faded away, as the Movement was broken by bloody industrial battles, internal feuding, betrayals, armed clashes with the law.

Hunted down in America, disillusioned remnants scattered far and wide to nurse their dreams and wait for their day; and hand on, as he did, the torch of faith and hope.

Some survived less well than others. Like Larry Slade and Hugo Kalman in *The Iceman Cometh*, they chose to sink to the bottom of society rather than compromise with the System. Or perhaps they did not know how to compromise and remain pure? Jimmy, perhaps harder or shrewder, more worldly and detached than he presented himself to be, plainly did know. At Carbeth he lived in gypsy style, but there were hints of a large house in Edinburgh and unspecified business deals that took him away for a few days now and then. During such absences someone from the Camp would look after the little shop for him.

There was always someone there to do the odd job. It sheltered what amounted to a little colony of drop-outs, a sturdy *maquis* living in the shadowy purlieus of the System or, as Jimmy grandly put it, 'a brotherhood at the bottom of the heap'. In those doldrums of unemployment, especially during the long summer emptiness, to stay at the Camp was as good a method of pushing time away as hanging round street corners or at the Broo. If you were resourceful, you could exist there without any money in your pocket at all, You did simple maintenance jobs at the Camp, or some fetching and carrying for Jimmy, in return for basic rations, the odd can of beans, loaf, portion of sausage meat, a few eggs, some milk. At night you might go out and lift some potatoes or other produce in the surrounding farmland. Taking food 'within reason' wasn't really stealing! In this manner a few hardy fellows even survived at the Camp the whole of the winter.

Sometimes they tried to lord it over us wage slaves. They were beating the System, they arrogantly affirmed; doing that you raised yourself above it. They were not beating the System, and I sometimes wondered whether the assertion was no more than a comforting pretence. Jimmy, a merchant, apart from his other enterprises, was part of it, indeed exemplified it, and doing jobs for him was to stay within it too. And as for 'lifting' produce from the fields, they did not like to be reminded that someone had worked hard to plant and cultivate it, 'So much the worse for them,' they would retort, 'for working to maintain the System!' In a small way they were predators, speciously justified according to their lights but predators none the less. Indeed, I argued, at one remove they preyed on *us*. But that was too strong medicine for them.

All the same there was something attractive in their seeming independence, a romantic, picaresque quality.

'But what happens,' I asked one of them, 'if things get really hard, and you can't make ends meet out here?'

He was amazed at the naive question. 'Ah jist thumb a lift back tae Rose Street an' move in wi' the family again!'

I felt like saying: 'So your family, the wage slaves, bail you out? So that's what your high talk about independence and not compromising with the System amounts to?' But what was the point?

Wage slave or no, the job at the factory was a life-line, a thin one, but I was lucky to have it at all.

Sometimes we arranged with the boss to work late on a Friday instead of going in on the Saturday; that meant we could leave for

Carbeth straight from the factory that night, giving us two clear days of escape. But it could mean that it was midnight or even later when we made our way across the Muir. No matter how late, even in the small hours, from far off we saw the yellow glimmer of Jimmy's oil lamp. We kept it in view, dipping and rising and veering as we followed the windings and undulations of the familiar track. Up on the hill the Camp was asleep. All around us to the invisible horizon no farmhouse showed a light. His never dimmed. Whatever the hour we could knock on his window if we needed a can of condensed milk, a pan loaf, a small tin of beans. Out he would come in trousers and the torn khaki shirt:

'Come on and join me! Take the weight off yer feet. I'll blow up the fire. There's tea in the skilly. Help yourselves.'

When was there not tea in the skilly?

Those arrivals in the night were uniquely wonderful, filled with a sense of home-coming, to a place where your lungs lustily drew in new air that was your very own. And the darkness emphasised the sense of personal mystery. On our way across the brooding wilderness we trod the earth in a kind of dedication, celebrants straining towards a secret shrine of the spirit. Hearts newly freed from the hammering of the factory, we felt wrapped round and comforted by the silence, the touch of air that carried freedom on light wings, caressed by the scents and little sounds of the sleeping land, rush and ripple of burns and flowing ditches, sudden flap of a disturbed bird, distant hoot of barn owl, rustle of a small animal in the bushes.

He seemed to need company then more than in the day. I pictured him sitting up into the night fiercely wishing to hear the sound of plodding footsteps, the rattle of billy-cans in rucksacks.

Not only talk but disciples. The individualist creed must spread, the doors of freedom must be opened, violence the only key. A latter-day Bakunin. How certain he was that he would see the awakening of the world's workers, and the mass slaughter of the privileged! Yes, *mass* slaughter. *They* did not deserve the luxury of the private tumbril! The Great Day of the barricades. This time the Communards would be vindicated. Their spirit would triumph the world over.

'The Great Day will come! Oh yes it'll come all right, when we storm the armouries and arm the people and mount the machine guns opposite the Stock Exchanges and the banks and mow down the exploiters, every man jack of them. Then we'll be free of them for good an' all.'

After such a pronouncement he would

183

lean back on a bedraggled car seat wedged against the back door of the old coach and regard us proudly, a warlord after a harangue to the faithful, but also quizzically, testing us. Perhaps, through us, he searched for weaknesses in the testimony? The yellow rays of a storm lantern that hung from a hook over the door above his head illuminated a narrow patch of beaten earth where the brazier stood, and touched a branch and a nearby bush; and the downward rays picked out his lined features in a bronze radiance, an oracular chiaroscuro. He lifted to his lips a carved meerschaum pipe with a thick silver ring round the flared bowl, and a silver strap about the stem inset with little glittering stones. Catching my interested glance one night, as the stones flashed in the light, he said:

'Sure, diamonds me lad! It came out of a raid by some o' the Movement boys, out near Houston I remember. To get money for ammunition and explosives, an' – yes, an' livin' expenses. This thing was too identifiable. Nobody wanted to risk tryin' to sell it! I "found" it, ye might say!' He showed blackened teeth in a hard grin. 'Stashed it away till I got back here. We called the raids "reappropriations", like Lenin called the bank raid at Tiflis and other places. What we take from the boss class is simply takin' back

184

what they stole from us, see?'

Stories of riding the rails across America, of meeting Robert Service and Daniel de Leon. America the golden land, the melting pot, where the System was at its most savage. And perhaps, being new, at its most vulnerable. Days of turmoil and hope, of blows struck and groups scattering, to lie low and come together again and plan the next blow, or the next reappropriation. The present was only a hiatus. The Movement bided its time, its spirit nourished so long as here and there in the wilderness disciples tended the flame – of righteousness, liberty, and nemesis for the exploiters.

Innocents, we were uplifted by this gospel of the victory of benevolence. Probably none of us took his talk of the need for bloodshed seriously. It was an abstraction, rhetorical emphasis.

Bernard would not have taken it seriously either, but for different reasons, had he ever come with us, but he never did; for him the Camp itself was not serious. It was for 'milk and water socialists', for drifters and dreamers, for ineffectual drop-outs.

But for Jimmy the drop-out – the 'bum', as he called him – was the virtuous standard-bearer, the independent spirit fearlessly following a glorious star. Plainly he saw himself as one, sidestepping the fact that he had become a prosperous entrepreneur.

That incongruity certainly occurred to us, but in youthful excitement at touching new ideas we did not linger on it; or perhaps we shrank from being tactless enough to question him about it.

As we sat round his brazier in the dark hours, mugs of tea in hand, we sang softly with him:

'Hallelujah I'm a bum!
Hallelujah bum again!
Hallelujah give us a handout,
To revive us again...'

Fellowship of the night; a time for innocents.

The track across the Muir passed a stretch of old Roman wall, said to be Agricola's – to the casual glance simply a hummock covered with scrub, bracken, thicket of bramble and hedgerow flowers. At one point, where a shallow declivity had been bridged by deeper courses of massive stone, hidden by stunted oak, was an embrasure roofed by slabs of granite, originally perhaps part of a storage chamber in the fortifications. Presumably it had been uncovered, many years before, in an archaeological dig that had run out of funding. In it on fine summer nights, if we were more than usually late on the road, probably having done sixteen hours that day in the factory, and felt too tired to go the remaining three miles or so to the Camp, we often slept.

Visions of those times reappeared, hovered, heavy with regrets unappeased, as I walked again over that ground, or where it had been, many years later, a whole world away. Now there was nothing recognisable. Where were the vistas of rolling moorland freely mingling in yellow and brown and green, trees leaning under the west wind, ranks of bracken standing stiffly, and the golden scented broom waving, long neglected dry stone walls dipping and winding, a wild-running demesne owing discipline to no one? All erased. Choked now beneath a labyrinth of villas, semi-detached houses, military lines of council houses, one-storey shopping parades, the standard arrays of off-licence, newsagent-cum-sweet shop, self-service grocer, dry cleaner, launderette, garage. In the withdrawn mood induced by pacing between endlessly similar suburban walls, from whose peeling stucco and marl and brick the hard sunlight struck back and pounded the mind, I turned a corner and stopped abruptly in a cul-de-sac that ended in a high bank of sun glazed foliage and brilliant wild flowers.

I knew.

Compelled as in a dream I parted a clump of giant sunflowers. Deep in the green shadows, sun-dappled, I saw the venerable greys and browns and slatey greens of sleeping stonework. Behind splintered fencing and bits of old cars was the Roman storage chamber, our cave. I had stepped into the past. On one of the blocks marks were visible. Elbowing further through the rank greenery, I picked out the incised words, tracing each mark upwards and downwards as my lips formed them. And once again, as in my mind's eye I had done so many times over the years, I saw her knuckles tighten as she gripped the sharp flint she had picked up, her tumbled fiery hair falling over her face and sweeping the paleness of a slender pointed shoulder, and with parted lips entered her name and her moment in this record of history and slow time.

For her a beginning, and an end.

'Annie Dalrymple came here, 21st June 1936.'

I stared at the word 'came'. Discovery and self-discovery! Had she ever returned? Stood before that block of stone, and reflected, as I did now, on our broken history?

9

A LETTER FROM OXFORD

For many months after I had overheard Annie and Phil at the ashpits at the back of that close, at unguarded moments of the day and night, her loud whisper echoed in my mind: 'Ah telit ye ah never minded when tha' happened!'

The combination of intimacy and calculation in her voice burnt like acid. This was not the Annie I had known. For her sake, for both our sakes, I mourned a many-stranded tragedy. The road she had chosen spoke out loudly, like a Greek chorus lamenting the future – mine, hers, the destinies of all of us.

Especially poignant was her implied verdict on me and on my worldly prospects. She had chosen Newton Mearns – not Phil, but the prizes his road would bring her. An old, old pattern. Her forecast for me was probably right. I was not the stuff that captains of industry were made of, even if I had had Phil's advantage of a family business to start from. But where now were the principles we had once shared – as I had thought – when we swore to each other that we were important for what we were and not for what we possessed? Now it was Newton Mearns and to hell with what you were as a person.

Had my faith been so hopelessly astray? Or was it simply that for her, at last, the pull of the world, the corruption Bernard inveighed against, was too strong?

One day these thoughts were driven totally from my mind. A letter arrived that I had not expected, or rather that I had told myself not to expect. It was from Oxford:

I am pleased to inform you that you have been appointed to a Special Category Open Scholarship on your performance in this year's Essay Competition. Please inform me as soon as possible whether you are willing to accept the appointment. If you are, would you also confirm that you will take up residence in College on the first day of Michaelmas Term next?

That morning I had left home for the factory at five, long before the post came. I found the letter when I got home about seven in the evening. While I read it I bolted my tea as usual. Then I read it again, a message from a distant planet, with its strange, sonorous, processional language. 'Willing to come into residence...' you didn't go and stay, you went into *residence!*

I tried to think clearly. What could I possibly have to do with Oxford, or Oxford with me? I had to stand away from the idea to see it at all. Could it be a hoax? Me, of all people? Oxford! Oh, yes, I *had* written that essay. I *had* sent it off, an arrow shot at a venture; best forgotten.

But the Fates had decreed that I would never forget that essay, or rather its theme, which must have touched profound sensibilities within me; in diverse disguises it would be a *leitmotiv*, especially in my writing, in all the years to come: 'Has Science Increased Human Happiness?' In the essay my answer was 'no', as it would continue to be.

I felt breathless; there seemed precious little air in this kitchen of ours, steamy and yet cold too, smelling of stale fat, decay, damp.

I shoved the letter into my pocket, snatched towel and swimming briefs, and hurried out to the Baths. In the street I threaded automatically through the evening bustle, seeing no one. Thoughts whirled and rocketed about, would not be controlled; it was like being drunk for the first time. The world was upside down. How do you start thinking about a bombshell like this, that breaks through everything you're used to, asks you to decide something you've no precedents for? A stupid question hammered away in my mind: 'Do I dare tell anyone?' It would be a long time to keep it to myself. What they called Michaelmas was nearly a year away.

I turned out of Bedford Street and went along Gorbals Street, and as I came near the Baths entrance I was remotely aware that Annie was standing there, apparently studying the notice beside the arched doorway that gave the times of opening of the various departments and prices of admission. In my indrawn and bewildered state I idly noted her presence, nothing more, felt no special response. As I came near, she turned and seemed to notice me with surprise. Suddenly she stood in my path.

I suppose my mind was too full to wonder about this coincidence. Later I did, and reminded myself that most people who knew our group could easily discover that we now met at the Baths on three nights a week, on Monday, Wednesday and Friday. This was Wednesday.

At the factory I had seen her only from a distance. I may have noticed her more often of late. Yes, I must have done. I had caught myself looking at her, bent over the drumming sewing head of her machine, hands and arms in feverish motion as she steered the edges of cloth or lining material under the whirring needle, hair curtaining pale cheek, half-shielding her eyes. Pools of green fire I had known so well. Memory unnerved me again and again, till I reminded myself how it had ended, abruptly, like a light switched off, which was how it felt; but with lingering pain, made worse by the sense that on her part it had been a decision coolly reached.

In the last few days I had sometimes caught her glancing in my direction in a puzzling, equivocal manner, but it had not occurred to me that she might be trying to catch my eye. There was no reason why she should. So I had let the glance slide past me. We had not spoken.

Now, coming near, she greeted me with her old welcoming smile:

'Wha' a coincidence! Ah was just thinkin' aboo' ye! Whit d'ye think o' that?' Turning her face half away and tossing her head, looking at me from the corners of her eyes, she added: 'All that long time ago? Remember?'

She came close, and her green eyes gazed luminously into mine.

The letter in my pocket held my thoughts. Her words barely registered. I heard myself reply woodenly:

'Aye, Annie, a long time ago!'

'Too long!' She went rushing on, 'Far too long! Aye, ah've been thinkin' a lot aboo' us – and that time, ye know?'

'What d'ye mean?' I asked dumbly.

She turned to stand at my side, put her arm through mine, and to my surprise pressed close. A cloud of scent enveloped me. That was new. She never wore scent when we went about together. Beneath it, surging through to me compellingly, came her familiar sweat, touching my senses and my mind with the soft magic of her flesh, so sweet in memory, which I would conjure up as long as I lived whenever that fiery spirit of hers called to me across the years.

She spoke in my ear to compete with the rattle and bustle of the street, the voice hot and urgent: 'Ah've go' so much tae say tae ye! Oh please listen tae me! Ah've been meanin' tae talk tae ye like this for long enough! Oh ah'm sorry, real sorry for wha' ah did! Ah'm beggin' ye tae forgive me. Ah must have been mad tae leave ye! Ah've loved ye a' the time, an' ah didnae know it till – till – well ah know it now right enough! Ah really mean it, dear. Come wi' me! Come up tae oor hoose. They've a' gone tae ma Granny's. We'll have the place tae oorsels an' we can talk? Ah want tae make i' up tae ye. Ah *know* we'll be happy taegither. We'll be happy for ever. Happier than we ever were. Ah promise. Ah really and truly promise. Oh come wi' me now?'

The heat of her body as her loins pressed upon me as if she would enwrap me in her flesh, those secret fumes pulsing up into my head, were near to sweeping away all sense.

Then some perversity interposed itself. That personal vapour of her, once irresistible, awoke the past and revived the hurt of rejection. The letter in my pocket reasserted its hold on my mind, and everything here became distant. Close to me as she now stood, I saw her on the far side of a barrier, and I had no room in my mind for what lay beyond it. I wanted desperately to think about what that letter would do to me. Nothing else.

Only part of me stood here on the cold pavement in the Gorbals that was the only world I knew, suddenly aware that my time here was being foreclosed. The rest of me stood apart and read the letter again and again, incredulously seeing myself in a perspective that stretched away to a wider world I knew only from hearsay, that I had never seriously thought I could enter, apart from the freakish impulse that had made me shoot that arrow into the blue months ago, and had now brought me the letter. That world was the preserve of people not of my kind, who I must meet on their ground, not mine. Far, far away. Another life. Distant trumpets! Stuff of new dreams, new fears.

Now that that unattainable mirage had become beckoning destiny, I had the dizzying feeling that time itself had accelerated and was whirling me away from everything I had known here, too fast for me to think about. Too fast for me to hold in check. And then the next moment it seemed that it was this world of the Gorbals that was being pulled away from *me*, as the quay recedes from one who stands at the rail of the departing ship.

In this state of separateness the fever and feeling and urgency in her words were like the sound, overheard from a distance, of someone knocking on the door of an empty house, a summons addressed to someone else, no concern of mine. Above all I did not *want* it to be my concern. Even though her flesh sang to me, dizzied me, I had no room in my mind to rehearse the past. An urgent voice told me that I must move away from her. I searched for the right words.

A few minutes ago I had resolved to keep quiet about the scholarship in the coming weeks and months, the instinctive impulse to avoid ill humoured murmuring: 'He's giving himself airs isn't he?' No doubt my uncertainty nudged me too. What if I simply couldn't take up the scholarship in the end? Best not to talk about it till I was good and sure.

But I was flustered and off guard. I blurted it out: 'It's too late, anyway. I'm going away from here. I've won a scholarship to Oxford.'

She entwined herself tighter still, searched my face with the intentness of unbelief – and fear.

'Too late?' Colour faded from her face. She mouthed the words again as if the meaning would change if she did so. 'Too late did ye say! Oh don't say that! Please, dear, it cannae be too late. Oh it mustn't be! Ah'll do anything tae make things good for ye! Anything. I promise. Please!'

Amidst the turmoil in my mind the command to move away from her became insistent: 'Leave this alone! Get away from it! It's dangerous!'

Gently I loosened her arms from about me. 'I'm going away. My time here's over. Something very important's just happened to me.'

I was tempted to be less definite, temporise. But that would be cruel, weak – and false. The truth was that I distrusted my feelings. Yet that inner voice told me to say an unequivocal 'No'. What my doubts were I did not know. But I knew in my bones that I must draw away from her. I said weakly, repeating myself:

'Something very important's just happened tae me. Let me go now. We'll speak together again. Yes, afterwards, in a little while.'

She would not let go.

'Aw come wi' me now! This minute! If we

197

don't it might be...' She turned her head away. Then, correcting her course, she faced me again, brows puckered in supplication: 'Please. Ah can't bear it!'

'Not now. Not now!' I clung to the words as to a lifeline. Then added desperately: 'Listen. If it's waited two years it can wait a bit longer. The most important thing that's ever happened to me, maybe that ever will happen to me, has just happened. And I've got to look at my life all over again. Let go now.'

The terror in her eyes puzzled me, but I dared not pause to speculate about it. Stupidly searching for something considerate to say I muddled on: 'You mustn't think I don't – I mean...' How to finish the thought was beyond me. Lamely I said: 'We can wait. We – I mean – I *must* wait and – and see what happens to me.'

What on earth was I saying? What did I mean: '...see what happens to me.'?

'Oh but ah cannae wait–' She bit off her words, hung her head, began to sob. She no longer pressed herself against me. She leaned for support. Tears streamed down her blotched cheeks and soaked into the lapel of my coat.

No one took special notice of the sad tableau we must have presented there on the edge of a circle of yellow gas light from a street lamp. Women came past from the

Steamy bent low under their loads. Men returning from work trudged heavily by, huddled into old army greatcoats or other cast-offs, dirt-encrusted boots thudding on the pavement flagstones, lunch cans dangling at the wrist. Others, coming out for the evening having rested and eaten, strode past aiming for one of the dozen or so pubs near the Cross. A woman weeping on a man's shoulder was a common enough sight, the causes common too – drink, debts, infidelity, children's delinquency, general despair, the wear and tear of living. Best not to show interest. There might be a fight, families and allies taking sides. That was how neighbourhood battles started.

She raised her head, seeing defeat but not quite accepting it. In a low voice, throaty and broken, she said: 'Ye might be askin' me tae wait too long. The way ah feel now ah cannae wait at a'!'

I put my hand in my pocket to touch the letter again. For one mad moment I wanted to give it to her to read. I felt I ought to prove that I was not being carelessly unfeeling. My life *had* changed.

No, that would not do. It would draw her into my affairs at a moment when I was pushing her away. And then it struck me that the letter was irrelevant. Why? I had no idea. But I was sure it was.

Her voice broke into my thoughts, but so

softly that I missed the first words: '...that ah love ye. Ah always have. Ah see that now. I want ye tae know that.'

She pushed herself from me, turned away and went quickly along the pavement in a pale shadow of the old hip-swinging, proud and preening gait. I would recall that moment again and again, as well as the thought that pierced for an instant into the turbulence within me: 'How tired she looks.'

10

LOST ILLUSIONS

Sometimes the factory was a refuge from the world. The noise that battered you on every side could also protect you. Normal talk was impossible. Communication needed a tremendous effort and some ingenuity. You had to pitch your voice high, condense your message to the barest minimum, supplement shouted words with gestures. A question. A request. A warning perhaps. First you alerted the person, shouted to make him look up: 'Hey Alec!', or Ian or Jimmie, and if he remained oblivious you might even throw something, preferably soft like a piece of cloth, to land on the table in front of him. Looking up at you and studying the gestures and expression with which you supplemented your words, he would decode what you said, only partly heard if at all: 'Hey! Throw me that bundle of facings!' or 'Here's that iron-holder you wanted – catch!'

Apart from such signalling you were enclosed in the noise as effectively as a hermit in his cell.

Since our encounter outside the Baths I had not consciously avoided Annie at the factory. It was the busy winter season and we were hard at it for sixteen hours a day producing garments for the spring trade. You came to work in the dark of early morning, walking half asleep past bakeries just finishing the night shift, where white-clad figures stood in the doorways having a drag before going home, the sweet smell of warm dough and yeast and new-baked bread wafting round your head in the keen night air and uplifting the heart; and stables where the big Clydesdales stamped and clattered as the hands began to groom them and clean out stalls and yard and get the carts ready for the day's haulage. Wet cobbled streets were empty, pools of yellow gaslight disturbed only by a few other lonely figures hurrying to work, or a prowling cat drawing its tapering shadow along a wall. When we left work in the evening, numb with fatigue, feet and ankles stiff from standing, it was dark again, the streets crowded with office and factory and shop workers heading home, shoppers, theatre goers, in a roar and clatter of buses and trains and horse-drawn vehicles. By chance or design Annie's arrivals and departures did not coincide with mine. An encounter could easily have been brought about if one of us had decided to linger, choosing the time, by the factory door on the Broomie-law, the quay on the north side of the Clyde at the Victoria Bridge opposite the Gorbals, or on the stone staircase leading up to our long workroom. But that did not happen.

I had replied to the letter. Yes. I would 'come into residence' on the first day of Michaelmas Term next year.

That certainly was a hostage to fortune, for I had no idea how I was going to get together all the things needed to present myself there – money, clothes, books and, perhaps most uncertain of all, myself. Still, there was nothing for it but to pretend that I *was* certain and do my damnedest to get ready.

Obsessively I wrestled with the practicalities, most of them only dimly understood. I worried about the things you needed in order to be a student at Oxford. In answer to my letter of acceptance, I was sent daunting information, including lists of clothing I ought to bring with me. I had practically nothing but what I stood up in. With amazement I learnt that I ought to have at least three suits of pyjamas. I had none at all. How strange to put on special clothes to sleep in? I had no suitcase, for I had never travelled anywhere. There was a long list of books to be read. I had no books at all. I had done all my reading in the Mitchell Library, a fair distance from both the factory and our house. And being so busy at work now, there was not much of the evening left in which to get there and do any solid reading. Somehow I must find the money to buy some books and get some reading done at home. For this and all the rest I could not possibly save anything like enough money in the time. Soon, when this busy season came to an end just before Christmas, there would be a slack time for about six weeks until we started another hectic busy season producing for the summer trade. I could manage, just about, if I could borrow a few shillings here and there on the strength of the scholarship money to come.

In secret I sought out Aunt Rachel. It had to be secret, for father, angry because she had helped my sister Mary to leave home, and taken her into her own house to live, had forbidden all contact with her. I showed her the letter that had told me I had won the scholarship.

Aunt Rachel, mother's younger sister, little and wiry, was round-shouldered from years of bending short-sightedly at her sewing in Uncle Salman's tiny clothing repair workshop in Norfolk Street. Within herself, however, she was strong and upright. Brown hair, gathered to a tight bun near the crown of her head, framed fresh rounded features and a high forehead. She spoke sparingly, always after clear thought. Her attitude to life was summed up in a favourite saying of hers that stuck in my memory from early childhood: 'Speech is silver. Thought is gold!'

With her shiny black apron she cleaned her Woolworths' spectacles, thick lenses in metal frames with wire side pieces, and read the letter, screwing up her eyes.

I said, 'I don't know if you can manage it, but do you think you could lend me a little money to get a few things I need? Clothes and books? I'll pay you back as soon as I get the scholarship money.'

She looked up into my face with great intensity, then bent her head and read through the letter again. She tugged the spectacles off her nose and went to a tall dresser and stood on tip-toe to see into the top drawer, took out a folded handkerchief and held it by a corner and shook it out. She kept her back turned, but I had seen the tears.

She dried her eyes, blew her nose, refolded the handkerchief and tucked it away in a pocket in her black skirt, and studied me again, many feelings revealed in her changing aspect – pleasure, pride, wistfulness, concern at yet another demand in a burdened life. 'You're a good boy, and it's a credit to you, what you've done. An Oxford student! Who would have thought it could happen? You deserve it. We'll do what we can. But it'll be only a few shillings, mind!'

'Thank you, Auntie. It'll be a godsend. You'll definitely get it back as soon as I get the money from the college.'

She shook her head, and looked away, fumbled for the handkerchief again. Her voice was unsteady now: 'I wasn't thinking of that. If only your mother could have been spared to see you turn out like this? Her beautiful baby boy she had to leave so soon! Still, I must not say that. It was God's will.'

Tactfully she did not ask what father was doing to help. She knew how badly things stood.

Apart from the things to be bought, I worried about the adjustments I had to make within myself – outlook, prejudices, ways of thinking and conducting myself; what was needed I could only guess.

And the letter burned in my pocket, a secret, magical flame. I carried it wherever I went. A talisman. Proof that I was not the victim of a powerful delusion. It became so tattered, coming apart at the folds, that I pasted it on to a piece of the stiff paper the cutters in the factory used for marking out patterns. All thought turned inward.

As for Annie, a shadow must have remained at the back of my mind. Now and then, idly looking round as I stood at my pressing board – the 'donkey' – I saw her raise her head from her work and turn in my direction, but in the steam and dust and dim light I was never sure whether the look had any important meaning to me. If it did, I probably did not want to see it, for reasons I preferred not to examine. In retrospect a signal there must have been. Getting no response, she did not come near.

I kept the world at a distance. Not much of it was real to me. The letter had raised a dust storm within me in which all things became indistinct, even these I knew so well, the work I did like an automaton – seams opened and pressed flat, edges and shoulders and shapes manipulated and fixed in place with accustomed care and skill – the daily routine of factory, food, and sleep, and the Baths, the visits now shorter to make more reading time, familiar streets and tenement stairs and closes, all experienced and seen, but not seen.

And always Oxford hung perplexingly on the horizon. Alien territory. Preserve of the boss class!

Standing at my pressing board one Monday morning, I was roused by a commotion over by the sewing machines. I caught only one word, but it was one that always sounded a note of profound alarm among us: 'Hospital'. I may have caught that word because, unawares, I had been expecting it. Something important must have happened for hands to leave their piece work in such agitation: a shocking bit of news.

At his work place on the opposite side of the pressing table Alec Birrell was mouthing words at me in the exaggerated manner we employed to help each other lip-read through the noise. This time I failed. I shouted at him:

'Hospital? Who? Who is it?'

He had just spread a damp rag over a piece of work, the long front edge of a coat. Lined with soaped canvas, that edge needed plenty of steam followed by heat to fix canvas and cloth together and make the edge hang straight and clean; the damp rag was a large sheet of cotton soaked and wrung out in a water bucket that we shared at the end of our table. As I shouted he was in the act of banging down upon it a newly heated iron. A cloud of steam sizzled up round him and hid his face. Head inclined, manoeuvring the big iron with his right hand, he swung his left arm to the side at shoulder height and pointed to the nearest bank of sewing machines. I saw an empty place there. Annie's.

I put down my iron on its metal rest beside the donkey and went round to his side of the table. The story, in essentials, was nothing out of the ordinary. Yesterday, Sunday, Annie had drunk a whole bottle of patent medicine, a specific for clearing the bowels.

Some time later, seized with violent vomiting, and probably delirious, she had dragged herself out of the house and staggered down the spiral stairs in her close making for the lavatory tucked into the concave wall, lost her footing on the overflow of excrement and hurtled down a whole flight of the jagged stone steps.

Our shower room group, in the scabrous and cruel musings of the young and green, feeding sexual fantasies, had often dwelt upon the ironies of a woman locked in contradictory battle with her flesh, on the crude antitheses of desire and the grim prudence that life demanded, on pleasure and its capricious consequences. We would never have admitted to being puritanical, but in an ambivalence of open glee and private censure we gloated over sin with imagery that glistened with the sweat and heat and lubricity of primordial passion, as in Somerset Maugham's 'Rain' the missionary, Davidson, was perversely obsessed with Sadie's flesh. Unlike Davidson, however, we knew, being very young, that we need not fear sin. Youth is invulnerable, immortal. In imagination *we* could play with fire, with sin, safely. But deeply hidden in this dream talk was a disturbing mixture of envy and fear of woman, the unattainable, unknowable, dark magic that dwelt in her. Her power to conjure life.

'Funny! Whit it must be like for a hairy when she's been reamed oot wi' a big prick! Wonderin' if she'll ge' 'er monthlies next time, eh? An' then she doesnae ge' them, and starts prayin' tae God it's a mistake! An' then she doesnae ge' them the second time, oh Christ is she in a panic! Nothin' for it bu' a bliddy great dose o' strong clearin' oot medicine or somethin' drastic like that tae gie her insides a bashin' an' ge' 'er wurrks started again! Some o' them get sae desperate they try a fall doon the stairs. Sometimes the shock does the trick ye see? Or she has a go wi' the auld knittin' needle! Or if she can ge' a few shillins taegither she goes tae Maggie O'Reilly in Rose Street to dae it for her. Aye, an' then in a wee while there she is in the back close, red hot in her hole tae ge' reamed oo' again! Aye, there's allus plenty mair where the last yin came frae.'

The ambulance had taken Annie to the Royal Infirmary. Some of the girls from her bank of machines would go in and see her there this evening after work.

Stupidly unaware still, I stood there staring at him. For one chill moment, fool that I was, it crossed my mind that she might have attempted suicide because I had rejected her plea. Yet it was not such a stupid thought. The romantic Annie I had known, or felt I did, would have been

210

capable of it.

'Christ! What came over her to do a thing like that?'

He studied me wonderingly, then broke into a sarcastic grin: 'Ye cannae be serious!'

'What d'ye mean?'

'Whit's the ma'er wi' ye?' he asked despairingly. 'Hiv ye no' wakened up this mornin' yit? It's as plain as plain! That lassie had 'er caird stamped good an' proper!' He shrugged. 'An' she drank up tha' stuff tryin' tae bring on 'er monthlies! The auld, auld story! Some jaunty lad refused tae feyther the wean in 'er belly!'

He nodded knowingly. He knew who the jaunty lad was, and assumed I did too.

And then it hit me hard, the truth of what she had done to me, or tried to do and failed. Not trusting myself to speak, I turned away so that he should not read my face, I went back to my pressing board and lifted the iron, which now seemed to weigh much more than its eighteen pounds, and blindly carried on working, hardly knowing what I did. The sweat felt cold on my back.

Had my mind not been so full of that letter – and innocence – surely I would have put the pieces together? How could I have failed to be alerted by at least a grain of suspicion when she waylaid me at the Baths and coolly – I saw it now – tried to make me go home with her?

211

With these thoughts came such a surge of fury that my head seemed ready to burst. Oh to destroy something, anything, shatter, rend and tear and batter into dust! If Annie had stood in front of me at that instant? God help me, what might I have done! I slammed the iron down on its steel rest, dug my nails into my palms to keep control.

I thought of my father and his frightening rages. Was this what they felt like? Were they my inheritance too? And the misery that provoked them?

Some control returned. I looked round to see if anyone had noticed. The weak electric bulb hanging before me, under its dusty green shade like an up-turned soup plate, cast a patch of miserly light on the donkey, but the spot where I stood was in shadow, deepened by the clouds of concealing steam about the pressing table. In any case everyone had his head down working away for dear life.

And then, to my surprise, I felt sorry for her. I remembered how pale she had become when I said 'Too late,' with no idea of the other meaning those words had for her.

No wonder Alec was amazed at my stupidity. Phil Emet had turned his back on the stamped card. That was obvious. In panic she had resorted to me. Had I gone with her that evening, how transparent her plan was now? At her home emptied of her family, in a bogus reconciliation, her contrived euphoria would have swept aside any thought of being careful. French letters were not cheap. Some fellows carried them around all the time or claimed they did. I didn't. And then some days later she would have come to me, in desperation then totally understandable, to place paternity at my door and demand, sweetly but determinedly, immediate marriage.

Premature births were common among women of the tenements.

As Alec had said: 'An auld, auld story.'

At the Baths that evening Phil remarked with detachment: 'Aye it's a real shame about her. She shouldnae've panicked like tha'! *They* know whit tae do, don't they? Plenty gurrls've gone tae Maggie O'Reilly in Rose Street hiven't they? An' been none the wurrse!'

Tactfully the talk was deflected. Phil knew as well as we did that girls had died after a visit to Rose Street. And some were left permanent invalids. No one wanted to dwell on such thoughts. Behind the bragging and the coarse jests, the shadow remained. One day, any day, their turn might come. Would they, like Phil, have the nerve to shrug and walk away?

Annie had fractured her skull, cracked a vertebra at the top of her spine, broken her jaw and her left arm. She was lucky, they said, not to have broken her neck. As for the stomach and bowel damage from what she had drunk, she would suffer from it for the rest of her life.

Nothing was heard of a pregnancy, so in that respect she had succeeded.

I could not bring myself to visit her in hospital, or send her any message. Over and over again I wished I could blot out what she had tried to do to me, and think of her again as she once had been. And then the shock would return and resentment burn again as I thought of how close I had been to the snapping of that trap, forced to turn my back on the door that had been opened by that letter from Oxford.

The enigma of the female. No wonder the Sphinx was a woman, and all who failed to divine her riddle paid with their lives.

Behind the shower group's gallows humour was a frightened huddling together before that Sphinx, her secret feebly guessed at in the callow terms in which they saw life repelled as I often was by their savage simplicity, they seemed to me to speak for the received view, and when I was with them my insecurity was temporarily stilled – though in calmer moments I knew that they were as insecure as I was. How profoundly separate was the woman s vision, doomed in the end to be mortally opposed to ours! The ripening seed in the womb – *or the unthought desire for it* – imposed its own laws, its own expedient calculations, its egoistical assumptions about right and wrong, refracted all vision, changed all perspectives. To use the man, or failing the one chosen *any* man, to fulfil her destiny was simply to implement a natural law, ruthlessly if necessary, carelessly to invoke the life force!

But these primitive sophistries cloaked apocalyptic ironies and I wanted to reject them all. For me the truth was simple, and nothing could excuse it. A sense of right, of trust, had been violated. What harm had I done her? None whatever. It was she who had rejected *me* – suddenly, without warning, from one day to the next. Was it simply caprice? Or some inadequacy in me unexpectedly discovered? In some ways either reason would have been bearable, or at least accepted as honourable. The truth hurt because it was shabby, and because it meant that judgement, faith, vows, had been worthless.

Yes, the truth was simple and in its way understandable, the compulsion of a higher fancy she could follow only with someone else. Very well. That was her business, not mine. Desperate she may have been when Phil turned away, but how cruel to try to gull *me*, struggling so hard to do the best I could with my life, into becoming a victim

215

of *her* miscalculation?

It did not occur to me till much later that I too could have turned my back on a stamped card. Why not? It happened often enough, which was how Maggie O'Reilly got most of her clients! That, in its way, was part of the received view too. No, I couldn't have done that. I was not Phil Emet and that was that. It was an aspect of me that Annie knew she could depend on. Her judgement of me had been accurate – unlike mine of *her*.

Alec Birrell remarked thoughtfully: 'If we could tell how many couples got wed this way, aye, an' went on tae live guid lives taegither efterwards, ah guarantee we'd be very surprised! Efter a', who are we tae judge?'

The auld, auld story. Did it really matter that much? Yes it did. I was sure of that. These were deep waters, too deep for me. Alec was paraphrasing an old saw: 'The heart is not troubled by what it does not know!' Maybe. But *she* would have known it! And knowing that I did not, she would have betrayed me every day of her life. And who knew what intuition might plant the dark thought in my heart, unknowable and unprovable, to haunt me through the years?

How could I ever have forgiven her if that had happened? And how could I forgive her now for having attempted it? She had tried

216

to exploit my trust. And my love. Alas, love would remain. I would never escape from that. She knew it. And for her to have acted on that knowledge, if nothing else, made her deed unforgiveable.

11

BERNARD, SPAIN, DISENCHANTMENT

In Spain Bernard was wounded, a bullet in the side of the neck, luckily in the muscles at the join of the shoulder. When he was out of hospital he was given a 'political guidance' job. He went from unit to unit in the shifting fronts, up and down through the command organisation to get 'appreciations' and provide political briefings, attending high-level policy meetings to adjust his political tuning to shifts in the party line and changes in directives to its cells in the military and governmental structure. Subtly, his role changed, from the revolutionary sage giving political perspective, to the inquisitor searching for deficiencies in faith. It shocked and oppressed him to discover that, like the inquisitors of old, he carried the power to invoke death.

He saw the purity of the cause as diluted. Too often he found himself compelled to defend a party policy or, worse, the behaviour of highly placed comrades or groups, that betrayed the faith he had come to Spain to fight for. In his travels, physically across the war-riven country, mentally up and down the shaky political and military levels, from the fighting men on the ground living hard, to the well turned-out politicians meeting in gilded salons, he saw most of the game.

He was to tell me of Russian generals living high, who in the intervals between orgies critically influenced strategy and the movement of supplies – sometimes, he suspected, their stoppage – and the fate of leaders, in the interests of a remote *realpolitik*. He spoke of doctrinally divergent groups fighting one another, the strife taking precedence over the efficient prosecution of the war, doing Franco's work for him. They behaved like states within the state, leaders strutting like war lords, bargaining for supplies, for politically advantageous positions in strategic plans, sometimes at gun point. They executed comrades on flimsy excuse, not only as supposed dangers to the cause but as possible rivals in the power struggle within it. To kill people of your own side in order to promote your brand of salvation became commonplace, and to dispose of anyone who shrank from doing so an accepted necessity. Dark statecraft hung menacingly over everybody.

With a hardening clarity that turned him

into a dangerous man, Bernard was coming to the conclusion that if it ever had been a workers' war for freedom and justice, with capitalism the sole enemy, it was that no longer.

He asked himself whether his role really had changed, or whether he had been too innocent to see it earlier for what it truly was? Presented to him at first as one of helping to strengthen morale in the International Brigade, in the hectic climate of fighting a war with amateur soldiers and a rickety organisation pitted against a professional army, in an atmosphere of make-do-and-mend and uncertain unity, he had reluctantly begun to see his role partly as secret surveillance, partly as that of a 'mind policeman', marking out the politically unreliable – 'deviationist' became the dread label – whose 'removal' would favour the party's potency in the internecine strife. Such men would end up on rubbish heaps or in ditches, a bullet hole in the back of the head. Like the French Revolution, the cause had turned sour on itself and was destroying its own. He had become one of the destroyers.

'Would you believe it?' he chuckled humourlessly, 'Yours truly going round with a forty-five in a shoulder holster?'

He could stomach no more and was on the knife-edge of deciding to leave it all, when something happened that made the decision for him.

He told me about it on another grey winter's day not long after he had reappeared from Spain. We had halted on the pavement in Castle Street, a steep hill that climbed towards the mound on which stood cheek by jowl two bastions of life and death – or vice-versa depending on your point of view – the Royal Infirmary and the Necropolis, surrounded by an assembly of churches and religious institutions of many shades of doctrine, gospel halls, mission halls, evangelical rooms, Band of Hope meeting halls, supporting troops. A wag once remarked that the party must have been 'guided' to site its headquarters, which sheltered behind its bookshop in Castle Street, in the midst of these strong points of faith, in order to hedge its bets. 'Aye! Maybe we should call it the Karl Marx Band of Hope Rooms!'

The hill became dangerously slippery under frozen snow and slush. People broke bones, in the elderly the injuries could be fatal, and the Royal Infirmary, only a couple of hundred yards up the hill, was conveniently near.

Horses fell, and as often as not were shot on the spot.

The Necropolis, filled with elaborate Victorian tombs and funerary statuary, was now in the main a civic monument, but up there on the crest of the hill adjoining the Infirmary grounds, with the grim visage of John Knox on his column dominating the whole *mise en scene*, it jolted the minds of people visiting patients in the Infirmary with thoughts of death and damnation.

'Did *you* have to do any of that dirty work?' I asked him. 'I mean kill people like that yourself?'

'More of that some other time,' he said. 'I'll only tell you this just now. Because – well, I have to talk about it to somebody, and there's no one else I can tell it to – not yet. How it all came to an end for me there.'

He had acquired a tight-lipped manner, wary, laconic. The once full face was now lean, almost lantern-jawed, the ruddy features leaden. The wound had left him with a permanent tilt of the head into the left shoulder. The battlefield surgeon had cut deep.

The most noticeable change of all was that the old ebullience of the street demagogue was no more; he had retreated into himself. He had aged twenty years. The once cheerful black eyes were stilled and watchful, the face concealing expression, spontaneity suppressed. A sad man.

Before he continued he looked about him as if searching for something that should be there, or which he feared was there, with an expression as chilling as the air about us.

'Sometimes I can hardly believe it myself,' he said, his lip curling in an attempt at a smile. 'Anyway, this is the way it happened. I had just got to a small town on the northern coast on a job. I had a few hours to wait for a meeting that night, and I had the desperate feeling that I must get away from people for a bit. There was never any end to people and meetings. Watching points every moment of the day, analysing this or that statement or action or even mannerism, signs of motives or attitudes that needed looking into. I was hardly ever on my own. My head was full to bursting. I needed to think things out.

'So I went out of the town. The shoreline was deserted. Not a soul about. The sea empty. I walked along for about a mile. The day was hot and the gun felt especially heavy and the holster strap was hurting like hell, cutting into me at the place where they had dug out the bullet. I found a shady spot down by the water, under an overhang of the cliff. I tucked myself well down among some rocks. It was second nature to pick yourself a good defensive position wherever you stopped. And I sat there staring at the water. Thinking what to do. From force of habit I cleaned and oiled the gun. In the life I was leading you did that regularly. It wasn't healthy to be slow in getting off a shot.

'The things life can do to you! If anyone had told me the day would come when I would go around with a pistol under my coat, watching my back, ready at any moment to draw and get a shot in fast, I would never have believed it.' He nodded thoughtfully: 'Yes. And sleep with the gun ready to hand.'

I said nothing. I felt I knew what was coming and was sickened in advance, responding perhaps to the residual shock I sensed in him.

'As a matter of fact,' he said, 'I discovered I was a naturally good shot with a pistol.'

He shrugged. 'So I re-loaded, and went on sitting there with the gun in my hand, thinking through everything, my political position, how things had moved from what I had expected, and from what they had been when I came to Spain. I kept on coming back to the same point. What had happened to the principle I had come to Spain to fight for? I certainly hadn't come to kill my own comrades simply because some top party men didn't like their opinions, or their faces. Some of our lads would never get back across that water because of me. I'd been manipulated into doing terrible things. I wasn't the only one, but that didn't help. So far I'd been lucky. All I'd got was a nick from a Fascist bullet. But now it was a fair bet that I'd get one in the back from somebody on my own side. After all, directly or indirectly that was what I was doing to others. That was the life I was leading. Sooner or later my luck would run out.

'I thought of many things. What hope was there now? Was there any way forward? Could all this confusion, this fighting and killing inside our ranks, this corruption of a great cause, be stopped in time? And by whom? Individuals like me wouldn't have a chance in hell if we tried to stand out against the people pulling the strings at the top. And not just in Spain but far away behind the scenes in Moscow. We'd be got rid of – no question of it. I should know: who better? That's what they were using people like *me* for. So what was I going to do? Every line of thought brought me back to the same dead end. And over and over again the question hammered at me: "What good was I doing?"'

He pushed his lower lip up, and seemed to contemplate the evening crowds hurrying home from work, hunched up against the wind. He was looking far beyond them.

'I must have sat like that for hours. The scar was aching. It does that at night sometimes. I thought that was what had roused me. But I wasn't sure. The light was fading. The sea and the sky had turned grey. It was time to go to the meeting. From force of habit I checked in all directions before I moved. It was as much as your life was worth not to do that. All I saw was the line of cliffs and the narrow pebbly foreshore stretching away to the dark smudge of the town in the distance. Not even any birds. I waited another minute or so. Nothing moved. Not a sound. Feeling a bit stiff from all that time I'd been sitting, I began slowly to stand up. I caught a little clinking sound, like a pebble falling against another, and by instinct I ducked down again. And if I hadn't done that I wouldn't be standing here talking to you now. I heard the shot and felt the wind of it going past my head. The round ricocheted off the rock next to me and on into the water a few feet away. He fired another three rounds rapid, which gave me his position exactly. He had crept up to about twenty-five yards of me, and was in a crack in the cliff face to the left of me. He was between me and my way back into the town.'

He drew his breath in quickly with a small whistling sound, eyes narrowed like a hunter's.

'His gun must have jammed. Trying to clear the action in that tricky half-light he must have bent his head forward. Just for a second I saw the dark curve of it outlined against the pale cliff face. And I got off two rounds and saw him go down. It was an instinctive reflex. You don't *think* when you're under attack. You just act. I think I dropped him with my first shot.'

He shook his head slowly.

'I went over to him lying there. I recognised him. Curiously enough that didn't surprise me. Can you understand that? As if I had been expecting it. But it shocked me all the same. We'd drunk a glass of red wine together many a time. A decent fellow. From South Wales. A miner. Doing much the same job as me in the group I had been sent to purge. Yes, purge: that was the word we used. What d'you think of that?'

I didn't say anything. I knew he didn't expect me to.

'And why were they after *me?* God knows. Maybe the leadership in that group had got nervous about my visit and decided to get me first, and so send a warning to the central committee to leave them alone. Or maybe the group had been given the word by the central committee to get rid of *me*, and I had been sent there like a lamb to the slaughter. That's how it was done sometimes. That was the kind of scheming and double-dealing that went on all the time. You had to watch your step. You had to be very, very careful, like living in a spider's web. I thought I had kept my doubts to myself, but maybe I hadn't been careful enough.'

He laughed with teeth clenched. 'Now I

knew what it was like to live in Russia! Anyway, I never found out why he had been sent to kill me, or by whom. I was too busy *running*, believe you me!'

He did not tell me how he had got out of Spain and made his way back home.

'One day I will,' he said, 'when it's safe to talk freely. I mean,' he added quickly, 'don't take this the wrong way. It's not that I don't trust you. It's only that you may let something out without meaning to.'

He had left the party. Officially, he was described as expelled, for no one was allowed to resign. He got his job back in the factory, and we saw his idealism turn in another direction, working hard in our trade union branch. Then, after a few months, the union gave him a job as organiser for the West of Scotland. That was a step up in the world. Now he was a brief-case man in a bespoke blue serge suit and smart snap brim hat, and he wore a clean white shirt every day – the kind with the newly fashionable attached semi-stiff collar – and a tie: an ambition of many a Gorbals man with calloused hands.

He commented on that shift in status one day. 'Between ourselves, I did feel a bit guilty, moving up from the standard of living of many of my members. But here's something else Spain taught me. Self-abasement can be a kind of hypocrisy, cynical window dressing, almost a kind of arrogance, like Peter Kerrigan wearing that open-necked grey shirt in the dead of winter.'

Kerrigan was party leader in Glasgow and British representative on the Comintern, a hard-liner who dutifully defended Stalin's murder of comrades. Bernard was not the only one who saw that open-necked shirt as a carefully selected symbol of unity with the proletariat.

'You might as well live decently,' Bernard went on, 'not in luxury but decently, in the way you'd like everyone else to live in fact, so that you can think clearly and give of your best.'

'You don't have to explain yourself to me!' I wanted to say, but plainly he felt he did. What he expressed was more than a political feeling. It was innocence; in seeming to distance himself from the people he cared about, he might unwittingly betray them. I would understand how he felt, but for different reasons, one day soon. But that was hidden from me.

He moved away from the Gorbals with his family, to one of the more respectable tenements near Charing Cross at the western end of Sauchiehall Street, at the back of the Mitchell Library, on the fringe of the University area.

The Mitchell Library! My private temple.

My Aladdin's Cave. There and at the
Socialist Camp at Carbeth I was more at
home than at the house in Warwick Street.
The Library drew me like a magnet, after
work of an evening in the busy time, and for
whole days in the slack season. I could have
found my way there with my eyes shut. Even
now the feel of those hard mahogany chairs
in its great arched reading room returns
instantly, all the hours and days I sat in
them; as well as my envy of the students
sauntering in and out without a care, who
treated it as a social club, a place for
assignations, or to sprawl away a waiting
hour in tennis flannels on a summer
afternoon. What an irony, I used to think,
that they did their stint at these reading
desks *force majeure* as I did at the factory,
thinking of it as hardship. What did they
know of hardship?

Bernard, fortuitously, remained in remote
contact with the party. Union work took
him to meetings of the Trades Council, on
which the party, through 'underground'
members, sat in strength. Council com-
mittees sometimes met in a mission hall a
few doors away from the party bookshop.
One day I arranged to meet him after one of
his meetings and we had our first long talk
since his return. Absorbed, we paused on
the pavement a few paces from the shop.

In its tall narrow bowed windows, with

small panes set in rounded wooden glazing bars, were tall jars of sticky Russian sweets, red and yellow and green, standing like lonely glass towers amid pamphlets bearing the faces of Lenin, Harry Pollitt, Bernard Shaw, copies of *Ten Days that Shook the World*, and the innocently named *Labour Monthly*, the party's ideological journal edited by the glacier-minded Rajani Palme Dutt. He it was who dismissed Stalin's purges and mass slaughter as 'a spot on the sun'.

In a back room the Agitprop Committee met, the party's key operations group for Scotland. Agitational propaganda stood for destabilisation, Machiavellianism from below, the selection, or creation, of 'issues' on which to agitate for wrongs to be righted, whereby the party would be seen in shining armour, the only true champion of the underdog. Issues chosen, self-evidently worthy like bad housing, were tools to win support, no more. Until his 'expulsion' from the party Bernard had been a member of the Agitprop Committee.

Perhaps he had never stopped to question the cynicism of Agitprop, but had lived with it only for the sake of his higher dream. The end justifies the means. When, in Spain, he had finally questioned that principle, feeling, inescapably, that the human price was too high, it had nearly cost him his life.

Yet when I thought about the tenements, one water tap for six families or more, lavatories overflowing yellow and brown down shattered stone steps, rats in full possession, and people skimping and scraping to be allowed to live in such places, why should one be disturbed at the party's Machiavellian motives? Surely Agitprop must do some good even if the party did use it, and us, for its own purposes of power?

We stood without speaking, stamped our feet and blew breath into cupped hands against the cold. Clydesdale draught horses, white hair hanging over their broad feet like dainty aprons, slithered on rounded wet cobbles as they tried to slow the long cart of coal or cement on the steep hill, massive legs quivering with veined muscle, flared nostrils blowing jets of steamy breath, while the driver held the brake lever hard back and the steel-rimmed wheels squealed and held and squealed again, scattering sparks. Wonderful, noble, patient beasts. What a shame they could not change their condition.

That was the truth for all of us.

And so Bernard searched for another faith. And I was moving too. From where, towards what? I was not looking for anything as grand as a faith, but for confidence in *something*.

He might have been listening to my

thoughts. He bared his teeth in that humourless laugh: 'Are you saying that is what we both want? Have faith and forget the truth, just like the old religions.'

I said: 'In a way you were happy then.'

The thought echoed between us, and faded away.

He chewed his lip, and watched another team of struggling horses go past.

He said: 'You were right in a lot of things. Remember that night in the close near the Workers' Circle, when the fellow in the back with his girl told us to fuck off? The last time we talked hard about things before I went to Spain? And you trying to pin me down with my own doubts? That worried you at the time, and maybe still does. Don't worry! You probably did me a lot of good and might have saved me... Well, what's the point of saying "If only"? If only I'd listened. I didn't want to believe what I'm sure I knew already, or suspected. Or maybe I did believe it but thought – no that's wrong, I didn't *think*, not properly. I was blinded by feeling. Impatience. Desperation. Christ, how naive I was! I didn't bargain for the callous and clever and dangerous men who would be operating when the chips were down, What sickens me most of all is the corruption of the *will for good*. And I can see no way out of it.'

Softly he said, unbelievingly, as of a

miracle: 'And I nearly didn't live to tell the tale.'

As if startled by the words 'tell the tale', he looked quickly up and down the pavement. Astonished and dismayed, I saw that he feared to be overheard.

It began to sleet. Passers by turned up coat collars and pulled caps lower down over their faces and quickened their steps. We retreated from the edge of the pavement and hurried for shelter to the nearest close mouth; as it happened it was next door to the bookshop.

It occurred to me that this might be too near for him. But the sleet was heavy, and my coat thin. He was wearing a fine new heavy trench coat with a wool lining and a smart trilby and was well protected. He made no objection. We might not have to shelter here long.

Incongruously, I thought about his reference to Annie and Phil by the ash-pits. Had he identified the voices? It was strange that he should have taken note of their presence then, at a moment when uppermost in his mind was the challenge of Spain and battle. And of all things to speak of it again now? I wondered if he had known about me and Annie in the past. We had talked confidentially on many things over the years, but for some reason I had kept Annie – winning her and losing her – to myself.

He said: 'And I'll tell you this. These fine gentlemen next door here, the party apparatchiks, they wouldn't hesitate to serve you the same as they did me in Spain if they ever got power in this country. And to think that I used to sit in that back room with them! God help me, I'd have to do the same if I were still one of them. What am I saying? I *did* do the same, in Spain.'

He brought up his right hand, and flexed the fingers once, and looked hard at the palm.

The power and fury of the gun. Death had been the only sure victor in that holy battle.

'Yes, I do feel guilty for some of the things I had to do in Spain. No, "had to" is wrong! I didn't *have* to. I did them willingly, at first anyway, even with a sense of doing the right thing for the cause I had gone there to fight for. I believed they were necessary. I must have done! I feel a bit empty now.'

Suddenly he moved, in a light springy step that had menace in it, like a hunter delicately placing himself in killing range, to the very edge of the close mouth and glanced quickly to the right, at the glass door of the shop. This time there was no mistaking the reason. He drew back and turned to face me again, and a dark cloud of fear moved over the strained features. The street was full of the clatter and rumble of carts and lorries, the clang and jingle of harness, the shouting of drivers, the hubbub of loading and unloading at a warehouse at the corner, the bustle of people, a mad syncopation bouncing back and forth between the facing tenements. No one could possibly have heard his words, least of all in the bookshop. He managed an apologetic smile. But that fear had been real enough. Momentarily, for his sake, I shared it, or tried to. Spain had wounded him more deeply than the bullet in the neck. It had found his heart.

I would probably never feel disillusion with the sharp edge that he did. In a sense I had foretold it, but that gave me no satisfaction. He at least had tried to do something, bravely, with a good heart. He had put himself into the hazard. If he had not done that, how would he know?

I too felt an emptiness. If there were no answers to be found, anywhere, what should we do? What should anyone do? Did it matter?

That was the most depressing question of all.

12

THE DEVIL YOU KNOW

Alec Birrell was tall and lean, ginger haired, with long bony features and a jutting lower jaw. He had a natural elegance even in his working garb of fustian coat and trousers and off-white woollen muffler. And an easy charm. He gave the impression of uncaringly letting the current of life carry him where it would.

But he had his share of worry. Nearly every shilling he earned went to the care of his ailing, widowed mother, and a half-crippled sister, who hobbled about lop-sidedly because of a defective hip, victim of rickets; a sweet and kindly girl, her chances of marriage were small.

He was not a deep thinker in any formal sense. For him the world had been set on a certain course for better or worse, and whatever balance it had, having been set through uncounted ages, had better be left undisturbed; any alternative, untried by time, was certain to be even worse. You learned to live with that balance, whatever trials it brought you, made yourself familiar with its idiosyncrasies, for life to be possible at all.

And yet in his fashion he did ruminate on the ways of the world, the fitness of things, manners, choices.

His relaxed exterior could be dangerously deceptive, for within he was hard as steel. Not easily roused, his fury could be white hot. One day Jimmy Gillan from the far end of our pressing table, a beetle-browed and surly fellow in his thirties, started teasing him about sticking to his Roman Catholic faith. Jimmy, a lapsed Catholic, was already set on the familiar road of blotting out life with drink, a negative soul who found Alec's accepting and pragmatic personality profoundly irritating. Religion was a risky subject to joke about. Jimmy had been at the factory longer than any of us and should have known who he was dealing with. If he had not been drinking at the lunch break he might have had the wit not to provoke Alec, or having done so, known when to stop. He stood at Alec's elbow as he worked, and sneeringly, with the foulest of language, persisted in the attack.

The rest of us read Alec's face and saw the danger signs. Superficially, he appeared unperturbed. He kept his head bent to his work, banged the bulky iron down on the damp rag, ran it back and forth to steam the cloth all over, lifted the iron and ripped the rag away from the garment, then turned the iron upside down in the air and touched its silk smooth dark foot swiftly with the palm of his free hand to make sure it would not burn the cloth, then swung it down and moved it back and forth briskly to dry the coat, skimming its surface with the lightest possible contact to avoid creating a sheen that would take the bloom off the cloth.

Failing to get a rise out of him, Jimmy fell into a frenzy of frustration and began to lard his curses with obscene blasphemy, forgetting that even though people might pretend to be indifferent to religion they usually drew the line, superstitiously maybe, at insults to the Holy Family.

After some minutes Alec looked up, slowly turned to face Jimmy, jaw thrust out, and shouted: 'That's *enough!* Ah'm tellin' ye!'

Fearing a fight, some of us moved round the table towards them, ready to separate them. Not that we cared that they might knock each other about – they could do that outside after work if they wanted to – but a fight in the factory interrupted the flow of work and lost us piece work pay; we might have to work extra hours to push through enough work to recoup the losses.

Apart from Alec's now evident fury, the sight of us closing in should have warned Jimmy that he was going too far, but he ignored us and went on: 'Why don't ye go

239

an' tell that priest tae shove it up 'is Holy Mother fuckin' arse! Like *ah* tellit 'im masel?'

Alec put his iron down carefully on the metal rest beside the donkey, folded his damp rag, hung up the garment he had been working on, turned to him again, his face pale as death:

'Listen you! Ah'm here tae knock oot a livin' an' that's a'! Ah'm no' here tae listen tae your fuckin' nonsense. This is ma last warnin'! Jist yew let me alone. Understand?'

He turned his back on the other, reached for another coat from the pile at the end of the table between his workplace and mine, threw it flat on the donkey and draped collar and shoulders on its rounded end ready for pressing.

Jimmy did not understand. He backed away a pace or two, eyes glazed, a face with a numbed brain behind it, and yelled a retort: 'Yew go an' fuck yersel' ye great big Holy Mary fucker!'

Alec was not, to use his own words, 'much of a religion hand'. He hardly ever went to Mass. But foul language about religion upset him. He turned and stood rigidly facing Jimmy, who was now giggling tipsily, and spoke slowly: 'Don't say ah didnae warn ye.'

Bony jaw held tight, Alec turned his back on him again, and carried on working quietly for the rest of the day.

Jimmy lurched back to his work place at the far end of the long table, the grin somewhat forced now, trying to catch our eyes for support as he passed by. We all bent our heads to our work. We knew this was not the end of it. No one knew what to expect, though some had their suspicions. Better not to appear to take sides – yet. If at all.

The next day Jimmy did not come in to work. The word went swiftly round. The previous evening he had been set upon in his close and beaten up. We never learnt who his assailants were. These attacks, normal events, were seldom random; they represented rough justice according to *someone's* lights, the working out of long-running feuds, passing quarrels, drunken sessions of insult like this one. The culture fed on its primitive passions.

Jimmy was off work for three days.

He had a wife and two young children. Three days off was too short a time for one to qualify for sickness benefit, and the loss of half-a-week's wages could be catastrophic. Alec went to the parish priest, we heard later, and begged him to help; and Father Millan made a collection among his flock and gave the few shillings to Jimmy's wife to buy food and coal while he was off work.

More important was the danger to

Jimmy's job. We were in one of the busy seasons and the boss might reasonably have taken on another presser in Jimmy's place, concerned as he naturally was about meeting delivery dates, and therefore anxious to avoid hold-ups in the flow of intermediate processes – machining and button-holing, for instance, that required phased pressing – and bad feeling among the piece workers. Alec, with his quiet charm, persuaded him to take on a temporary presser for the few days and have Jimmy back.

When Jimmy did come back the following Monday, Alec behaved as if the incident had never happened. The matter was never mentioned again.

Alec was *l'homme moyen raisonnable*. 'Ye mus'nae ask too many questions o' life. There's never enough time tae wait for the answers!'

Hidden in the near future, he was to be proved right. He did have too little time. In the D-Day landing, ashore in one of the first waves, he silenced a German pill-box whose accurate fire was working havoc on the crowded shingle. According to the citation, 'Corporal Birrell on his own initiative, and with great coolness and total disregard for his own safety, went ahead on all fours till he was below the gun's level of fire, then ran to the emplacement wall and stood up and lobbed a grenade into the firing slit.' Then he fell dead. In the hurricane of cross-fire, death could have come from friend or foe.

He was content enough to work hard at the pressing, 'ge' a lassie in the back close' whenever chance offered, play billiards, and look after his mother and sister as best he could. Grinning, lips drawn away from big white teeth, he would say: 'Ye live a bit, eat a bit, fuck a bit, an' sleep an' wake up the next mornin'! Whit else can ye ask for?'

One evening a few weeks after Annie had gone into the Royal Infirmary, we were doing the usual clearing up in the factory after working late; we each dried our damp rag and the cloth cover of the pressing donkey with a hot iron, sorted the work tickets for the garments worked on that day, made up the piece work tally and handed in the counterfoils to his cousin Bunty in the little glass-partitioned office, turned off the gas in the ovens that heated the press irons, swept up round the work place. Looking round I saw that Alec had finished and was sitting on the edge of the pressing table waiting for me. We went down the stone stairs together into the evening crowds.

Hands deep in trouser pockets, he whistled softly as we picked our way along the pavements littered with debris from fish and fruit and vegetable stalls, made the more slippery by recent rain. I waited for what he must have on his mind.

He began cautiously: 'Ye willnae' mind me talkin' a wee bit *perrsonal*, will ye now? Ah mean it for the best. Ah've heard aboot ye goin' away tae Oxford. Ah've been thinkin' a lo' aboo' tha'. Ah'm wonderin' if ye're daein' the right thing? Efter a' ye've go' a guid trade here in yer hand! Whit guid's it goin' tae dae ye bein' a student? How're ye gonnae ge' back intae a job efter? These are bad times ah don't need tae tell ye! Wi' a' the unemployment. Ah know it's an honour yew winnin' a scholarship tae Oxford. All credit's due tae ye! Ah'm jist a bit fearful ye might be *verry* disappointed in the end.

'Apart frae anythin' else,' he went on meditatively, 'it's a gey different wurrld ye'll be goin' intae. Well-to-do fellers frae hames where naebody ever wanted fer anythin'! Wi' different ways an' ideas. Yew're no' goin' tae understand *them* an' they're no' goin' tae understand *yew!*

'Or I should say,' he added, 'won't go out of their way tae understand ye!'

My thoughts had swung away. How did he know about the scholarship? I had told only my father and Aunt Rachel, and sworn them to secrecy, for there were a great many things to settle before I could be sure that I could go at all; and I was superstitious enough to take nothing for granted. In any case, even if they had let the news slip out, their links were totally different from Alec's and it was inconceivable that he could have learned of it by that route. And then I remembered that I had blurted it out to Annie.

It was easy to see how it might then have leaked out further. Desperate when she had staged that meeting with me outside the Baths, my news, if it had touched her mind at all, would have been pushed aside as irrelevant. Later, after the accident on the stairs, lying in the Royal Infirmary ward and slowly resuming awareness, I could imagine that resilient will of hers collecting itself again, turning her fate over and over and wondering what had gone wrong with her plan to entrap me, passing in review every possibility, running the film back and forth again and again. And then there must have come back to her, like an unheeded murmur of the Fates, the words I had let slip: 'I've won a scholarship to Oxford!' and understood at last. The unforeseeable factor?

Unburdening afterwards to one of the girls visiting her – by chance it could even have been one of Alec's lasses – she could well have mentioned it, the cruel stumbling stone! And that friend had passed it on, an interesting piece of gossip. For someone to win an Oxford scholarship, after all, was an unheard of thing to happen in the Gorbals.

How many days had Alec meditated on it, standing there opposite me on the far side of our work table, studying me, before deciding to speak? And now, gently, stepping carefully, he was bringing into the open the very unknowns that worried me. Or most of them. Oddly enough, fear that I might not get a job was not among them. Something quite different, much more crucial and personal, returned again and again to nag at my mind. He had put it delicately: 'it's a gey different wurrld ye'll be goin' intae.' Not one question mark but many. Would I fit in? Could I stand the pace in that foreign culture, among people who had come straight from public schools and grammar schools at eighteen, my schooling having been chopped off at fourteen? How isolated, how inadequate, would I feel?

So his intuition was accurate. More astonishing, and touching, was that he should show concern at all. We were not exactly friends. We knew each other only from the factory. Out of it, our paths diverged. Except on pay day sometimes, when after work a few of us had a game of billiards at the saloon a few doors away. Threepence per head for an hour at the table. I had given this up in recent months, for though I enjoyed the game the others preferred to play for money – sixpence a corner – and I never would. To tell them why would have been to betray father's gambling addiction.

Alec in kindly fashion had tried to reason me out of my scunner against playing for money:

'Ye've nae call tae be afeart ye know? Yew play a guid game! Look how many times ye've beat me?'

Praise indeed, for he was a fine, thoughtful player. Sometimes, humouring me, they agreed to play without the corner bets, but I could see that this spoiled their pleasure, and I found excuses not to join them.

He went on: 'Ye see, ye could fin' yersel' verry unhappy there. Ye'll have thrown away the wurrld ye know. Och we know things are bad here in the Gorbals, but at least *yew* know where ye stand here. Ye can make real relationships here – well, yes, good and bad, I know, ye don't have tae tell me! – but ye make 'em wi' yer ain kind. There ye'll be a freak! A brainy freak, they'll see ye're brainy right enough – aye, an' maybe hate ye for it – but it'll no' make ye one o' *them*. Never. They'll make sure o' that. An' that'll hit ye hard because yew're no' the kind tae tell 'em tae go an' fuck 'emsels! So ye'll be caught in no man's land. An' as fer ye "goin' native" – I mean *joinin'* them an' beatin' them on their hame ground – well!' He gave a sad laugh and shook his head, 'Ah wouldnae put money on yer chances that's a'. Will ah tell ye why? Because ye're no' callous enough! Ah'm no' sayin' tha' for any discredit tae ye mind. It's a guid thing in some ways. So long as ye never let the other side get tae know!'

Here was an unsuspected depth to Alec, so down to earth, reflecting on all this with such care, speaking out for my sake. Here was a sample of the warmth he was talking about. Perhaps he guessed that he posed a question I did not want to ask myself. Was I really following my star? Or a will o' the wisp?

He said: 'I hope ye don't mind ma sayin' these things? Ah've seen a lo' o' lads who couldnae ge' away frae the Gorbals quick enough, an' then they found the wurrld ootside wis *wurrse!* But it wis wurrse in a way they could never understand. It wis sae cauld an' everybody kept ye at a distance. An' then, thinkin' back, they see tha' some things here are be'er – sma' things, the way ye talk tae people, whit they think o' the wurrld, things ye never notice when ye *are* here – an' that's jist 'cos ye *know the score here!* But then, if they try tae come back here, in a way it's too late. 'Cos this wurrld, the one they knew here, wull've changed as well! An' the things they missed an' came back tae find again willnae be the same any mair. Och, ah don't know if ah'm talkin' sense! Or if it's ony use? But that's why ah'm sayin' it anyway.'

There may have been another motive,

hidden even from himself. When someone goes away, those who remain are forced, uncomfortably sometimes, to re-examine where they stand.

As if he had overheard my thoughts he added: 'Here ye know where yew stand. Oot there ye'll know none o' these things. An' yew're the kind that needs warmth.'

How much did he know about Annie and me? If he was right that I would not make relationships easily 'out there', it might not be for the logical reasons he advanced, but because I would cling too long to the emotional debris of the past.

I said: 'I don't know where to begin. One thing I do know, I appreciate you saying all this. I didn't expect it. You're right, it'll be a different world. Apart from everything else I'll be lying far back in the race. All the same I can't see how I can *not* go. It's like Fate taking a hand. I never expected anything like this to happen. I just went in for it saying to myself: "Well, why not? Who knows, it could just happen!" And now that it has, I can't turn my back on it. I've got to chance my arm.'

13

PRIESTESS OF THE NIGHT

Now that he had moved north of the Clyde, Bernard never came to the Baths; in fact he was seen in the Gorbals rarely, when Union business brought him, as when he attended inter-union meetings at the Workers' Circle that had a bearing on the garment industry, or met union members from the few small garment workshops south of the River. The latter discussions were usually held after the workshop closed for the day, on the pavement outside it or in a nearby close, occasionally at the Workers' Circle. The days of doing Union business in the boss' time and on his premises were in the future. When this work was done he never lingered. I had not seen him for some weeks, since before the letter from Oxford.

I never asked him directly why he seemed to shun the Gorbals. Thinking about it later it was obvious. For him the place rang with a voice he had abandoned, that of the confident evangelist of Red Revolution. Spiritual wounds were still raw.

New traits showed in him, one of them a

self-mocking irony, as when he remarked: 'Maybe it's better to work from the ground up as I'm doing now, dealing with 'issues' of hours and conditions, Trade Board regulations, proper lighting at the work place, washing facilities and lavatories and toilet paper! Nothing grander than that. Instead of from the top *down*, taking the God-like view, as I used to think I could. It was easy *then*, get the big questions settled and the little ones will take care of themselves!'

Thus he confided his sadness. Where was the old exaltation? 'Give me one fixed point and I will move the world!' Remaking the world is a job for giants. I too can walk among them. I too can see to the far horizons of time.

Not for him the long littleness of life, the bread and dripping of ordinary things. He listens to the music of the sibylline winds. He carries their message to the groundlings. Oh to breathe that rarefied air once more!

Gradually he strengthened his new self in the course of dealing with the 'day to day realities' as he called them, in contrast to 'the basics' he used to take his stand upon.

'Maybe' I said, 'there really is nothing else?'

With the stooped stance his wound had left him with, he had to make a special effort to raise his head and look at you, so that his regard seemed more intense than before,

251

conveying the feeling that everything one said needed profound probing before an answering word could be let slip. That was another important change. Where was the old mercurial talent, the swift scalpel swoop of the mind? All that had surely not vanished altogether, only gone underground.

Unbelievably, the word 'humble' came into my mind for this new Bernard, modest, practical, attentive to mundane detail, who now placed supreme value on personal feelings and relationships, sensitive to the subtleties, who did not rush his thoughts at you like battering rams as he once did. I preferred to think of this time as an interlude in which he digested Spain, tempered his soul in his own internal fires, and that a new spirit, feeling and responsive, willing to speak his heart with power, was arising within, grooming itself to emerge.

In what Avatar?

He was seldom at his desk. Recruiting, interceding with employers in the dozens of garment factories in the Glasgow area, going to meetings all over the city, he was always on the move. Sometimes, late in the evenings, he might be found at the union's district offices in the Saltmarket not far from our factory: but to do so without prior arrangement meant hanging round their dingy entrance after work on the chance of catching him.

And that, with the mind turbulent and the flesh hot, could be a disturbing experience.

The Saltmarket and the little streets running off it, on the north bank of the Clyde near the Albert Bridge, constituted a distinct quarter, of fish and vegetable and meat and grain merchants, warehouses and workshops and small traders. People mentioning the Saltmarket often meant the quarter as such, rather than solely the street of that name. Strewn with refuse, rotting produce, horse droppings, the quarter stank high in summer and mouldered foully in winter. But rents were low on thc upper floors of the warehouse buildings.

Alec propounded a different reason for the union offices being there. Close to the main business area, its ill-lit side streets deserted in the late evenings, loading bays and adjacent railway arches providing shelter and many dark corners for privacy, the quarter was a favoured place for street prostitutes to get and serve clients.

'Ye mean tae tell me the union heid yins didnae know tha'?' His long bony face half-serious, he elaborated with relish: 'Aye, never any shortage o' cunt *there!* Dozens o' them. Jist yew imagine a' them skirts swingin' free, knickers stuffed intae their handbags, ready an' waitin' fer ye! Hiv ye no' seen them hingin' roon the door at night when we come oo' o' the branch meetin'?

253

That's real *serrvice* fer ye! Nae wonder them meetin's are well attended!'

Keepers of the sacred labyrinth,
Priestesses of the stream of life,
And of the night.

We were walking home from the factory late one night, about ten o'clock, the streets stilled. Something in his mood suggested he wanted a cue to talk.

I said: 'Have you ever had one of them?'

'Aye, a few times,' he replied in assumed indifference, 'when ah've been hard up for ma hole. That wis where ah had ma first hoor, when ah was aboo' fifteen. Ah wis jist this minute thinkin' aboo' 'er! In fact she comes tae mind many a time. She wis ma first proper fuck!' He fell silent. 'But that's no' the reason. She wis, ah don't know how tae put i'. She wis warm an' understandin' an', well, she was genuine. She wanted me tae be happy! She made me feel ah wisnae jist *anybody*. Ah'll never ferrget it. Never. A wee thin-faced lassie wi' red hair, verry pale, shiverin' in the cauld wi' a thin coat an' skirt on. A guid bi' older than me she was, aboo' twenty-five. An' wi' a weddin' ring on.'

He pushed his lips out: 'It wis one payday, an' it wis snowin' an' cauld, an' ah wis comin' away frae the workshop late at night dog tired an' for some reason ah don't remember ah wis gaun hame through the Saltmarket an' no' thinkin' aboo' anythin'. An' suddenly there was this lassie beside me an' she caught haud o' ma hand sayin': "C'mon ah'll show ye somethin' wonderful!" An' she pulled me intae a big dark archway an' before ah knew anythin' she'd put ma haun' up 'er skirt – Jesus ah can feel it this minute – an' she'd got haud o' me an' a couldnae stop masel'! Christ wis ah ashamed! Bu' she said, quiet an' soft: "Never yew mind. Ah'll wait. An' ye'll be fine wi' me in a wee while." And she held me light, an' kissed me as if she really meant i'. An' efter a minute she shivered and said: "Ah'm sae cauld! Ah'm tha' hungry. Will ye gie me a sixpenny piece an' ah'll go an' ge' a bag o' fish an' chips?"

He snorted, 'If a hoor said that tae me the noo ah widnae trust her tae come back! Bu' ah wis ony a boy. An' she'd been sae warm and gentle wi' me. She looked sae peaked ah wanted 'er tae have somethin' tae eat. Ah gave 'er a whole shillin'. Ah'd have tae tell ma mither ah'd lost it on ma way hame. In a way that wis true! She took tha' shillin' in baith 'er hauns it could've been a gold sovereign! An' she said: "Yew jist wait here an' rest yersel'. Ah'll be back in a wee minute."

'An' ah wis left standin' there all flustered an' lonely an' wonderin' whit was happenin' tae me. Ah felt ah wis seein' this wurrld fer the verry furrst time. Aye, seein' a lo' o' things fer the furrst time. Ah thought of 'er walkin' aboo' hungry in tha' God forsaken place, through the piles o' rubbish an' horse shit dirty white wi' the snow left lyin'. A' the emptiness an' loneliness. And the bitter cauld that had driven a' the ither hoors hame. An' her sae desperate. Grabbin' hold of a boy tae ge' a shillin' aff of, for a bag o' fish an' chips an' pennies fer the gas an' the price o' a pint o' milk! An' *her* bein' nothin' tae me, an' *me* bein' nothin' tae her. An' the next minute ah thought: "No. That's wrong! I' is somethin'! If it wis nothin' ah wouldnae be carin' at a'! It's got tae mean somethin'!" Ah started shiverin', standin' there under the arch, the freezin' cauld creepin' up ma legs frae the pavement. Ah wanted tae feel 'er warm body pressin' against me again, an' 'er gentleness, sayin' nothin', jist *bein' there* wi' me. An' then ah started wonderin' if it wid be different fuckin' her than blockin' ma sister.'

I should not have been shocked but I was, and I must have shown it, or at least that I was surprised, perhaps by the slightest shift in my step or a questioning turn of the head, for he looked at me in astonishment. 'Yours've done it wi' yew surely?'

I shook my head, not sure what words would fit.

'Come on!' he said, disbelieving, 'Yewr sisters must've shown ye whit's what? Ah'll lay ye odds o' a hundred tae one ye'll no' find a feller, who's go' an older sister, who's no' been intae 'er – aye many, many times, sleepin' in the same bed night efter night! Hiv ye really no' done i'? Ah'll no' tell on ye mind!'

'No. It really is true.' I searched for a bland excuse. 'Maybe it was because they were so much older than me.'

Most Gorbals parents, trying to instil the standard prohibitions, fought against impossible odds. Girls and boys were not even supposed to undress in each other's presence after a certain age, but in most families they had to share bedrooms and as often as not beds, and so the rules were dead letters. In our house they were of little relevance for a different reason; when Mary started having periods I must have been only about three or four. By the time I was old enough for sexual experiment, she was adult, her interests outside the house. In the tiny room I shared with her, hardly bigger than a bathroom in a present day council house, father rigged up a dividing screen that folded away during the day; on one side of it she slept in a chair bed – a wooden armchair that opened out into a single bed, its three cushions of velveteen cord laid end to end as a mattress – and on the other I lay on a narrow flock palliasse on the floor.

I have a dim memory of Mary, every few weeks, sleeping with mother for several nights in the alcove bed in the kitchen, and father occupying the chair bed. After mother died, Mary still went for those few nights to sleep in the kitchen. I never got a satisfactory answer to questions about this monthly shift of sleeping arrangements.

Father said: 'Girls get a bit unwell once a month.'

He called it 'the change'. He was not especially prudish for his generation; he felt, probably, that it was a waste of time explaining such things to a child, that I would learn about it all when I was ready.

How could I even begin to explain all that?

Alec paused for only a moment: 'Aye, ah see whit ye mean. Maybe that's it.' He dismissed it. 'Anyway, *ma* sister went at i' wi me fer years. She used tae play wi' ma prick in oor bed even before ah'd go' any hair on me; an' after ah grew ma bush an' started comin', she go' me tae take 'er maidenhied.'

The memory jolted him: 'Christ tha' wis a night an' a half! Wonderin' whit tae do aboot the big bloodstain in the bed. Though at first when she saw it she was sae overjoyed – no, ah mean light-hieded like she wis drunk. Ah couldnae understand it.'

He thought about it: 'Whit *do* ye understand at tha' age? Ah wis only thirteen or fourteen ah suppose. She's no' married yet, an' maybe never wull be, crippled like tha'. An' maybe – God help her – somethin' telit 'er she'd better ge' a' the blockin' she could frae me?' He sighed. 'Well, anyway, in the end we decided she'd pretend she'd had a freak early monthly! An' ah'm no sure tae this day if ma mither believed 'er! Still an' a', nothin' wis said. Efter tha' she go' me tae block 'er over an' over again, nearly every night sometimes! But it wis never a proper fuck 'cos she never let me come inside 'er. She always knew when ah wis goin' tae come an' pulled me oo' jist before. Well, she stopped a' tha' when ah was aboo' sixteen. Ah've go' an idea tha' Father Millan, seein' ah was gettin' tae be a big lad, had a quiet word wi' 'er one day in Confession, an' telit 'er it was bad for her immortal soul! An' mine too. How 'e knew, well, ye can guess. Them priests! Aye, them priests. They're on tae everythin' that's goin' on. Too bliddy much.'

I wondered if he was about to branch off into that familiar pastime, scurrilous talk about priests and female parishioners. Not this time. The encounter in the Saltmarket long ago, shining within him over all the years, needed to have its say.

'Anyway, as ah wis sayin', ah stood there under the arch freezin'. It wis snowin' again. There wisnae a soul aboo'. Every single

259

hoor must a' given i' up that night. An' ah did begin tae wonder if she'd come back. An' then ah heard the quick steps muffled in the snow, an' ah smelt the chips an' vinegar, an' the next minute she was pressin' against me there in the dark. Shiverin' an' movin' against me tae ge' the warmth. An' d'ye know? She'd waited till she was back wi' me afore she started to eat any! Ah could tell she wis real hungry 'cos she ate them fish an' chips as if she hadnae had anythin' tae eat fer days. Ah hadnae the herrt tae take a chip frae the bag. Bu' after she'd had most of i', she stood there leanin' close an' put chips in ma mooth one a' a time till the bag was finished.'

We walked on for several minutes in silence and I thought he would reveal no more. He needed to, but couldn't.

At last he did, quietly, sombrely: 'Well, as she'd said, ah' wis fine wi' her in the end. She showed me many things. Aye, many things. An' then she came! She really did. A lo' o' hoors jist pretend tae come so's tae make ye feel great. Aye an' tae make ye think they're enterin' intae the spirit o' things an' no' jist standin' there thinkin' aboo' the gas meter! Anyway ah'd never felt anythin' like i'. I' made me feel – ah don't know how tae say it – i' made ma herrt feel full tae burstin'. An' then she went very quiet an' hung on tae me all limp an' said: "Haud me up dear ah cannae stand.'"

It had all been said sadly, far from the bragging manner of the shower group. He might have been pouring out his heart for a long lost love. His silence could have been of mourning, and reverence, for the lost bounty of innocence and revelation.

I had never been with a whore. In all the shower room anecdotes about them there had been nothing to compare with the enrichment he had spoken of. I thought of Annie. Would I, ten years from now, still cherish that experience as he did this one, and see all else as dross?

'No, it was a' different,' he said at last. 'It wasnae like wi' ma sister at a'! Ah suppose ah should've known tha' anyway! It was – it meant more. Somethin' important. I mean important for the baith o' us. It's hard tae explain.'

'Did you see her again?' I asked.

'Whit did ye say?'

He had fallen into reverie once more.

'Did you ever see that hoor again?'

'See her? Ah wish ah could've stayed wi' 'er for ever!' The words rushed out. He stopped and looked at me, in wonder at himself.

He turned away and we walked on. When he spoke the emotion had gone underground again. The tone was different. He had moved away from re-living the experience, perhaps in flight from it, from regret at how far away it was, the simple closeness, with its freeing of emotions so precious but so beyond his power to comprehend and hold.

'Ah never fucked 'er again if that's whit ye mean. Bu' ah've seen 'er plenty o' times. She's lived a' the time in the next close tae us! Married wi' two kids. Her man's on the booze, an' knocks 'er aboo' regular. He's given 'er tha' many black eyes she cannae see tae wurrk. She used tae be a button hole hand. *They* always ge' bad sight, bu' gettin' a' them black eyes as well must've buggered up 'er sight good an' proper! She cannae see tae thread the needle any more. Come tae think of i', if 'er eyes'd been be'er she'd 'ave recognised me in the dark that night afore she'd got hold o' me. An' maybe left me alane? Anyway, bein' hungry an' cauld, whit can ye say? She needed that shillin'.'

And now, to free himself from the attachment, attempting to denigrate the quality of the experience, he feebly essayed to kill the emotion, ordained to be out of time, a taste of something that would remain out of reach for ever, an antidote to bitterness.

The truth was in the words he had spoken before: 'If it wis nothin' ah wouldnae feel anythin' aboo' 'er at a'!'

A lost love. Or rather a love that might have been, if the dissonances of age and circumstance had not put it out of reach. Her continued presence in the next close kept the emotion fresh, and the pain too. She must now be a worn shadow of what she had been, but still able to sustain the memory of the tender, caring, courageous soul who had come towards him and awakened him long ago. That was the image, glowing in its indefinable sympathy, that would remain inviolate in his heart.

'Somethin' important. It's harrd tae explain.'

14

FEUDS

Since so much of Bernard's work was done out of the union offices, and out of office hours – in the evenings and at weekends when union members could attend meetings – there had to be a way of reaching him at home. And so he became the first person I knew to have a private telephone, and it was in trying to reach him, not long after the letter from Oxford, that I used a phone for the first time. I needed to hear his reaction to my news. I had brooded on it alone long enough. Knowing more of me than Alec did, and with the crucible of Spain so recent, Bernard might have a different, more courageous view.

A telephone kiosk had recently been erected near the monument at Gorbals Cross, resembling the ticket collector's wooden hut at the boating lake in the park. Walking past it every day on my way to and from the factory I never saw anyone actually using the instrument. Sometimes a meths drinker went in and subsided on the floor, knees up to his chin, and slept away a morning, that is if he was not evicted by a passing bobby. Luckily the kiosk was placed next to the steps leading down to the public lavatory, and it was only occasionally used as a toilet.

One evening I got two pennies ready and went to the Cross, and gingerly pulled open the green painted door. The interior smelt so strongly of a recent cleaning with carbolic that my eyes smarted, and I kept the door open an inch or two with my foot to dilute the vapour with fresher air. I lifted the long black receiver from its sprung hook at the side of the little brown wooden box on the wall, and was startled when a girl's voice sounded in my ear, amazingly fresh and close. I asked for the number at his new home about a mile and a half away across the river.

There came a distant 'Burr-burr', like an other worldly rat-a-tat on the door of their house, then the girl said briskly: 'Press Button A please!'

I did so and the two pennies clattered down into the recesses of the long black box. Bernard's mother said: 'Yes? What do you want? My son is not here.'

She was in her fifties, small and dark and energetic, with an oval face and bright, inquiring, blackberry eyes – houseproud, thrifty, always neatly dressed in shiny black blouse and skirt and a newly pressed white

265

apron, busy at her sewing machine when she was not looking after the house. Her husband, a skilled cutter in one of the high-class men's bespoke tailoring workshops, was slim and distinguished looking, with finely chiselled features and sensitive mouth. Cutters were the elite of the tailoring craft. A dignified figure in clerical grey suit and wing collar, he typified, too, the working-class intellectual. For years he had been much in demand as a lecturer on Kropotkin's life and work, as well as on his own brand on 'gentle nihilism'. But these appearances had become fewer, for of late his consumptive condition had worsened. Whenever I saw him he seemed thinner, walked in a stooped posture and with effort, and coughed with a deep rumble of phlegm.

Bernard, now able to support his parents, wanted him to give up work, but hesitated to press him.

'He says he would die quicker if he gave up work than if he stayed at it. He may be right. I don't like trying to force him in case it does him harm. And mother would never go against anything he felt so strongly about. It's hard to know what to do for the best. It breaks my heart to see him dragging himself about like that, coughing his lungs out, back and forth to the workshop. It makes you wonder what life's for.'

Mrs Lipchinsky shouted down the phone

at me as if she were leaning out of the tenement window to address me in the street below: 'What are you doing out there? You must come 'ere and knock at the door, like you used to! Tell me, 'ow is your father keeping? And 'ow are you keeping? We never see anybody after we move here. It is all strangers 'ere. It feels so far away!'

'Please, Mrs Lipchinsky, it's hard to go visiting after working late, with you living there now. Yes I will come soon, with Bernard. Please give him this message; I need to talk to him about something important. Can he meet me tomorrow evening after I finish work if I come to the union office, say about half-nine? Tell him to leave a message for me at the factory.'

'All right. I tell 'im. And you be sure to come with him here! It is not good to be wandering about the streets, you hear?'

'Yes, I hear.'

'An' tell your father good 'ealth from me! You hear?'

'Yes, I hear.'

There had been a tremor in her voice. I knew why, and she knew I did. It was something we had never talked of openly, and probably never would. In the years when I was growing out of childhood, shedding its egocentricity and looking outward, piecing together adult utterances overheard, I had been saddened to feel that some people blamed father's gambling, his manic melancholy, his lacerating rages, for hastening mother's death – if not actually causing it. To accept this opinion was unthinkable; a Gorgon's head that must not be contemplated. However wounding our quarrels, no matter how much I longed to grow up fast to be free of them, I needed to honour him.

For all I knew it was he who merited sympathy, caught in a maze of wrong vision and wrong action. I longed to help him escape, but had no idea how, and even if he had brought himself to air his problems to me, as a child they would have meant nothing, and when I reached my teens too much had happened. And he was too far off course. So I grew up in conflict.

Mrs Lipchinsky's undeviating respect and sympathy for him always uplifted my heart. Though she and mother had been close friends, she never accepted that simplistic verdict on father, indicating, without actually saying so, that mother's personality must be brought into the account too, *her* method of dealing with life, her responses to his longings and dreams, action and reaction, all understood in their wholeness together; it was wrong to see their life together as one-way traffic, from him to her but not the reverse. And so it was unjust to see his behaviour as wilfully evil or determinedly egoistical, but rather as a response, inadequate or mistaken though it might have been but sincere, to life as he perceived it.

Integrity, she maintained, was his outstanding feature. He might have been happier had he been a better opportunist, less open with people, readier to dissemble and manipulate them. The apportionment of blame was not for us. Life's purpose remained an enigma. We must contend with it forever.

She permitted herself one explicit judgement. Life had given him too many knocks. 'To be left a widower with a family! What can he do?' she had exclaimed more than once. 'What a pity it is.'

Her view of him, balanced and detached as far as I could tell, was important to me. She could surely not be alone in it? Many others must see light in him too.

People spoke of his charm. Did that explain some of the sympathy? I could never see it. Perhaps he let it flow freely only for outsiders, and when so minded? But alas not enough!

Father had started his working life in the craft of bone and wood turning at a time when gentlemen sported walking sticks with turned and carved handles in bone and ivory and fine woods. That market was in decline. Replacing it was an increasing demand, extending down the social scale to the better-off workers, for umbrellas. With two brothers, he opened a shop in Dalmarnock Road to sell and repair them. At first the business prospered. Then came quarrels. Father, I learnt much later, suspected his brothers of swindling him, and scheming to squeeze him out. They accused *him* of neglecting the business and borrowing its cash for gambling.

One evening, I must have been about five, I was in the shop when a fight started between the three of them, two against one, my father alone. The savagery of it, and the awesome sense of sacrilege, as even my child's mind saw it, of brothers raising their hands against one another, would return again and again through the years in all the furious movement and thunder of those few volcanic, terrifying minutes. In panic I hid behind the counter near the street door with its glass panes black against the night, furthest away from their hurtling bodies. I had often seen drunks fighting outside the pubs and taken little notice. But the sight of my father and his brothers hurting each other broke my world to fragments. It was unbelievable, yet there it was happening, the sickening crunch of blows, blood streaming from faces and hands, their great frames falling with a noise like thunder and rising again and leaping to the attack, wild eyes willing destruction. Counters and show-cases were smashed and stock scattered all over the floor, much of it reduced to bundles of broken umbrella frames and torn fabric, amidst splintered wood and shattered glass. My cries of terror reached them at last, for suddenly they stood still, like huge puppets arrested, and turned and stared at me. Perhaps they felt a moment's shame at what they had shown me of their adult world? They bent over me, gasping for breath, looming black giants dripping blood onto my face, united now in guilt.

I sensed the continuing rage burning within them, and that was as frightening as the fighting had been. My uncles seemed to be condescending to father, insulting him. Why, oh why was it happening? Tears flooded down my face, fear for myself, for father, for the whole world, the only appeal I knew. Words sparked between them like fireworks, the meaning going over my head but plainly loaded with fury and hate. Father at last turned his back on them with a contemptuous shrug of his broad shoulders, lifted me up in his arms, held me strongly, comfortingly, his bruised hands oozing blood onto me, and carried me out of the shop into a dark rainy night.

When I was old enough to think sensibly about it I could never be sure, in the tangle of family anecdote, what were the true facts.

By that time my two uncles had emigrated to America with their families, taking with them, according to father, money from the shop that was rightfully his. The trail had gone cold. In any case the sadness of the past as I remembered it was enough; I had little desire to probe for more detail. But anger and shame and pity for father's sake never left me.

He had forbidden all contact with the brothers or their families; and when they went to America no correspondence was allowed. On a small child the latter prohibition had no impact, but as a result, by the time I was grown up the links of kinship that *might* have been re-forged, at least between the younger members of the families, were lost. In my twenties, turning my back on the past, that was of no consequence. In any case the business of living crowded out any thought of seeking them out; abstract, possibly interesting, but a luxury one could ill afford. In later years the sense of isolation grew, and I regretted letting that happen. Whether the regret was well-founded, except on the principle that family ties are self-justifying, there is no means of knowing. I often said to myself: 'If there was so much poison between the brothers, could their children have escaped infection?'

That fight finished the shop. From then on

mother seemed to recede from life, as if she knew her course was set and how little time was left to her, sad only that she must abandon her children, mourning our fate in advance. Apart from that I am sure she did not sorrow to go. Her face, remembered as beautiful and full of dignity, vigour and blithe courage, bright with intelligence and humour, became drawn and fixed; and gradually turned yellow.

One day she came back from hospital accompanied by a woman neighbour who brought with her a brightly polished brass jam-making pan. I overheard her tell mother:

'Aye, the doctor says if ah could lend ye a brass pan like this, polished up, an' ge' ye tae look intae it often, tae use i' as a mirror, it'll make ye ge' bc'er quicker, ye see? So don't yew ferget tae dae tha'. Ye mustnae use an' ordinary mirror at a'. It's nae guid fer tha'. Yew use this a' the time, see?'

Little as I was I wondered about that. In my teens the truth burst upon me with a terrible poignancy. If mother saw her reflection only in that brass pan she would not know how yellow her face was becoming, and this ignorance might slow her decline. Or, delaying awareness of it, comfort her.

Cloud of unknowing.

I doubt if mother was deceived. I never

273

saw her use the pan as a mirror.

Father and mother were proud souls, he mercurial, impatient, explosive, she with greater control turning the pain of life inwards.

He too must have begun to go downhill then. There were other business ventures, dry-cleaning, electrical goods, local delivery, all ephemeral, whether because of ill-chance or bad management I never knew. Luckily, with his natural understanding of mechanical things, and his skill with tools, father could turn his hand to most practical tasks. For many years, in the fallow periods between these attempts to become – as he put it – independent, he made good money doing maintenance work in the garment factories. Each problem differing from the one before, he enjoyed the challenge. His care for quality of workmanship, imprinted during his days as a high-class craftsman in the walking stick trade, was well-known and he was in constant demand.

But always he would be drawn like a somnambulist to the faro table at the gambling club in St Vincent Place, in the heart of the business area near the Royal Exchange, and there, too often, he left his wages.

I never heard them quarrel, even when he came home skint and there was not a scrap of food in the house. In our cramped flat we would have heard any words of anger or reproach, but there were none. Was it simply the self-discipline born of their pride? Or was it love, more powerful than misfortune, weakness, foolishness? Often in adult years I told myself that that is what it must have been; I did so wistfully because I should have liked to have understood it while they both lived, and been old enough to express my tribute to their love.

That must have been the vision of them that Bernard's mother had, and timidly tried to convey.

They loved profoundly, simply, unquestioningly, acceptingly and, in their own fashion, with integrity.

One day of calamity, when the only item of food left was some cocoa in the bottom of a tin – no milk, no sugar, no bread, nothing – must have stuck in my memory because with a little child's single-minded discontent I blamed Mary, who was alone with me in the house, and kicked her hard on the shin for it. She must have been about thirteen, in puberty consumed with perplexities she could not possibly have shared with me, and therefore more forlorn than I was. Certainly she must have been every bit as hungry and frightened. Her pale round face, beneath its plaited corona of dark auburn hair, twisted in pain as she doubled up clutching her leg. She picked up a long bread knife and held it out, the handle towards me, saying through her tears: 'Go on then! Kill me if you like.'

I thought she meant it. She probably did, the way she felt. And now fear and horror at the imagined deed – I couldn't have done it but it *seemed* that I could – drove away the pangs of hunger. Drove everything away, except dread and despair in our isolation and powerlessness. What if no one came back! We sat in oppressed silence and, as the day waned, in darkness, for there were no pennies for the gas meter and no candles; and in increasing cold, for there was no coal left. We climbed into the alcove bed in the kitchen and huddled together for warmth under the blankets. At last, well into the evening, father came in with a few little parcels of food wrapped in newspaper, and a small bag of coal. Mother must have been at the hospital. Lilian was out late as usual.

In moody silence he busied himself getting a fire going in the kitchen range. Gradually the wintry dampness thawed out of the air. He put a few pennies in the gas meter and soon the little gas mantle on its thin metal bracket high above the fireplace spread its meagre yellow light upon us, its hoarse guttering competing with the crackle of the sticks in the grate and the coal on top of them spitting and sparking as the red and orange and blue flames licked and danced. For me, if not for Mary, it was his capable presence as he went methodically about the kitchen, more than his care in bringing food and warmth for us, that made the world come alive again. He peeled some potatoes and put them on the gas to boil, cleaned a few herrings and laid them out to cook on a griddle over the fire. Soon, with hunks of black rye bread, we ate and were comforted and felt delivered. My infant soul ardently focussed on the single moment, I soon forgot my hunger and despair, or thought I did, but Mary put each morsel of food into her mouth with an air of doing so under duress, with a kind of defiance, as in her emergent womanliness she essayed to judge him as a man, and made her verdict plain. Forgive him she never did. Years later she would tell me that she blamed him, not me, for that kick on the shin.

In her implacable nursing of wrongs she was very like him. Alas she knew it. And in other ways too. She was torn between her love for him and her hatred of his defects that were hers too.

Father often did save the day by forcing himself to leave the faro table while he still had a few shillings in his pocket. Had mother been at home he would have handed over the money to her, and *she* would have gone out to buy some basic food and a little coal. A silent message would have passed between them as he handed over the few coins. I often wished that I could have read his thoughts at such a time. Did he not see that this recurrent struggle on the frontier of survival was his own creation?

With his high earnings we could have lived comfortably by the standards of the time, not in the slums of the Gorbals, or in the Gorbals at all. Did he really feel, as he appeared to sometimes, condemned to lift the heavens single-handed, bemoaning a cruel fate like lonely Atlas? Not that he ever complained aloud; I could only guess. And now, standing at the sink there in shirt sleeves and braces scraping the scales off the herrings, with the eyes of two starving children boring into his back, what *did* he think of himself? Capable of great sensitivity, a compassionate and good-hearted man, how could he not read Mary's face, pale with fury and disdain and contradictory love? How could he not see that I sat there in fear, aware of a brooding despair in the air, racked with perplexity for I was aware – and feared the knowledge – that this was too heavy a burden, wondering what I *should* be making of it, knowing that whatever it was I had no power to change a jot of it?

When he came home not partially skint as on this occasion but totally so, and stood ashen-faced in front of mother in the kitchen, she stretched out a hand to his cheek in brief comfort, no word spoken, no sign of disappointment or reproach, then turned away and moved slowly, short of breath, to the curtains of the alcove bed, leaned on the wall and lowered herself carefully to her knees. With little gasps she reached under the bed and drew out a battered brown tin trunk, opened it with a key from her purse, and took out a beautifully embroidered tablecloth, treasured from her dowry, a silk blouse, or some other pawnable item from this emergency reserve. Dark head bent, breath coming hard, she closed the trunk and locked it and pushed it with obvious difficulty, nearly empty though it was, back under the trestle bed. Then, clutching the front timber of the bed, with a little groan she pulled herself upon to her feet again, spread the item on the bed cover and scrutinised every part of it to make sure it was in good condition, for if not its 'pledge value' would be diminished. If it needed ironing, that would be a worry, for as there was no money for the gas meter there was no way of heating the iron, unless a neighbour could be persuaded to put it on their gas stove for us. With such a crisis always threatening, mother must have regularly examined the trunk's contents to make sure that damp and mildew, or insect pests, had done no damage.

Ah that little key from her purse! Years

later I came across it and put it on my key ring. It fitted nothing, for the old tin trunk had disappeared long ago, but it touched my heart strings with memory, brought vignettes of their strange, deep flowing, abiding love, of the ways in which she strove to save him from himself. Whispers on the wind. Oh how well she knew him! She kept that trunk locked as an iron control over the last reserve of pawnable items, lest in his despair one day he raided it to feed not us but the faro table.

The day would come when I would wish I had followed that example.

The trunk's contents did not long survive her death.

During this ritual of dragging it from under the bed and deciding what could be pawned father stood apart, not because he would not assist her – he was always attentive to her in the home – but because a certain nicety restrained him from seeming eager to join in the plunder of treasured things to rescue us from his folly. Mary and I stood huddled, wide-eyed with wonder and fear; somehow we must have known that this enactment was at the very edge of existence, the commitment of our only reserves to the battle.

While Lilian lived at home such total crises were few. Father must have been less sunk in melancholy, and therefore less enslaved by the faro table, or luckier. I think it was the former. Even so she must often have got us out of trouble by contributing extra money for food when father came home skint.

As time went by another reason may have deepened his depression and tightened gambling's grip on him. After Lilian began to practise as an accountant, her income must have risen far above what he earned. While her success must have pleased him it must also have added to his conflicts, for he must have seen it as underlining his failure.

Lilian's going hit him hard – a judgement upon him, a desertion. A betrayal of *mother* he called it, though this was about three years after her death. I suppose he was too proud, or in his heart too clear-sighted, to call it a betrayal of *him*. He was also implying, unintentionally I am sure, that even in death mother was in some way still the linchpin of the family as she had been fully in life, and that he could not take over from her alone. How much lower could he cast himself down?

I never knew how much money Lilian contributed to the home. When she left he forbade all contact with her. Did he not guess that Mary and I could not go against our feelings, the attachment of blood come what may, and that his prohibition, apart from being futile, would distort our lives with anxiety and guilt? He even announced that he would never accept money from her; the pathos of that came fully home to me only when I was grown up, when I found out that for years after leaving home she often gave him money in secret to buy us clothes.

Why in secret? Even after so many years that thought could bring tears, that even in her continuing fury with him some tenderness made her protective of his pride.

Perhaps, too, she needed to protect her own? She could not bear to be thought soft. I once heard her tell Mary, after a furious row with him, 'When I leave home I'm not going to work my eyes out any more to pay for his gambling!'

Like many strong-willed people who think they have fought their way through only by suppressing sentiment, she affected to despise it.

For Mary and me as children, torn by awareness of father's torment, the reasons for it remained a mystery. Mary may at this time have begun to understand what gambling was, and perhaps what it could do to people. I had no idea. I hardly knew what money was, except that it consisted of round bits of metal, silvery or brown, that you handed over the counter to the shopkeeper; and, on pay-days, bits of paper that father and mother handled reverently.

Certainly neither of us understood the emotions that enchained people to gambling. We sorrowed for him, Mary less and less as she became a woman, or rather as her conflict about him, the tug-of-war between contempt and love, increased. But I wished and wished that I would wake up one morning to find that I had discovered the magic spell to cure his unhappiness.

Lilian justified her leaving us as an act of self-preservation. When I was about eight I overheard her tell Mary:

'If he thinks I've slaved all these years, night and day, to get qualified as a professional woman, and then let him drag me down like mother, then he's making a big mistake!'

While working as a typist and later as bookkeeper in Hieger's cloth warehouse, Lilian had become one of the first women in Scotland to qualify as an accountant.

I had no idea what 'drag me down' meant, but the corrosive vehemence in her voice sent a shudder through me. Father must have done something terrible if she could speak of him like that.

Not long after, one bitter winter evening, she packed up to leave. Since mother's death the place had had the air of life held in suspense, of little love, of stony coming and going, of grimly holding on. Lilian went to work about eight in the morning and returned late, sometimes around midnight. Father left a little after, usually accompanying Mary and me to school before going on to one of his maintenance jobs. Mary brought me back from school at four. That homecoming was the most depressing part of the daily round. Ill though mother had been for almost as long as I could remember, her simple presence when we came in from school radiated warmth even when the kitchen grate had no fire in it. These days the place was always cold. Each piece of our meagre furniture fixed me with a hostile eye as we came in, the kitchen range sullen in its neglected covering of ash and splashed fat, the only signs of life the glistening cockroaches scurrying in the shadows, and a scratching under the floorboards as mice hurried away at the sound of our footsteps.

Because Lilian was so much older, in fact had been a grown-up all my life, she appeared to my child's vision as a kind of parent; and so her going was in some way of the same nature as mother's, different only in the manner of it.

When mother died I remember standing in the darkened kitchen, not allowed to be near her lying in the alcove bed. Grown-ups towered closely round me, a forest of giants, seeming to wait for some signal from afar. Mother was making little murmuring sounds. And then there was a long hard deep sigh from her, followed by total silence. When I was a little older I understood that the murmuring sounds had been her struggles to breathe; the silence meant that the fight was over. The giants turned to each other and shook their heads as if puzzled. Women held each other and wept loudly. A few caught hold of me and keened over me and I wanted to push them away for they were disturbing my wonder at what was going on. 'Why,' I asked myself, 'are they making such a fuss? Mother is asleep, that's what they said would happen. She would fall asleep for a long time! That's what they said.'

Lilian's going was quite different. For one thing no one pretended. She was leaving us and I would not see her each day as before. But the most profound emotional difference, not fully understood till later but sensed, was that Lilian could decide *not* to go: Mother couldn't.

Though Lilian had been physically at home so little in each day, I saw her departure as the loss of one of the two remaining buttresses of our little family, a piece of adult strength I feared to be without.

The evening of her leaving the tension was almost palpable. Father sat at the kitchen table, shirt sleeves rolled up, bare elbows resting on the oil-cloth cover, and stared stonily at the range in its high black arch that filled most of one wall. The fire had gone out, and cold ash had spilled through the bars of the fire-cage and on to the hearth stone. While mother lived, the brass kerb had always shone like gold but it had probably not often been polished since her death, and was now a dull bronze flecked with droppings of fat.

Lilian called me from the little cubby hole she slept in next to the one I shared with Mary. Dressed in hat and coat ready to go, she stood tapping a foot, expressing the inflated self-justification that supports a violent act. Behind her on the wall the gas mantle at the end of its thin upturned pipe wheezed and sputtered, its tiny yellow incandescent shell throwing an enlarged silhouette of her on the faded white-washed wall a few feet away.

On the narrow iron bedstead lay an open suitcase, a large expanding one in brown fibre that was new to me, heaped with clothes, shoes, books, papers. Beside it lay a little pile of new, stiff-looking shirts and vests and pants and socks. She snatched it up and muttered through clenched teeth: 'Take these to father!'

She placed the bundle across my out-stretched arms. The aseptic, impersonal smell of new clothes somehow called to mind that last huge sigh of mother's, presaging silence. Now I was sure, if I had not been before, that she really was going.

Distant though she had always been I longed to reach out and cling to her, do anything she wanted, if only she would stay. Tears ran down my face and fell like rain on to the garments pressed against my chin.

'Oh come on now!' she hissed impatiently. 'You'll be all right. Go and do what I say.'

From her doorway across the tiny lobby to the kitchen was only a yard or so. She could almost have stretched across and handed them to him herself. But I knew that would not satisfy her. There had to be a go-between.

That realisation darkened everything. Something must have happened too terrible to be revealed.

I saw that in making me deliver this strange Parthian shot on her behalf – a shot it was, that much I understood – she dragged me into the crossfire of an incomprehensible adult battle. And this feeling that I was being thrown about by uncaring and savage forces far beyond my power to withstand cut deeply into me, a wound that would sting for many years. I would ask myself: 'Didn't she stop to think that I had feelings too? My own sister! What had I done to deserve it? Her quarrel with father was *her* affair, their affair, not mine!'

The fight in the shop would come back to me. If brothers could behave like that to each other, egoism obliterating the sympathy and compassion that close kinship was supposed to nourish, why should I be astonished at Lilian's cruelty to me? My feelings were irrelevant to her purpose and deserved no consideration. Where had I learnt that women were naturally kind, with a divine gift of sensitivity that made them tender and caring? Perhaps, like 'blood is thicker than water', that was an artful fiction too?

Something of these thoughts, or rather feelings, surged through me even then and fought to emerge, and because I could not properly grasp let alone formulate them, battered me inside. I turned away from her and went to father, and stood before him with the clothes lying across my arms as she had placed them there. That smell of new garments, so rarely experienced in our house, in spite of the deathly significance it now had, stirred a timid excitement. The child snatched at a morsel of comfort. We were to have new things to wear! How wonderful that was going to be! Then I felt the chill of father's stare, blank as of a face in marble, and my tears flooded out again.

I had the frightening sense of great forces fighting within him, and knew that he struggled to stop them roaring out in flame. Only in later years, turning over the experience again and again, would I identify them. Not so much anger as a rage with himself and with his fate, and disgust at her defection. And something else – fear. I smelt it. That *he*, my giant of a father, should be afraid tore the ground from under me.

Lilian had been the apple of his eye, brainy, articulate, lucent, confident, incarnation perhaps of the soul trapped inside himself, and secretly depended on to fight by his side, and with youthful dash and brilliance help him to realise the visions he had nursed from the days of his own youth. And now, with her going, a last hope would go too.

A premonition must have cast its shadow over me, to be understood years later. From this moment he would no longer confront life, only continue an unwinnable fight with himself.

Seeing me weeping as I held that apocalyptic gift out to him, he must have made a tremendous effort of control. He tried to smile:

'Listen to me,' he said, intending I knew to be warm and reassuring, but his words sounded hollow as from a tomb, 'what's happening isn't your fault. Don't cry. She shouldn't have sent you with this. She shouldn't have sent it at all! It's a guilt offering. You won't understand that now but you will when you get older. It's an insult as well if it comes to that. I mustn't lower myself to take it back to her, I mustn't even touch it. *You* must take it back. Don't say anything. Put it down in front of her and come back and sit on my knee. Everything will be all right, I promise you.'

How closed in they both were, unaware, or only partly aware? Defeated in a sense they both were, and both knew it, and yet they could display a regal pride and treat with one another as from within turreted citadels.

I stifled my sobbing and did as he said. If only I didn't have to!

She stared at me with something like the mixture of emotions I had seen in father's face. Yes, they were very like one another, ruled by a perverse, misleading, destructive pride.

Then she fixed her eyes on the bundle I had brought back. Terrified and desolate though I felt, hurled about in my whirlpool of emotions, I had a kind of pity for her – shattering for a child to feel about a grown-up – seeing the pathos and perplexity on her plump face, and the dampness glinting on her eyelids behind the thick rimless spectacles.

Her lips tightened and opened and tightened again as if she struggled to speak and no sound would come, in disbelief that what she had done could rebound upon her like this. She had misread him, as he had so often misread her. No doubt she felt diminished. A hard blow to that haughty spirit – as he had intended.

To his way of thinking, no matter how hard life was under the parental roof, a daughter must not leave it as long as she was unmarried. Duty to home, parents, sister, brother, was absolute. A professional woman must not live in a Gorbals slum tenement? That was no reason to leave home. Let her take the family with her! Where the family home was, there she must be.

Whether he knew of, or suspected, any of the intrigue that lay behind her going I never discovered.

Lilian was torn, like Mary, between profound love for him, as elemental as the wind and the rain, and contempt because he had wasted his talents – a cardinal sin to her, who gloried in the exercise of her own – and because he had stamped his failure upon mother's life, and probably shortened it. The latter thought oppressed her perhaps more than any other, for she feared that a similar fate awaited her too. An added reason, irrational and doubtless unconscious, to distance herself from him.

Her fear would prove well-founded. She too could not change her destiny. Leaving him would make no difference.

Perhaps her business ambition did have something to do with her leaving home, but not for the reasons she gave. Oddly for someone of her brains she blindly imitated the thinking and values of the rough and thrusting business people of the world in which she was making her way; and especially their superstitions. They had no time for the loser. He was to be shunned like the leper for fear you caught his infection, or lest other people imagined you had caught it and shunned *you*.

But these were minor influences. Years later, Mary would tell me of the crucial ones, sinister, cruel, destructive, in some of which she herself played a part.

Was father truly a loser? What *was* a loser? The tragic clown who could not accept that a course of action simply would not work despite failure after failure, and persisted in it? Or the man born under the wrong star, whose implacable destiny consigned him to ineluctable disappointment? Both descriptions turned on the observer's view of the desirable life. All they told you about the 'loser' was that he suffered.

Father was too complex a spirit, finely tuned, sensitive, to be judged simplistically. For him certain standards of his own were decisive, and if they could not be met he would settle for nothing else.

This was brought home to me with dramatic force when I was about five. I was with him in the Synagogue in Turriff Street near Eglinton Toll, at the point in the High Holy Day observances when the Cohanim, members of the hereditary priestly tribe, were about to ascend the dais and stand before the Ark of the Law, cover their heads and faces with their prayer shawls, and perform their ancient duty of conveying to the congregation the blessing of the Almighty. As a number of men rose to their feet from the wooden benches and began to make their way towards the dais, he took me by the hand and whispered urgently:

'Quick. We must go out now.'

We had been sitting at the end of one of the rows of benches only a few steps from the swing doors, and were able to slip out quietly. I wondered whether he had chosen to sit there with that in mind. Out in the draughty vestibule he turned up the collar of his coat and glanced back at the doors, apprehensively I thought, towards the worshippers we had left behind.

He said: 'We will wait here till they've finished that part.'

I studied his sombre face far above me: 'Father, why did we have to go out?'

His face assumed the distant look I knew well, when he sought to put subtleties into language I would understand, something he did with charm and ingenuity, and I loved him for that alone. 'Those men you saw going up there to the bimah [the dais on

293

which the Ark stood] are Cohanim, and we're Cohanim too, inheritors of the duty of priest, and they are going up there to give God's blessing to the people. As a Cohan myself I must not be in there when they do that.'

'Why?'

'Because I must either be up there with them blessing the people or be outside. And I can't go up there because I don't feel holy enough to bless the people on behalf of God.'

'Does that mean,' I persisted, with the cruel logic of a child, 'that all these other men going up to the bimah think they're holy?'

He stroked my face with a calloused hand and gave me a smile, partly of approval, partly of sadness. To try to explain might expose too much. And how could he, if he tried to answer the question truthfully, share with a little child the infinitely varied chiaroscuro of life?

'You ask hard questions my son. You don't know how hard! You'll have to wait till you're older – I'm sorry I'm always telling you that! And then you'll have to answer that question for yourself. Maybe they don't think they're holy. Maybe they're just pretending. Maybe they don't even think about it. Maybe they don't care. But I do care. And that's why I cannot go up there with them today. Maybe next year I will, only God knows that.'

A moral judgement on himself, the fruit of painful knowledge. Painful, too, to put it into words for his little son. Never mind what others did, *he* would not pretend that his soul was clean when he felt it was not, even if he suffered by the admission. Answerable, inescapably, to himself, and to God.

A child learns much by overhearing things. An innate shrewdness tells him to note in particular the unconsidered remark, and to discount much of what grown-ups deliberately say. In time he will learn to decode the prepared statements they use to conceal their thoughts.

'I made my own way,' I often overheard Lilian tell Mary, 'I worked late into the nights to pass my exams. Ruined my eyes to do it! He never paid a penny to help me. It was the other way round. It was me that came to mother's rescue many a time, to *his* rescue really! Who is he to tell *me* what my duty is?

'As for mother? He says I'm betraying her! How can I betray her when she's dead? What can anybody do for her now? If I don't get on with my professional career now, after all these years of bashing a typewriter and doing Hieger's books at night and studying all night to get qualified, it won't help *her!* She should've left him when she still had her health. But she was brought up in the old ways: "No matter what your man does, you stick by him!" Women are not thinking like that any more. But it's too late for her. And it'll be too late for *me* if I don't get away from him soon.'

Father dismissed such talk as a cloak for selfishness. Loyalty was all. A man's luck, good or bad, was not his alone but belonged to his wife and children as well. The good times were shared. So must the bad. You were all in it together. The Captain Scott dilemma: should the stronger members of a stricken group go on alone and save themselves, if there was no hope for their companions whether they stayed or not? Or remain and perish with them?

From what father from time to time let slip, he too had been tempted, long ago, to break away and go on alone. Had it been his own fierce principle – 'You go on together or perish together' – that held him back? Or, in a secret corner of his heart had he in truth mistrusted himself? And had that doubt blunted his will? Better the Devil you know...

Perhaps only part of him had stayed, while another part looked back over his shoulder at what might have been?

Wait for Destiny to speak.

Lilian's answer was different. She would

go forward alone and save herself. Or so she thought.

Standing trembling before her with the bundle of clothes resting on my out-stretched arms, I could not know what thoughts fought with each other behind those round flushed cheeks. Thinking of it with the knowledge of later years I fancy she too examined her standards, as father had just done; and like him, seeing that life refused to conform to them, could not or would not act differently. Her pride dictated an angry and blinkered response.

'All right!' she snapped, 'I'll take them back to the warehouse and get my money back. Does he think I care, throwing things back in my face? He's done that once too often, you tell him that. Go on!'

She seized the bundle from me, bent down to the suitcase, and with jerky movements, rage spilling over, began to pack the garments away, careful not to crease them.

Her anger had darted out like flame and scorched me. But her words meant little. This world of theirs, where a bundle of new clothes had the mysterious power to arouse fury, was too heavy for me to carry. I went back to him. He still sat there in his marble fixity. Mixed with my fear was another feeling, only later identified, new and unsettling; I was sorry for him.

He stirred and took me in his arms and

297

put me on his knee and spoke softly: 'Don't worry your head about all this. She may be clever and think she's very grown-up but she's got a lot to learn about life. She's spent too much time with her nose in books. Life doesn't happen the way the books say it does, all neat and tidy. She'll come to her senses one day. Let her go. We'll manage without her.'

As far back as I could remember Lilian had been distant, controlled, purposeful, building an incomprehensible life across a widening gulf of time and attenuated feeling. She could not, for all I knew would not, express affection through that life-giving alphabet of childhood, contact and warmth. Father expressed my feelings exactly when he spoke of her as always buried in books, almost sheltering behind them, at the kitchen table, or kneeling on the floor in her narrow room, wedged between the bed and the wall and using the bed as a desk, piles of books littering the blankets.

What dreams I fashioned about the mystery of those books! If only I could divine the magic communication that passed between her eyes and those pages? In the silence of the night something would waken me and I would know at once what it was and be drawn to it, the shadow on the wall in her room cast by the gas mantle, a brooding presence separate from her and also part of her. I would get up from my palliasse and creep to her door and stand there, ignoring the cold linoleum chilling my bare feet, and watch, not moving, hardly breathing. What spells did she weave in the quivering yellow light? What was that potent shadow on the wall commanding her to do? What was she writing, writing, writing?

Would that I could get near her, would that I could understand.

After a while she would sense my presence and swing round and each time I hoped she would say: 'Come to me! And I'll show you the magic!'

Instead she would take off her round glasses with an impatient sweep of the hand and rub her tired-looking eyes, and say crossly: 'I can't study with you standing there watching me! Get back to bed. Go on!'

Still, that was contact of a kind. Remote she had always been, but she was *there*, part of the fabric of my small world. Now she would go out of the door weighed down by that monster suitcase and make her way for the last time down the cold stone stairs into the street, to remain out there in some other world, far away. So another bit of my world would break off and float away, never to be seen again, as when father's two brothers departed and took aunts and cousins with them. And Charlie!

I could not foresee the furtive meetings in the coming years, planned many days before, when Mary would take me by the hand, swear me to secrecy, and take me to visit Lilian in a smart flat far away across the city. For some days after each visit I would be sick with guilt, fearing father's intuition. Certainly, for me, those meetings were stiff, hurried, miserable affairs, audiences given grudgingly. For Mary, as I learned many years later, they did have a dark importance.

Meanwhile, tearfully watching her go, I steeled myself again to the thought that life would always be punctuated by departures, bits of me lost for ever, everything transient. I would travel from one void to the next. Yet even as I thought this I knew that somewhere within me I did not, would not, believe it. At the next moment, the next turning in the road, I would see all that I had lost, the things I had clung to and thought I would always have beside me, the people I had loved and was going to hold close to my heart for ever, come racing back to me.

15

SISTERS' FLIGHT

I must have sensed that night that other forces, alarming because hidden, were at work. That awareness must have troubled me even more than the enactments I did see, especially because all three, father on one side and Lilian and Mary on the other, though ranged in conflict, appeared to connive at the concealment.

One feature worried me particularly, though it would surface in my mind explicitly only when much older. Mary was out at her evening classes. Why did Lilian choose *that* night, knowing Mary would not be at home, to pack up and leave us, an act that must have been prepared some time before?

Mary, somewhat nearer to me in age – Lilian at twenty-eight seemed as distant in age as father – could have been a comfort to me simply by her presence. Even at that age I felt it inconceivable that she did not know of Lilian's intention to leave. Obviously my sisters had settled the timing between them, and for some reason, whether for Lilian's interest or Mary's or both, had decided that Mary should not be present. Why?

Since all three of them were united to exclude me from knowledge, there was no one to whom to express my worries, or appeal to share them, perhaps even explain them away. Battened down, they gnawed away at me within.

Many years later, Mary would reveal the background, and I would come face to face with the truth of what, as a child, I had partially seen. All the details of my sisters' egoism and ruthlessness, clearly defined at last, would click into remembered places. Even with adult understanding doing its best to silence those memories, the pain would return as sharp as it had been long before.

The question remains, had I known it all *at the time* would I have been hurt the less? The answer must be yes. The unknown terrifies more than the known.

The adult wrestles with the logical, which usually means the superficial, and sees less and less of what lies beneath appearances. The child pierces straight through to the raw core of things, and suffers because he sees far more than he has experience to understand in its wholeness. He sees too much for comfort, 'Expert beyond experience'.

In my fashion I had perceived it all, the

paths that Lilian and Mary had chosen of escape and safety and worldly gratification, and a muddled urge to avenge mother's suffering by hurting father.

Though they rated their sensitivity highly, proclaiming in proof their heartache on mother's behalf, the fact – obvious one would have thought – that their strategy entailed suffering for their little brother, perplexed and defenceless as he was, did not occur to them. I had put the raw facts together and reached a harsh verdict, and set it down in the books as a debt against them. In doing so I tore at my love for them as at a sacred thing, and was wounded still further.

I could not have put words to their behaviour. In my memory it remained incised as twisted and wrong; and, sadly, as injury done to themselves as they strove to outstrip the Furies. I sorrowed for them too.

In their view, it seemed, the desirability of their goals justified any injury inflicted in pursuing them. For them too the end justified the means.

Both were naive emotionally, at least on the evidence of their personal lives. When it came to manipulating people in their business affairs, however, it seems they were sensitive and shrewd.

Obsessed with escaping mother's fate, Lilian set herself to be hard and mercenary, to use men solely to advance her career. She would sell what she had to offer them discreetly, with calculation. Not of course a unusual scenario: some might say it was justified, or at least the more understandable, bearing in mind that in the twenties and thirties for women to enter the professions, let alone advance in them unaided, was rare. It must be admitted, however, that the crux of the matter is the road the emotions want to follow, and for many women Lilian's choice would have done unacceptable violence to precious feelings and beliefs.

Such a profit and loss account had no interest for Lilian. For her the need to call the tune was paramount. She must not repeat mother's mistakes.

Even so, was hers the only way? If she had been kinder, less ferociously insensitive where her professional interest was not involved, would she have forfeited one moment, one iota, of fulfilment? One may doubt it. She might well have gained. I saw her always as steeled and tight-lipped, with no sign of happiness in her, no free laughter, no joy, only fixity, demons in possession. And that grim aspect continued even after she left home, when she had begun to practise, and to prosper.

With what irony, with what precision, do the Fates deal the cards? She was to die solitary, well off, her grudges unappeased.

Mary, too, longed for escape but also for safety. In some ways she was less single-mindedly mercenary. However, in her own fashion she was as detached as Lilian. And she too paid heavily.

She set higher store by emotional security, and thought she would find it with a man soft-hearted and caring and pliant, far removed, as she thought, from father's toughness and uncontrollability. In her most crucial relationship, in which she invested eight years of her springtime – from about seventeen to twenty-five – she discovered that, as so often with seemingly weak and dependent people, the man was strong and coolheaded enough where his own interests were at stake.

Both Lilian and Mary invested too much emotional capital in their opposition to father, whose influence naturally remained dominant, try as they might to escape; and this imbalance distorted their view of relationships and of the world. Self-doubt continued, defiance its obvious antidote. The secure person does not need such defiance. He presents himself for what he is and others are likely to accept him at his own confident valuation. Father did not intend to instil self-doubt into us, though he may have inadvertently transmitted his own. They misread him. They misread themselves.

Mary drew back the curtain during a reappraisal of what had been for her an exciting, careless time.

'D'you remember,' she asked, 'that I was out that night?'

'How could I not! I've thought about it often. Too often. I'd have found that whole business a lot less upsetting if you *had* been there.'

'I didn't *dare*, in case I couldn't keep it all in! We didn't know how much father knew, or suspected. About what we'd *both* been up to I mean! You remember how intuitive he could be sometimes? We didn't know how he was going to take her going. Remember his terrible rages? I couldn't have kept stony-faced like Lily could! We didn't want a whole lot of things to come out! So we decided she'd go that night when I'd be out at my classes.'

'What *was* all this you had to keep secret?'

'You mean to say you never guessed!'

I guessed now. Memories returned. Whispers overheard, glimpses of meaning looks; perplexity, helplessness, knowing and not knowing.

'How could I have guessed? I was only about nine! Don't you remember? So she was pregnant, was that it?'

'You sound angry.' Her tone reproached me. 'You can't still be after all this time? We couldn't help ourselves! You must understand that surely?'

For Lilian to have had any tender attachments at all seemed bizarre as I had seen her, cold, controlled, detached, someone in whom calculation always came first.

Later however, in adolescence, it did cross my mind that Hieger, her employer and patron and later a principal client of her accountancy practice, might also be her lover.

'Of course he was!' Mary was astonished. 'Though I wouldn't use the word love! Not with a crude man like that whose mind never got as high as a woman's belly button. Anyway, why d'you think he did all that for her? She paid him for it with her body. As simple as that! Well, no, it wasn't that simple, not for him I mean. He wanted her badly. Needed her rather, I should say. But he was only one of them. Whether he knew he was sharing her I don't know. I don't think so, not at the beginning anyway. Later on, when she had him where she wanted him, it was different. He probably did know. But by then she didn't have to care. He couldn't take back what he'd given her, and he had to go on giving her what she wanted. Anyway, I'm not sorry for him. He did get what he wanted from her, as far as it went. So she was entitled to everything she got out of *him*. You look shocked?'

'Never mind,' I said roughly. 'Tell me the

rest. I want to see the whole of it.'

'Try and understand how we felt, Lily and me. We used to cry together about the life mother had; how *she* got paid back for being nice and gentle and loving and long-suffering! From about the time I had my very first period, Lily kept on at me that that wasn't the way a woman should be. Oh no. *She* was using her body as well as her brains to get what she wanted. No man was going to get anything for nothing! *She* would always be in control! Men would pay through the nose, not only money I mean, or not the way you think. First of all to help her get qualified. That cost plenty, you know. And then money to set up her accountancy offices. And help in building up her practice, bringing new clients to her and so on, help in making useful contacts, and in moving into profitable deals on her own. She led them on till they were mad for it, till they would do anything she wanted. I admit I was a bit shocked myself sometimes, in the early days. Anyway it worked! She got what she wanted.'

Hieger was a man of many interests, property, cinemas, bookmaking, a shrewd wheeler-dealer who cheerfully sailed close to the wind. It was said that one of the sources of his wealth was the enhanced value of many of his properties which he rebuilt with the insurance compensation following fires. Such a man had useful contacts. For him to arrange for an abortion to be done discreetly in a private clinic was a simple, if expensive matter.

'Lily came to the office one lunch time and we went and bought some buns and milk and sat on a bench in George Square round the corner, near the drinking fountain where the meths drinkers sat, and she told me about it. Oh I'll never forget the look on her face! A sort of glory! No, that's wrong, it was wonder at what she'd done. I'll tell you – I was always frightened of getting pregnant myself but at that moment, in my girlish way, I was proud of her. Though she'd never said it in so many words, I knew that she intended to fix Hieger that way. And now that she was pregnant she would never look back. She was going to get everything she wanted.'

The pregnancy had been confirmed only the day before. Lilian radiated a half-incredulous triumph, and a fevered intensity. The soldier going over the top.

'She said it must be Hieger's. It was only then I knew for certain there were others. You knew he was giving her all that time off work to go to college, and paying her college fees? Didn't you?'

'No, of course not. I knew nothing about any college. I remember her saying she qualified by studying at night and doing a correspondence course. I suppose she didn't dare let on at home she was going to college or father would have wanted to know where she was getting the money from. Ah yes, she said she often had to work into the small hours doing Hieger's books for him.'

'God, that's rich! It wasn't his *books* she was doing at night but something else! At one time he was even saying he wanted to marry her, didn't you know that?'

How could a child have known any of these things? To assume that he did, and that he knew them with an adult's under-standing, must have been her naive device to escape guilt.

'How was he going to marry her?' I asked stupidly. 'It seems he made himself out to be a proud family man?'

'Well you may ask! If the way had been that clear to marry her he might even have done it. Anyway he talked big about making a settlement on his wife and getting free. That kind of talk. Life is not very original, is it?'

Epitaph for herself.

My image of Mary in her teens was of a lovely, graceful girl, with translucent creamy skin and dark silky hair long enough for her to sit on. Eyes wide in innocence and candour, a warm-hearted sprite. She tripped through the world seeking an equal innocence. The kind of girl of whom people said: 'She'll fall in love once, and that'll be forever. The sort that sticks to her man through thick and thin!'

From mother's photographs, she too had looked like that as a girl.

I must have been eight or nine when Mary let slip that she was 'going out' with a rich Indian student. She was about seventeen then; certainly it was before Lilian left us. Something new and wondrous and totally absorbing made her glow from within. I was aware of waves of feeling, exciting but enigmatic, radiating from her. But the accompanying secretiveness weighed me down. There seemed to be so many things father must not know! And how terrible these things must be. Fear of discovery by father added to my stock of nightmares.

The word love rang like the voice of a golden bell, but a muffled one, to be heard in secret, coming from Mary's lips breathless with enravishment. This love, whatever it was, must be something important to fill her with such glory! But it was also to be feared if father must not know about it?

It seemed that her lover, Gil, was gentle and caring, but indolent. He would marry her, he said, when he had finished his studies. That, if it meant getting a degree, never happened. Year followed year, of happiness and luxury for her, of timeless *dolce far niente* for him.

How she explained her frequent absences, trips to the country in the Bentley, down-river on his boat, days at the races and in his flat, I dimly traced to her references to the many girl friends she stayed with – difficult for father to verify in those phoneless days – and the midnight whisperings with Lilian. I smelled the guilt, and would carry it vicariously, faithfully, through puberty and adolescence. That I was acting out lies to father, blindly taking her side against him, keeping him in ignorance of things he had a right to know, I understood well enough. I feared to ask why. I feared to tell.

When I was older, and Mary had left home, it was too late to make a clean breast of it to father. He probably knew, and understood why I had not spoken. Even in his sadness and disappointment, he never once stooped to tax me with my complicity against him.

In the eighth year the family in India foreclosed on Gil. Or so he said. 'Come home. Time for play is over. You must now take your place here and marry your betrothed.'

This was his first mention of a betrothal, arranged by his parents long ago, he said, without his consent. Mary pretended to take the news stoically. She decided that, as the woman 'in possession', she was strong enough to restore her position to what she had thought it had been, his bride to be. Endlessly they talked about how to 'rescue' him; she assumed, alas, that he wanted to be rescued. Like mother, she tried to save her man from himself.

About sixteen then, I sensed her heartache only in the abstract; her agony seemed to me overblown. I felt, and in my callow roughness probably said it too bluntly, that she had chosen, almost deliberately, to play a game that she was certain to lose: what was predictable must have been intended.

It was so obvious: a gilded and feckless fellow from a totally different culture, language, outlook, destined to return to a country where she could not hope to slot into a place of equality, let alone tranquillity. In the grand tradition he had picked on her for totally different fulfilments, necessarily transient. Like father, she had *chosen* to be defeated, and to carry the mark for the rest of her life.

Gil insisted that he would obey the summons home only to lay his hands on his inheritance, and so possess the wherewithal to marry her. But he would also try hard to make his family accept her as his bride; failing that he would come back and marry her.

Fearing to part from him, she pleaded with him to believe that his money was

313

unimportant. She would be the willing sacrifice: 'I will work my fingers to the bone for you! We will manage. We will have each other!'

He had smiled sadly. Manly pride would not permit anything of the kind.

There came the classic farewell: 'I will send for you as soon as I can or come back to you. We shall be married come what may!'

His early letters were confident. He hoped to win the support of this or that influential relative. In time the tone changed; they were less and less specific. He would never give up the fight. One day he would come back and marry her. One day. The years passed. His letters ceased.

She never saw him again; she never married.

Lilian, at least by her own lights, played her cards better. As she had expected, Hieger, scared, ignored his previous talk of marrying her. Everything must be kept secret at any price. She knew then that he was at her mercy.

She imposed her conditions. He must personally arrange for an abortion in a private clinic, and make her a much bigger 'allowance', which must include establishing her immediately in a flat in one of the smart districts. He did everything she asked. Somehow she got hold of the receipt for his payment to the clinic. With that evidence, the threat she held over him was ruinous, and permanent. She would have other demands in future.

I said: 'So much for the talk about leaving home to be independent and to escape being dragged down by father! Somehow I must have seen through it, realised it was a smoke screen for something else, but not knowing what it could be, assumed it must be too terrifying to be told. No wonder I didn't believe in much after that time. With a flat of her own she could go into the clinic with no one around to ask where she was going. Afterwards she could operate more freely with other men. And of course a flat up west was a status symbol useful for business!'

'That's right. That was all part of the strategy. Hieger furnished the flat in real style. It was all expensive stuff, believe you me. Everything put in her name. The phone and all the other bills paid, everything.'

'And you too?'

'Me? No, he didn't pay for my abortion. Gil did. He was scared out of his wits his family would find out. I was scared too. It was one of those accidents. Anyway Lily got Hieger to make all the arrangements and write out the cheque to the clinic and get the receipt in his own name, which of course Lily took charge of.'

'The two of you! It's hard to believe.'

'Oh I don't know! Those were funny times, desperate times in a way. God knows how many times I've thought about it all these years. I don't *think* I was trying to trap Gil, I really don't. Sometimes I think it may have made him make up his mind the wrong way, who knows! Anyway, at least somebody benefited from it!'

'Who?'

'Lily of course. In that way, maybe in every way, she came off better than me. At least that's what I thought at the time.'

'What do you mean?'

'Well! With two clinic receipts in his name for abortions – they called them "curettages" but that wouldn't fool Hieger's wife or anybody else! Lily had him more than ever where she wanted him. How do you think she got the money to set herself up in style with offices and staff and everything? And got all those clients so quickly? *And* a finger in the pie in his big property deals? Stands to reason!'

'Very nice! Playing a wild game like that, no wonder she'd no time to care what happened to us small fry at home!'

That was a way of putting it. I knew, even as I said it, that I was ignoring many things. I was reacting impulsively, in the heat of the emotions her account had resurrected. It was as impossible for me, as an adult, to see into my sisters' hearts all those years ago, as it had been for me as a child at the time. Oppressed, fearing for themselves, did they see in flight and opportunist calculation their only hope? Who was I to judge?

16

PAWN TICKET

Mother took a clean pillow case and gently eased into it the items to be pawned, smoothed it out and wrapped it in a sheet of newspaper. Everyone in the street knew when a woman was on her way to the pawnshop, for even though it happened so frequently – the demand was such that there was hardly a street in the Gorbals without at least one pawnshop in sight – and 'respectability' constrained one to conceal the deed, a common telepathy made everyone aware of it. Or perhaps it was the ritualistic manner of the attempt at concealment? There was a special pose of unconcern as one approached the pawn-shop door, a pause at the window as if some item there had caught the attention, a shrug as if to say to any observer: 'Oh well, no harm in asking how much that cost!' and a quick entry. On the way there, the neat shape of the newspaper package was itself a giveaway, confirmed by its absence when the woman emerged.

Mother threw her old grey shawl round

her shoulders and tucked the parcel under it, not wholly concealing it, snatched up a battered shopping basket and put a string bag in it, and hurried out, still without a word.

Father stood for some minutes like a statue, heavy shouldered, lantern jawed, tight lips bloodless in the twilight. Collecting himself he moved to the long earthenware sink, threw off jacket, shirt, woollen 'semmit' – long-sleeved vest – and washed vigorously, blowing hard as the icy water shocked his skin.

How often did he scourge himself?

Mother might get ten shillings from the pawnshop at the corner. She went along the street and bought potatoes, bread and margarine, broken kippers – sold off cheaply by the fishmonger – or herrings to fry with onions and potato fritters, flour, oatmeal, sugar, tea, milk, and candles in case pennies for the gas meter ran out again, and a ha'penny box of safety matches. In the next few days we would eat. If father was in work, luckily he usually was, she would hope to persuade him to bring his wages home without visiting the faro table that week, and the next week, and so on for as long as possible. She would give him eightpence for cigarettes, the price of twenty Woodbines or a small portion of rubbed tobacco with which to roll his own; something he hated doing for it offended his pride. In the next few weeks, putting by a few coins at a time in a hiding place she alone knew, she would get enough money together to redeem the treasures from the pawnshop. And back they would go into the trunk under the bed.

To be fair, father would not need much persuasion, his abstention a tribute to her loyalty, her love, her sacrifice. By coincidence it usually lasted just long enough to get those emergency reserve items out of pawn.

Whatever the blows that fell, both observed a fierce nicety of behaviour. They would not expose their bitterness – and father, especially, his disappointment with himself.

Had my sisters and I been closer in age we might have helped one another to understand the feelings father and mother kept battened down, and made fewer demands on them. A child's worried dependence clouds parents' vision, triggers ill-considered action. Discord and guilt grow. Father, when he seemed to exclude us, was doubtless trying to clear his mind the better to wrestle with his perplexities. Mother's unwillingness to show concern might have been her way of protecting us, lest the depth of her suffering hit us too hard.

If only they had been open with us! We knew, and did not know, what worried them. The child's intuition illuminates random patches, uncertainly understood; and in the darkness that remains his imaginings conjure images far more shocking than the reality. Allowed to share their worries our love might have given them strength, and the burden of ill-digested experience we carried into adult life, there to distort our judgement too, would have been lighter.

As it was, their silence increased the uncertainty and wariness between us children; certainly between my sisters and me. Stretch out to them as I might across the gulf of age and experience, I could never reach them. And they, eagerly facing the adult world, did not try to reach me.

I did not abandon hope of understanding them. I would try to grow quickly out of childhood to be closer to them, faint yet pursuing. That the distance sometimes appeared to shorten proved, alas, a mirage. When I left school at fourteen Mary was twenty-one and Lilian thirty-two; she had been living away from home in her own flat for some years, a 'professional person' with a flourishing accountancy practice, a new woman. Mary had gone to live with Aunt Rachel and Uncle Salman.

We learnt to know when father, out all night, had been cleaned out at the gambling table. He brought home a paper bag of sugared buns still warm from the oven and breathing its magical aroma, bought with his last shilling at the bakery passed on his dawn walk home, only on 'skint' mornings! A pathetic effort, I realised in later years, to show his love for us, an antidote to guilt.

The buns, a rare treat in our house, were at first a delight, a sign of plenty. Then I found they signalled the opposite, lean times, even whole days without food, and they were like the ritual bitter herbs we ate at Passover.

Astonishingly in one who could be so sensitive, he seemed not to grasp that his morning bounty of buns, symbols of the riches he could *not* bring, had this effect on us, or perhaps he could not bear to, for he never failed to bring them.

One day he let slip that he sometimes had to 'borrow' that shilling from one of the men at the table. He said it ironically, as if he ridiculed his posturing self from afar, weakly defiant.

How could my father, so fiercely proud, court such humiliation? When I was about thirteen I once plucked up the courage to ask him. Why go on and on taking such punishment?

The grey-blue eyes darkened and he looked at me in sympathy, as a seer might regard a disciple not yet fully schooled to the higher understanding: 'It's hard to explain. All other ways are closed. I don't *know* what other way to go, maybe that's the way to put it. One day I must win. Really win. Everybody does sooner or later. And then I'll be free to do what I want.'

I wished and wished I was strong enough, *knew enough*, to lift him up. He was groping in the dark. Sadly I glimpsed in him what he had been long ago, a man of vision, of soaring imagination, confidently aware of his powers, sincere, creative, courageous. Somewhere along the road, long before the fight in the umbrella shop, life had hit him hard. He was a beaten man and knew it, yet struggled on, aimlessly now and with lessening strength, to gainsay that knowledge.

I did not have the heart to ask: 'And what *is* it you want to do?'

Young as I was, I saw it would be futile. He knew that he had not given me an answer. To do so he would have had to rehearse too many blunders which, like so many pledges in the pawnshop, were now unredeemable.

The very young have no past to regret, and no stake in the present. The future is their glittering possession, an amorphous treasure waiting to take shape at their command. An effort of will is all that is needed. Nothing is impossible. Why was it that father, in my eyes all-powerful for so long, would not make that effort? Would I understand, one day, why he punished himself?

Meanwhile I wept for him. I had no power to do more.

He had always worked hard. He liked shaping materials with his hands, carving, turning, carpentry, making things work. As a small child, seeing him bend over something he was working on, a broken chair, a bicycle, a sewing machine, seeming to grasp its essence by being close to it, in a kind of devotion, I felt that he perceived the world not by words and logic but emotionally, by sense and feeling, touch and form and texture, the elemental relationships of things, a lonely innocent.

In a world made up of people like Hieger, such a soul is buffeted without mercy, draws in upon itself for frail shelter, treads the shadows.

Farfalla in tempesta,
Under rain in the night.

In the market place the Hiegers will always win. That is, as the world knows winning. They have no inner quest, or rather turn their backs on the one they were born with. They despise the innocent for persisting in his.

The innocent asks uncomfortable questions. He reminds people of the spiritual essence they prefer to forget. The Hiegers ride over him.

From early days I knew that father's moments of fulfilment were few. I doubt whether he enjoyed even the flush times when he went on a spending spree, when he seemed possessed by a sardonic frenzy, threw his winnings in the faces of the Furies: 'You see! This means nothing to me! The prize I seek is greater, much greater, than this!'

When he did have a biggish win, forty to fifty pounds perhaps, a fortune to us, he brought back no sugared buns that morning! He brought nothing. But later that day he would start spending. For mother a coat and hat and blouses and handkerchiefs; boots and stockings and underclothes for me, shoes and stockings and knickers and vests for Mary. Lilian, who for as far back as I could remember earned her own keep, got luxury items like lace handkerchiefs or a silk blouse. He would bring lengths of cloth and trimmings for mother to make additional clothes with, sheets, pillow cases, towels, a tablecloth. And much food; though with no refrigerator there were limits to what we could store. The first item was usually a huge chicken, a wondrous treat, which mother would cook with dreamily exciting stuffing, and with various additions in the ensuing days make it last for many meals. There would be real butter, large duck eggs, many jars of jam. The coalman would fill our coal bunker, a wooden bin behind the front door, to overflowing even if it was summer; coal at least would not go bad.

Only when he had done all this would he buy anything for himself, cloth and trimmings for a suit and overcoat, shoes, shirts, socks.

The only times mother raised her voice above her usual controlled tones were when he was about to sally forth to the shops with that possessed look in his eyes: 'Don't throw money away buying things for *me!* And don't spend it all now. Put some in the Post Office for the future! For the children, for things that might happen!'

She would look into his eyes with hope, then turn away, shoulders drooping. Both knew, I suspect, that to spend the money was for him the only way of saving it. Otherwise it would go back to the faro table.

Some did find its way back, indirectly, through the medium of the pawnshop. That was brought home to me later, when I was about seventeen, in a manner so traumatic, so unbelievable, that the shock remained with me for years.

I was then earning about thirty shillings a week, nearly a man's wage. I decided to realise an ambition, to own a decent suit. For a garment worker that meant a bespoke suit, a fine quality 'other' suit. I saved and saved for about a year, and at last had enough money, four pounds or so. In the garment workshops, especially the smaller ones, workers collaborated to make the occasional suit or coat or pair of trousers for one of their number or a member of his or her family, in their own time – working on these private jobs in the factory early in the morning or late in the evening – but using the boss' sewing machines, thread, gas to heat the press irons, electricity for light and power. You bought the cloth, lining material, canvas, buttons and other trimmings, got one of the tailors to measure you and cut the garment, and later fit you and make adjustments, and a machinist, a hand sewer, a buttonhole hand and a presser to do their parts, paying each a few coins previously agreed. Most bosses tolerated the practice provided the workers were not making a regular business out of it.

In this fashion I at last had a proper suit, of the best worsted, made to measure. A high-class suit of charcoal grey with a delicate white stripe the width of a thread, hand stitched edges, four-button cuffs with real buttonholes. Every penny of it earned with my own hands. I was in glory.

One day in early autumn, not long after I

had got it, I came in from work tired but uplifted by pleasant anticipation; I was invited to a family gathering at Bernard's house that evening. There would be noisy, easy talk, the kitchen crowded out into the lobby, the heat intense, reddened faces blooming. Bernard's mother, dressed in shiny black with a fresh looking white apron, rosy with pleasure in her guests' enjoyment, would dish out simple wholesome food, devotedly worked on that day – as a child I often sat in her ever-cosy kitchen watching her cook; there might be baked rolled herrings, potato latkas, thick slices of her ginger sponge cake. A friendly, homely evening. The like of it in our flat, dimly remembered, had been long, long ago.

I would wear my suit!

Our flat had its familiar air of desertion, cold and grey and damp, of life stilled. There were only the two of us now, father and me. Small as it was, the flat was too big for us – to say nothing of the cost – but he would not move to an even smaller one. He would never have admitted it but I fancy he secretly dreamed of a day when the four of us would be together again. More deeply still, in his heart he could not bear to leave the place where mother died.

There was no fire in the kitchen grate, not unexpected, but on this grey evening its absence, emphasised by dead ash spilt down the fire bars beside the oven door, made the atmosphere more than usually cheerless. I would feel better when I had heated the big copper cooking pot full of water on the gas ring, emptied it into the sink and had a good wash, put on a clean shirt and my new suit.

The tiny lobby was little bigger than two telephone kiosks put together. Facing the front door was a press, a cupboard in the wall, where we kept our few clothes, bits of household equipment, boots, a few tools. I decided to get my suit from it and take it into the kitchen with me so that I could put it on immediately after I had washed. In the semi-darkness I half-opened the door of the press and reached in for the suit. My fingers touched the wooden coat hanger. It swung freely. The suit was not there.

I felt I had expected this. Had I conjured up a piece of negative sympathetic magic, hoping to persuade the evil powers to stay their hand? But I was hit hard, very hard. I was astonished to find myself trembling, gripped by fear and rage, fear of what my rage might do if I let it command me. And then, as if a breaker rolled in from a dark sea, I felt thrown down and helpless.

I was roused by the sound of a key being turned in the front door beside me. Before I could move, it was pushed open and jammed me hard against the press. Father stood in the doorway, his stocky bulk almost shutting out the grey evening light from the stair window behind him. Face pale and drawn, he looked at me in a kind of wooden apprehension.

All the winds of the world screamed round me. But in the midst of the tumult I felt an awareness unlike anything experienced before. I was responding in a manner totally new, reasoning with myself in a counterpoint that years later I would understand marked the beginnings of maturity. The expression on father's face, the lines at the mouth etched black and hard in the dimness, reached out to me, forced me away from my hurt and anger. I wanted to deny the appeal but my heart would not let me. Compassion hurt, yet it brought a small release from fury and self-pity. Other thoughts were admitted. I saw why I had half-expected this crisis. That morning, he had come home from a night at the gambling club bringing a bag of sweet buns.

He knew why I was standing there.

He said: 'I'm sorry.' It was the first time he had ever used those words to me.

He turned his face away quickly. But in the weak gleam from the stair window I caught the sheen of tears in his eyes.

Mine were damp too. In the midst of my racing anger I felt shame for him. To pawn his son's only suit – worked so hard for, saved and skimped for.

At Bernard's they would all be in their 'other' clothes. Of course it ought not to matter. Bernard would not ask himself: 'Why is he turning up in his shabby working clothes? Why doesn't he wear his other suit?' But to me it would matter. It would look like disrespect. I couldn't wear a notice on my chest saying: 'I didn't wear my other suit because my father's just pawned it!'

Not that it would have shocked anybody to say that. But you didn't flaunt your troubles. Everybody had plenty of their own.

I could not trust myself to speak. A single word, any word, might have released the violence bottled up inside me and God knows what I would have done. I doubt if I could have raised my hand to him, but I am sure I wanted to. I thought of Cain and Abel, but that was different. To strike your own father! Perhaps he blindly wanted me to. What deterred me, finally, was pity.

He brushed past me to the kitchen, half-turned, fumbled in a pocket, held out a small square of blue printed paper, the pawn ticket. I took it. He had some brown paper bags with him and went on into the kitchen and deposited them on the table.

Handing me the ticket was another clang of the doom bell, as if he said to me 'You'll be able to get your suit back from pawn before I can.'

His dreams of winning streaks, even of little ones, were fading. It would take me a good few months to save up the twenty-five shillings, plus interest, to redeem my suit.

A chair scraped on the bare floor planks in the kitchen. He sat there, back straight, hands clasped on the table, and stared in front of him. His sparse hair, once a vigorous ginger, now mainly silver, gleamed softly in the chill grey light that filtered through grimy window panes.

I remained there in the dark. If only I could walk away from all this! Now. Forever! Why not? What had happened belonged to a known pattern. It was one more blow in a long line. Was our family *so* different? Where were all those high principles of family life – love, loyalty, the cleaving together of parents with children, and children with each other? Or were they empty formalisms, products of habit, addiction to shibboleths, with no spiritual force? No, there must be more. Other families – Bernard's, Alec's, Meyer's, Phil's and the rest – seemed genuinely bonded together. Their members took thought for one another, willingly, unselfishly; they kept faith.

I thought back to when Lilian, and then Mary, had left home, and of how fiercely he had denounced their betrayal, how deeply he had been hurt. Why was obligation always from us to him? In pawning my suit had *he* not betrayed *me?* And was not his gambling addiction, even allowing that it sprang from pain within, a betrayal of us all?

Should I, could I, follow the example Lilian had set so long ago, and then Mary, and cut the invisible strings. I had never seriously asked myself this before. I did not dare answer it – yet.

I went into the kitchen. In silence I put water in the kettle and set it on the gas ring to boil, then made a pot of strong tea and placed a cup and saucer in front of him, put three lumps of sugar in the cup. I took from its brown paper bag the crusty loaf he had bought, cut a couple of slices and spread them with margarine from the quarter pound slab in another of the paper bags on the table, and put them before him on a small chipped plate with gold edging. Years ago there had been many more pieces of china with that gold decoration. Once upon a time, mother had told me, they had formed a magnificent tea service, part of her wedding portion. That plate and cup and saucer were all that was left of it.

On the cracked oil-cloth table cover I set out what he had bought, a pint of milk, bag of sugar lumps, bread, margarine, six eggs, a few herrings, about half-a-stone of potatoes, onions, a bar of soap ... pieces of my suit.

But this was not all surely? Some of my suit must still be in his pocket. Unless he had been back to the faro table in St Vincent Place already! Today was Monday, four days to go till pay day. If he were to gamble away the rest of my suit we faced a day or two of fasting after we had eaten what was on the table, and there would be no money for the gas meter even if we did have a spoonful of tea left. And on Thursday the factor would be knocking on the door for the rent. We could be put out on the street.

Why had he not told me that all that stood between us and hunger was my suit, our only pawnable asset? How could I have refused to let the suit go? Why did he have to take it without asking me?

A bizarre irony struck me. In pawning my suit and forcing me to make good his gambling losses he had in effect made me a partner. He had given me the right, in fact the duty whether I liked it or not, to say how money should be spent. I had no choice but to speak out. I tried to sound calm: 'Father, how much have you got left?'

He may have been expecting the question. His head jerked up and the liquid stare searched through me. He seemed ruffled by this shift in our relationship, but perhaps a trifle relieved too. I was trying to share the load with him.

'A pound,' he muttered.

'You'd better give it to me. I'll go to the shops after work tomorrow. It's the only way.'

I added: 'And we've got the factor coming for the rent on Thursday and there's coal to be got.'

He did not reply.

I poured out the tea for him. He took the cup and picked one of the sugar lumps out of it in a teaspoon and took it between his teeth to suck the tea through it, piping hot as always. Then, still holding the cup to his lips, he reached down into his trousers pocket, brought out a pound note and put it on the table and went on drinking the tea. There was a crackling sound as he crunched the sugar lump. With the money out of his pocket, some tension had gone too.

I picked up the pound. This was what mother would have done, except that she would not have had to ask for the money. And our plight would not have got this far. The iron reserve in the little trunk under the bed, grimly maintained, would have saved us.

I put the teapot in front of him and covered it with the red and white woollen tea cosy I had watched mother knitting long ago. A memory returned, one of my earliest, of sitting at her feet near the brass kerb at the cooking range, looking up at those nimble fingers, the only sounds the fire's crackle and the needles' click. Everything bright and cosy and warm and tranquil. A golden time.

He sat there, elbows on the table, the empty cup held in both hands near his lips, stilled. Perhaps he too thought of times past; did he think of good times, or only of other bad ones, to be compared with this one only in degree?

I took the cup from him and re-filled it and put it down before him. I went to the sink and stripped to the waist and washed under the cold tap, teeth gritted hard. The luxury of washing in hot water from the copper pot would have to await another day; the cold water was a fitting masochism. The tensions within me might explode any moment. The sooner I got out the better.

I put on a clean shirt, wetted my hair to flatten it, put on my tie, bought a week ago in Woolworths for sixpence on the day my suit was finished, brushed my working jacket and put it on again.

He was looking at me in an unfamiliar way. It was an appeal but I could not read it. Or would not. To whom? Not to me surely. What could *I* do for him, except, perhaps, forgive? That I could not do. Not now, not after this. Maybe it was an appeal to nobody in particular – to the Furies, to Destiny. For God's sake give me some luck?

Something in his look switched perception out of the present, into the interstices of time, where the blink of an eye seized a truth denied to ordinary vision. As in the theatre, when a change of lighting lifts part of the stage into dramatic focus and cancels all else, the table shifted and moved towards me with its cargo of tea and bread and margarine and sugar lumps, herrings and potatoes and the rest, and hung in a void, outlines edged thickly black as with a charcoal pencil, and I saw that it had become a still life painting, set at the edge of the world, the final darkness surrounding it. And father, in crumpled jacket and soiled shirt, stubbly face drawn in perplexity, those good square hands resting on either side of the goldrimmed plate and saucer, part of it, a prisoner.

Pawning my suit was the end of a road, and he knew it. Many other things had gone to the pawnshop and remained there 'unredeemed'. Ironic word. He saw that too.

And that pawn ticket he had given me was a kind of farewell, a renunciation, a seal on the past and the future, for me the end of that infinite optimism of childhood and youth when all things were malleable, all mistakes could be put right.

Nothing, any more, would be redeemable.

'Have your tea, father,' I said, 'It's getting cold.'

He put knuckles to his eyes to rub away the damp, and lifted the cup to his lips, and began to suck the tea noisily through another lump of sugar.

I went out.

17

SIREN DANCE

News from the hospital coursed round the factory each morning. Annie was improving. She had relapsed. Complications had set in, gastric, intestinal, kidney, liver. She would be out in three weeks, she would be in for a long time. So the weeks had gone by. Today she had 'turned the corner', was more cheerful, though pale and thin and looking ten years older. Youthful resilience might pull her out of the battle. Not, however, as good as new. An ailing survivor.

I too had turned a corner. I suppose I had needed these weeks to order my mind, cast the accounts. The books could now be closed.

In a sense only. A line could not be drawn under everything. She was part of me; her place in my heart might change but it would never disappear. Its power would continue, unforeseeable and perhaps unalterable. I asked myself how I could have clung to the secret thought that there was unfinished business between us which would contrive, one day, to command us to its fulfilment.

That illusion must have been necessary to me, and perhaps she knew it. Trying to exploit it she had erased it forever. What remained was a longing, unidentifiable, persistent, the voice of a potent genie stalking in the shadows; a longing not for her but for the enrichment of feeling I had known with her.

These days, however, it was pushed into the background. Obsessively I traced and re-traced that inner colloquy in which I projected myself to Oxford, rehearsed dreams and plans. Now and then I would waken from it, perhaps when I turned on my heel to slam an iron into the oven to reheat, or stepped over to the water bucket on its wooden stand at the end of the table to soak my damp rag and wring it out; and find myself in a different world, empty, cold, featureless as interstellar space. No, not really empty, for there were other people, many, many others, journeying helplessly, solitarily, with no warmth flowing from one to another, no signals from the heart. And then the longing would return in full force, a fierce and desperate hunger that gripped the soul with fingers of steel.

A different obsession sometimes took over, especially after the day's report from the hospital. Shifting shapes and landscapes, gardens, fountains, phantasms whispering, siren melodies tugging at the heart; mirages possessing me so completely that I would wake up from a morning's work not knowing what hours had passed. The sirens sang of a special state of being, misty yet effulgent, where magic reigned. Had I truly found it with Annie? The scenes would pass and repass before me. A time of golden light, of total understanding. 'Think each in each, immediately wise...'

True or no, I had breathed its rarefied air, clear, astringent, as on a mountain top when the rays of sunlight sing to you. No wonder the memory brought pain.

In later years I would know how seldom life enwrapped you in such glory; and how persistent and intransigent the longing for that siren land could be, and by what Protean mischief it deceived you.

Enclosed in these repetitive thoughts I shut out the enveloping thump and clatter of the factory, a hermit seclusion in whose creation we were skilled. But it was selective; a sensitive antenna remained active, so that when anyone approached the signal broke through to you at once. Some time during the morning after I had talked to Bernard's mother on the telephone, I sensed someone at my elbow. Driven as we were by the self-imposed pressure of piece working, one never stopped work unless for a crisis, an injury to someone, a fire. Continuing to move the iron quickly over the coat I was working on, shoulder and back muscles straining to hold the heavy block of hot metal in light contact with it, I shot a glance to my right. It was Bunty Birrell, Alec's cousin. Called the office girl, she sat in a glass-partitioned corner at the far end of the workroom, received the job tickets from the piece workers, tallied them and entered the figures in the daily ledger, did a little typing, answered the telephone, made tea for the boss and the master cutter.

She drew close and put her lips to my ear to make herself heard: 'Ah've go' a message for ye.' Little gusts of quick breath caressed my ear. 'Bernard Lipchinsky's just been on the phone. He says tae tell ye he'll meet ye the night as ye said, a' hawf-past eight a' the union offices in the Saltmarket. Did ah get tha' right?'

She was about seventeen, in the brilliance of her springtime, full bosomed, wide hipped, with fresh, clear skin, the long slender Birrell nose, cool blue eyes. Fluffy fair hair parted in the centre over a high smooth forehead gave her regular features a wondering, questing aspect in repose. Botticelli could have given that face to his Venus. And the earthy symbolism fitted the rest of her. She wore a white cotton blouse, crisp and blooming, and a dark skirt in the newly fashionable flared style tight over her middle, that fetchingly emphasised the womanly span of her hips and their in-curving sweep to the slender waist.

The long workroom was a place of patches of concentrated light shed by green shaded electric lamps hung low over pressing board or cutting table or sewing machine, each patch surrounded by dusty shadow. A lamp hung over the pressing board in front of me, but where I stood was in obscurity. Here, at one end of the thirty-foot table my back was to a blank brick wall, with which a short flank wall to my right made a secluded corner. Behind me against the main wall, an arm's length away, stood one of the low gas ovens that heated our eighteen-pound press irons, so placed that I could swivel on my heel and slam the iron I had been using, needing re-heating, into a slot in its front where it came to rest on a steel grid above a line of gas jets, then from an adjacent slot draw out a newly heated iron, which in a return swing I would bang down on the metal stand beside my pressing board. The jets burned all day even when slots were empty, and since this corner trapped their heat as well as that of the steam we produced and the radiant heat from the irons in use, I stood within a column of tropical air as if in an oven of my own. Even in cool weather some of us pressers worked stripped to the waist, as I did today; and sweat streamed down from armpit and neck and chest into the waistband of my trousers and the top of the short apron – made from a spare bit of cloth from the cutting table – we wore to protect the front of our trousers from fraying against the edge of the pressing board. By the end of the day every inch of clothing was sweat soaked, trouser knees caked with a deposit of expelled salt added to those of previous days.

I turned my head, and her face being still close my lips touched her cheek. She grinned happily and did not move away. In the high heat and humidity her body smell throbbed through me in waves as if I bathed in her enfolding flesh, and the glorious womanly chemistry went instantly to the senses and took possession. She smiled, quietly knowing. She put her lips to my ear again: 'Did ye no' hear me askin' ye? Did ah ge' the message right then?'

The message was a different one now.

The idiom was familiar, and powerful. It belonged to the ancient tenement rituals of sexual teasing, patterned measures that could be savage, even frightening, but always mysteriously alluring, that started for all of us in pre-pubertal days, and slowly progressed, with knowledge and confidence, to experiment and finally to tenderness.

Teasing intrusion, thinly veiled in play in the tenement close, was serious and demanding. Budding and ripening, the blood racing, celebrants pounced on those a shade behind them in experience, paying tribute to the myths of sexuality in an antic tradition, roughly, crudely. Tribal rites. The day had to come, and more than once, when a boy ran the gauntlet of a group of nubile girls who plucked at him as they heaved him in mid air from one end of the close to the other, their exultant cries all but drowning his yells, first of fury, then mixed with growing excitation, overtaken at the last by orgiastic confusion as they triumphantly wiped hands on his gaping trousers; and similarly, but in some ways chastely, a girl with boys, till her shrieks brought grown-ups to her rescue, usually not before the boys had seen if not touched.

Preliminary skirmishing. Heat of new knowledge, new because outside the home and thus far more intoxicating than any experience within it. Preludes to teasing singly, confidently. And so, in due time, to the shrine at the ash-pits.

Her play now, in the mood of that ritual dance, threw out its maturer challenge.

The impetus taking her onwards, she added breathlessly: 'Bu' *ah'll* meet ye in the Saltmarket masel'! Any time! Ah dare ye tae!'

The word Saltmarket made the play totally unambiguous. Eager, simple, primitive, and in its way pure.

I looked across the wide table. Standing in his own patch of shadow, head bent, Alec stolidly worked away,

Her lips, moving from my ear, as if by chance brushed my cheek, and at the same moment her hip pushed hard against me. A minute or so before, I had taken from the oven an iron so hot that it nearly scorched my hand even through the iron-holder's six layers of heavily stitched cloth. Both hands were occupied, my right in moving the iron close above the damp rag, here and there letting it rest on a chosen patch with a hissing burst of steam as it made contact and almost instantly rendered it bone dry, then raising it and passing on, my left in smoothing and shifting the damp rag and the coat to prepare another patch for the iron; I must not allow it to rest on one spot for more than a second or it would burn through the thin cotton sheet and scorch the coat. Thus entrapped, the determined leverage of her hip, forced like a wedge between me and the table, half turned me to her.

Thinking about it afterwards, that hectic moment had a comic quality, though I was too flustered to appreciate it at the time, for with the fiercely hot iron needing swift and careful manoeuvre on the coat, apart from safe handling, I was at her mercy as completely as the boy being plucked in the close. I arched my body sideways a little away from her but the hard contact of her loins remained. Glancing to my right I saw that her blouse had a damp patch on the left where it had pressed against my sweat-damp skin, and the firm dark nipple showed.

'Ye cannae dae anythin'!' She laughed delightedly, cheeks pink and damp in the heat. The knowing look changed, touched now with a kind of gravity. The time had come, it said, for the play to move on.

I needed to put the iron down to rearrange the coat, but fearing to hurt her with it in this close contact I exclaimed: 'Watch what ye're doin'!' not thinking how droll the words were in the circumstances. But since she was the only one to hear it hardly mattered; they might even have added spice to her play. But in truth I was worried that the iron might burn her as I swung it over on to its steel stand on my right, for she stood in its path. Burns on the arm or hand, from getting in the way of a presser's iron, were common.

I pushed her aside with my right elbow, hastily but not too roughly I hoped, and brought the iron over and set it down. With surprising strength she resisted, moved hardly at all, simply leaned a little backwards to let it go past, maintaining her body's pressure. In the second or so that the

347

iron was in its transit only inches in front of her, its radiant heat stinging face and arm like a fiery breath, she did not flinch.

'There!' she shouted in my ear, 'ye see?'

'Watch!' I shouted, alarmed, 'ye could've made me drop it!'

The words were out before I saw the other, slang, meaning. She laughed as she seized upon it: 'Och no! Tha'd never do! A great big feller like you's no gonnae drop 'is iron for nothin'! Whit wid a lassie do then? Come on, ah'm sayin' i' again – ah'm darin' ye?'

Matching her tone I said: 'The Saltmarket's no' a place fer a respectable lassie tae mee' a feller! Whit wid yer cousin Alec say if ah did mee' ye there?'

I was only half drawn in, but as I said the words I knew I moved further. I added: 'He'll no' like i' mind?'

'Och him!' she said. 'He'll no' say anythin'!'

She spoke confidentially now, joining me to her in complicity.

The play was part of you. It was always there, awaiting its time. It spoke to the willing heart if the moment was right. And what was happening now was a link in the chain of its endless regeneration, prompting us, drawing us in, poised to take us forward if we were both ready. That was not the wonder. With a fury of innocence not to be

348

denied, with intuitive precision, she had *found* the moment.

Or with her power created it,

'Anyway', she said in my ear, 'Alec's go' a great opinion of ye. He says ye're gawn tae Oxford! Ah like clever fellers. There aren't too many o' them abou'!'

She added: 'An' that's why ah'm darin' ye like this. Ah'm no' afraid. Ah'm no' afraid o' anythin' tha' might happen. So there!'

I can be a match for you. I can be what you want. Don't doubt me. Before I could answer she moved away a few inches. A shade anxiously she was looking towards the far end of the workroom. There, through the steam and dust, I saw a portly figure appear at the office door and look searchingly about him – Bompert, the boss. She said urgently in my ear: 'There 'e is wonderin' where ah am! Ah've go' tae go now. Don't yew forget ah'm darin' ye. The Saltmarket or anywhere else. Come on! Will ye see?'

Intent on rearranging the coat on the pressing board so that I could work on its other facing, I stretched out my right hand automatically, without looking, to lift the iron again, and touched her middle in passing.

Laughing she said: 'Ah'll take tha' for "Yes" then, eh?'

Her eyes were a wonderful china blue. I would have liked to see her smile like that all

349

day, for ever.

And still I would not move quickly: 'I'm not staying long,' I said, meaning in Glasgow. 'So long as ye understand that?'

To my surprise I had spoken as if my doubts about Oxford were over. That made me hesitate. Before I could continue, she said quickly: 'Ah know! Alec's told me. He thinks maybe you shouldnae go. Ah don't know why he told me about i' at a'!'

She put her hand to her lips as if she had said too much. Hurriedly she went on: 'Ah don't care. Ah want tae... Oh ah've go' tae go the now, the boss wants me there! Will ye see? Will ye?'

'Yes I will.'

18

NETHER WORLD

The union offices were on the third, top floor of a building that had fallen from grandeur, that had known the expansive days of the tobacco lords and other merchant venturers and traders to the West Indies and the Americas. You entered it by an ample doorway with fluted pilasters, a tri-glyphed lintel, and a timber canopy with classical pediment, supported by wrought iron brackets in a thistle and leaf design. Four stone steps, worn hollow, led up from the pavement. On either side was the dark cavern of a loading bay, in whose depths could faintly be discerned the raised platform, like the stage in a darkened theatre, the whole emitting a powerful stench of horse manure and nameless decaying matter. From within their impenetrable shadows, as I ascended the front steps, came little rustling sounds, masculine grunts, quick clear female voices chiding, comforting, hastening: 'C'mon if ye want it!' – 'There ye are, that's ma fine man!' – 'Och away wi ye! Ye've had yer shillin's worth o' me!'

The heavy panelled front door hung half-open, its great brass handle and knocker gleaming dully in the light from a gas mantle in a grimy glass globe high on the wall of the square vestibule. Beyond, this solitary point of light grudgingly revealed a spacious and lofty entrance hall with corniced ceiling, its timber floor knobbly from long wear, crowded with packing cases. In a far corner of it, as one advanced cautiously through the spectral obscurity, one came upon what must have been in its day a stylish staircase. A wide wooden balustrade, carved with foliage, much dented, topped iron railings thickly interwoven in floral clusters, vestiges of paint curling off. Broad wooden steps were partly covered with metal tread plates; these, burnished by much traffic, showed faint silvery gleams. On the wall that rose beside the stairs the last covering of some dark paint, its colour unidentifiable now, had almost disappeared among the many paler patches, presumably dirty white in daylight, where broken plaster had received minimal repair.

On the first floor were offices of tramp ship owners, and a customs agent whose brass plate announced that he was also honorary consul for one of the Baltic

352

Republics. Outside his door were stacked several empty liquor crates. On the landing above, the gas jet had lost its gauze-thin mantle and the naked blue flame, weakly shining among the jagged remnants of a broken glass globe, cast a sepulchral light. Here were doors whose painted name boards, contemplated in these dismal surroundings, prompted questions much more than they gave information: South American Hotel Agency, Argentine-Scottish Friendship Institute, Mrs Parchment's Governesses Ltd. Rumours about the white slave trade to South America were persistent these days. Could there be any significance in the siting of these enterprises here, on the edge of dockland, in the territory of the night walkers?

From the top landing came no light at all; the gas tap, as I found when I got there, was turned off, probably because of a break in the thin pipe extending beyond it to the mantle, a common occurrence. In the meagre light from the blue flame behind me I mounted gingerly through the gloom, straining to see outlines, guided by the balustrade, encouraged by sounds from the union offices above, murmur of voices and the rhythmic rattle and slap of a duplicating machine, and on the final steps by the rays of electric light escaping round an ill-fitting door. As in many buildings in the poorer commercial districts, the old gas lighting persisted on stairways long after electricity was wired in to the offices.

I found Bernard in a small bare room whose walls had once been distempered cream but were now darkened to a pale tan colour, with a grey stain round the narrow iron fireplace. No fire burned in it. On a slate coloured hearth stone stood a gas fire in a shiny black metal casing, unlit.

A thick grey overcoat round his shoulders, Bernard sat at a brown wooden desk much pitted with cigarette burns. I wondered idly about the burns, for he had never smoked and, naturally fastidious, he could be relied on to insist that visitors used the two metal ashtrays stamped: 'Smoke De Reszke' and bearing a begrimed image of the renowned singer in evening dress and cloak. The desk was either inherited from another union official or bought second hand in a 'disposal' auction – where the equipment of bankrupt business was sold off – in the Gallowgate nearby.

A green metal cabinet stood in one corner near him, and four brown bentwood chairs were ranged in a stiff rank against the wall opposite the desk. It was the first time I had seen him in his working quarters, and this aspect, orderly, austere – almost military, the coat flung round his shoulders like a campaign cloak of old – was an astringent reminder of how far he had travelled from the ecstatic visionary, disdaining lesser things, of two years ago. When I came in he was looking at some papers in an opened file, the only object on the desk besides the two tin ashtrays. He looked worried, greeted me with no change in expression, and signed to me to close the door. Then he snapped the file shut, stepped over to the cabinet, unlocked it with a key from a bunch he took from his trousers pocket, put the file on a shelf within and locked it. Facing me again, with a jerk of the head he motioned me to come round the desk to the window, the point furthest from the door.

'There's something I want to tell you,' he said quietly, 'but you've got to keep it to yourself, *absolutely* to yourself?'

I nodded.

'That file I was looking at. Government are putting to us arrangements for rapidly turning garment factories over to making uniforms! Wanting union co-operation "in the event of an emergency", as they put it. Mealy-mouthed bastards! Trying to be jolly decent chaps to the unions. We're expected to do our bit to make things run smoothly when war comes. In the national interest. That's where things've got to. That's how near it is.'

Side by side we looked out at the black night.

'Yes,' he said. 'Fucking near. God curse them. What a hopeless world we're living in. And it's all been for nothing.'

Spain. The fight extended. But whose fight? The people who got it in the neck were always the same, the groundlings, people like us. There was nothing to say.

He said: 'What about you? I know what this must mean to you. Oxford. Pulling yourself up out of this. Who knows how long any of us have got? It's why I'm telling you this, warning you in advance. When are you due to go?'

I did not answer immediately. For one thing I was disconcerted to find that he knew about Oxford. Ahead of me in much more than years, sophisticated, hardened by Spain, long committed to following his own line while I was only now beginning, I suppose I had naively hoped to take him by surprise with my news, note his reactions and chew them over. But his apocalyptic revelation pushed all that aside. It was a greater shock than it should have been. I had chosen not to see what was happening, believing it was pointless to think about it, unalterable anyway. Oddly, now, the thought of 'taking the King's shilling' came into my head, a potent echo. The uniform. Marching to war. Glory. War to end War.

That shilling bought *you!* What did *you* get?

356

And the woman's voice from the loading bay rang in my ears: 'Ye've had yer shillin's worth o' me.'

Down in the street a man in a dark overcoat and bowler hat emerged from a black doorway and walked quickly away into the deeper shadows. Almost immediately a female figure darted out of the same doorway, long skirt swinging, and strutted slowly along the pavement, looking behind her now and then. In the eerie, shut-down street other skirts swung and floated, or paused and turned idly about, in the yellow discs of light round the infrequent lamp posts.

Away to the south, over a tumbled expanse of roof tops outlined like black teeth against the glow in the sky beyond the Clyde, the orange flame flared high over Dixon's Blazes. For me it had always proclaimed the unfeeling sovereignty of the iron forces of the world. It was also a reminder of departure, the end of things. Charlie long ago. And my turn soon: if not to Oxford, then out into the void, dressed in the khaki our factory would soon be turning out?

Recent events in Europe had passed as a freak nightmare, its menace in innocence disbelieved. Miraculously, reprieve had come. Magic had worked. And now, standing here staring at the black window panes, the world came roaring back;

newspaper headlines I had seen but not seen: the faltering negotiations with Russia, double-dealing in the international poker game, the party screaming that the imperialists did not want to stop the dictators in their course.

Stumbling towards the unthinkable. Flanders fields all over again?

'October,' I said. 'If I decide to go in the end.' The Furies seemed to have plans of their own. 'What will happen to you?' I asked.

Watching his back still, he looked over his shoulder at the door. 'Let's go.'

Down the dark stairs he cantered confidently ahead of me. On the first floor landing, out of earshot of the people still at work in the union offices, he planted his elbows on the balustrade and looked down at the ghostly assembly of packing cases in the hallway.

Almost in a whisper he said: 'Even though you've seen it coming all along you can't believe it when it's staring you in the face. What am I going to do?' He shook his head, addressing an inner voice; a hint of something I was to divine presently.

'It's a strange feeling for me. I've been there before – or something like it. But when it comes – when, not if – it's certain to be different, worse and longer. A few days ago a comrade from the garment workers in

France was here and he had a fine turn of phrase for it: "It will be *une guerre kilométrique*" – going on and on and on. What d'you think of that? That's what we've been born to live through. If we do.'

'Spain's getting on that way,' I said.

'Perhaps it *was*. But it's really over. Franco's rolling the whole thing up. And by God I want him to do it quickly now. The misery's gone on too long. And with the big war looming over the world, the *guerre kilométrique*, things in Spain will settle down; something not too good, not too bad.' He paused, and when he resumed his voice had an unexpected tenderness. 'And I can't wait for that to happen. I need to go back there.' He stopped abruptly, perhaps surprised at what he had allowed himself to say, then hurried on: 'I mean – well it's a long story. It'll keep.'

I was reminded of his telling me, in a few opaque words, of his escape from Spain: 'One day I'll tell you, when it's safe...' Safe for whom? I had assumed he meant the people in the apparatus over there who had helped him get out of the country. Something in his tone spoke of attachment, yearning: a distant flame, the sweet helper on the frontier, the waiting heart.

'And now,' he spat the words out with sudden ferocity, 'this fucking war's going to shut the gates one way or the other. God knows when I'll get there.'

In his evangelist days I was seldom aware of him taking girls out. Essentially a private person, he had kept his amours to himself, a defensiveness doubtless strengthened by his mother's match-making proclivities. Since his return, digesting Spain, drawn even further into himself, and in the last few months living away from the Gorbals, I knew nothing at all of women in his life.

At least *he* had someone waiting! Alas, far away, but someone.

In different ways the Furies had hit us both: sod's law, waiting to trip you up.

'Spain was a war of principle,' he said ruminatively. 'Or so we thought. And I went willingly. Even in a sense joyfully. This one's going to be infinitely worse, and it won't even have the excuse, the great shining cause, we thought justified us going there to shed blood. Like the Great War it'll be another case of supposedly clever and civilised people stumbling into savagery. And just as futile. Greed, arrogance, lust for power, stupidity; and the leaders – my God, what leaders! – pandering to people's lousiest instincts, driven mad with power. And the cynical game the Russians are playing's no better. But the hell of it is, once you're in it, people like us can't back away and pretend it's no business of ours, that it doesn't matter if we're defeated and taken over. As the pacifists want us to believe. This is our place, where for all its faults we're a damn sight freer than in a lot of other places – Spain, Russia, Germany, Italy. We're stuck with the job of stopping this country getting trampled down and going the same way. You know how I feel about war? And it'll sound strange to you when I say this – it's strange to me too – but it's true. War when you're in the thick of it is an intoxicating, passionate thing: it draws you in.'

'So you'll go?'

He turned away from the balustrade and faced me and the thin yellow gleam from the gas lamp in the hall below touched his broad face with timid highlights, and it seemed that he breasted the darkness and pushed it away from him, in a lonely affirmation that recalled his apocalyptic ardour in that last talk before he left for Spain. But there was also a steely desperation, the fighter with his back to the wall. The battle would have no victory, for this time there was no new dawn in prospect, only the hope of preserving a little light in the darkened world.

If you've got to go down, go down fighting.

'There's something else, isn't there?' he said. 'Haven't you seen the refugees coming in from Germany? The union's been doing something to help. Old men, women, children, degraded, bestialised, by those fucking bastards over there, Hitler and his gangsters. People from their concentration camps with numbers tattooed on their arms. Numbers! Not people any more. What sort of animals are those Nazis? We've got no choice.

The ardour faded from his voice and he said sadly: 'Maybe bestiality's what the whole world is heading for? The rough edge of man's nature will be all that is left.'

He glanced up into the dark reaches of the stairway, then turned abruptly to lead the way down: 'Let's go. The others will be coming down any minute.'

On the entrance steps the damp river wind crept between the ribs. He shrugged deeper into his coat and raised the wide collar up to his ears. I pulled my muffler higher under my chin.

A few yards to the right, in the cone of thin yellow gaslight from a street lamp, two women strutted back and forth, no doubt as much for warmth as display. As we stepped down on to the pavement they lunged towards us and took post one on either side of us as if it were an assignation. The one who linked her arm in mine was about twenty-five, with bleached hair falling in crimped waves down to her shoulders, turned up nose and small pouting mouth; she reeked of crude perfume and cigarette tobacco and also, as she leaned close, of beer from her clothes, presumably from the breath of her last client. The other was about thirty, with dimpled cheeks, a pointed nose and full lips darkly rouged. Smooth black hair curled inwards at the shoulders and a fringe, 'bangs', partly curtained deep-set eyes.

Mine said huskily, 'Come on an' enjoy wha' ah've go' fer ye! Here ye are.' She pressed close and the pubic bone bored into me.

Her companion, in a chuckling whisper, said something in Bernard's ear.

To my surprise he knew their names. 'Now listen to me Kirstie, Jeanie,' he said good-naturedly. 'Don't waste your time. Anyway I've got some business to discuss with my friend here.'

It crossed my mind that he might be a client; but it was just as likely that he knew them from encounters like this as he came and went.

Kirstie gave him back in practised style, half-mocking, half-kindly: 'Och, yew're a right saint aren't ye now? Ye cannae kid *me*. Yew know ye could do wi' a bi'! An' *ah* know ye could! Ye're a normal healthy feller! Come on an' ah'll gie ye yer pleasure dear. Ony a shillin'!'

She made to reach under his coat and he gently pushed her hand away.

363

'None of your tricks,' he humoured her. 'I mean what I say.'

'Och, away wi' ye, ye don't mean i'. Ah can see ye don't. Come on, ye can have a free grope tae start wi'!'

She seized his hand and at the same time took hold of her skirt below the knee and began to pull it up.

'None of that I told you!' he said in that gentle, coaxing voice.

In mock despair Jeanie exclaimed: 'Kirstie, they're sae pure!' She turned to face me squarely, her back to the light from the lamp post so that her front was visible to no one else: 'Here, ah'll gie ye a free look.' Swiftly she gathered up her skirt to the waist. 'It's a' yours. Wha'ever ye like, see? A shillin' that's a'. Come on then!'

Remembered afterwards, this nocturnal encounter, imposing a harsh yet magnetic counterpoint on his words on the stairs, had a bizarre, inferno quality, questioning life to its limits, testing the spirit and the will.

Nether world of flesh and calculation; exquisite torment of proffered bliss one was doomed to refuse.

The shower room's callow and superstitious view of life was confused about whores. They excited primitive attraction one moment, revulsion the next. They were an irritant. They debased conventional attitudes to women, yet confirmed them too. They placed themselves in the twilight of society. They degraded a sacred essence by commerce. They were branded with guilt. But they exercised an arcane power, and were objects of appropriate awe. Supposed exemplars of finished excellence in the arts of the flesh, they threw out a teasing challenge to manhood; but, alas, life was so unfair that to accept it brought the high risk of getting a dose.

I could not have said which of these influences doomed me to refuse; probably none specifically. Inner tumult pulled me away.

'Listen,' I said, 'this isn't the way I want to get it, that's all. I'm sorry.'

I wondered if I had sounded priggish, unmanly. What matter! Those priestesses of the night must surely have heard every variation of excuse many times over.

It was her turn to be patient and kindly: 'Think of i' like this, dear. Ye'll ge' yer pleasure wi' nane o' the bother ye'd ge' efterwards frae one o' them stuck up respectable lasses! Nae tears, nae worries, nae naggin' ye fer promises tae marry them! Nae bother at a'! An' a' fer jist a shillin'. Aw come on!'

Kirstie snuggled up to Bernard: 'Ah know *yew* appreciate a wumman tha' understands whit ye want eh? Yew're fine an' strong an' randy. Come on show me whit ye can do!'

She turned her head to survey the street. Her tightened features, crudely limned in shades of darkness, spoke her anxiety: 'Shall I persevere? Is something better coming along?' It was about nine o'clock, peak drinking time in the pubs. Not another man in sight. In a new tone, one of comradely seriousness, she appealed now to both of us:

'Ye can be *free men* wi' us! Ye can say anythin'. *Dae* anythin'. Whit yew want's on'y *natural*, ye see! An' ye'll get a' the understandin' ye want. An' when we've sa'isfied ye, an' ye're at peace wi yersel' ye walk away an no' a soul in the wurrld's goin' tae know a single thing aboot i'.'

Oh world where the wish is law; siren land.

Seizing on our silence, she went on eagerly: 'Ah've go' a wonderful idea. If ye want a bi' o' comfort, there's a fine boardin' hoose near here. A big room wi' two double beds for five shillins. Nice an' cosy an' warm. An' dead secret ah promise. Ye can do wha'ever ye want wi' us there! An' ah mean tha', *anythin*'! That's right isn't i' Jeanie?'

'Aye, anythin' at a'! A' the things ye've ever dreamt aboo' doin' wi a wumman an maybe never dared tae say! Come on let's go there, eh?'

Bernard's clipped soldierly tone returned, finishing it: 'We're not in that league. We'd sooner get it for love. No offence, Kirstie. Jeanie. You're good women and I like setting eyes on you when I come out of here. So we'll leave it at that.'

Kirstie shivered, accepted it, hugged him again, this time for warmth. 'All right, dear. But mind ye gie us a turn while ye're waitin' fer yer love! Ah know ye well enough! An' ah'll keep mind o' yer friend here as well. We'll be here when ye want us right enough.'

'There's serrvice for ye!' Alec had said.

In silence we walked to the end of the street and turned north and went on into Argyle Street. In that long defile of dazzling light from shops and department stores, there was little traffic this late in the evening, but crowds of window shoppers moved slowly along and dreamily contemplated fumed oak sideboards and gate-leg dining tables, leatherette three-piece suites, bed-settees, radio-gramophones in tall mahogany cases with gothic bas-reliefs, suits in the Fifty Shilling Tailors – fulfilment on the never-never.

The scene was no different from any other night. Naively I wondered why. The nether world we had just left belonged to a distant, immutable universe. But in *this* day-to-day world as it lurched to war, surely the collective mind must concentrate? One should feel *something*, a tremor of fear, a closing down of perspectives, a post-ponement of hope? Why didn't they stop everything, as people did when the end of the world approached?

We crossed and entered another hinterland, of long narrow streets where we passed beneath cliffs of darkened office buildings, once more among shadows, but not as profound as in the Saltmarket, for in this better class business district lamp posts were closer together and lighting brighter. An electric sign and warmly glowing windows announced the presence of an upper-class restaurant; and at a nearby corner a little group of nightwalkers strutted and whirled, on faithful watch. Here was a different caste, fashionably dressed in fitted tweed coats with fur collars, toque hats, silk stockings, high Cuban heels.

'Five shillin' touches!' Alec called them, 'But ye'll get tae lie in a bed, an' she'll gie ye bacon an' eggs efter, so it's probably wurrth it!'

As we came near, two of them, young, poised, debonair, halted and assessed us, hesitated, then turned away. Bernard with his trilby and smart coat and shiny leather portfolio would have met their standards, but I saw that my muffler and cloth cap and scruffy working clothes ruled me out. Off-balance as I was, I resented the rejection. It recalled Annie's long ago. She too had assessed me as a poor economic prospect and turned away.

Would I in the future become sentimental about Kirstie and Jeanie? Unpretentious, kind in their fashion, surely they must be the salt of the earth.

Bernard, head sunk at a slant in his coat collar, spoke in a low, troubled voice: 'Sooner or later they make you question your feelings, your integrity. I used to see whores simply as a social problem! Not a bit of it. It's a state of mind. We'll never understand it. Don't dare to perhaps. It would mean destroying too many illusions. Why do we feel shame for them sometimes? And for ourselves for wanting them? We have an idea of woman that's almost a religion on its own, and as unrealistic. We want her to be tender and caring. We want constancy. We demand that a fuck should mean love, on *her* part but not always the other way round! It had to be a man who wrote:

'Man's love is of man's life a thing apart,
'Tis woman's whole existence.'

'But come to think of it, it's in the woman's interest to say that too, to make us feel guilty if *we* fuck without love. But we don't feel guilty, not often anyway. We blame it on the Old Adam. At the same time we don't like a woman to think of *herself* that way.'

Oh waiting heart on the frontier! Will *you* be constant?

'I'm not cut out for abstinence,' he went on. 'But I can't stomach the idea of pretending I care for a woman simply to get her. That *would* make me feel guilty. Sometimes when the pressure gets too much I feel there's a lot in what Kirstie says. Take what she offers and walk away free. Well, free in a sense.'

'The soldier's way of looking at it?' I said too quickly, and then wondered if I had touched a sensitive nerve.

He wasn't put out: 'You're right up to a point. But it's more than soldierly savagery. In war you feel your manhood's in jeopardy more than life itself. That may sound absurd but it's true. Having a woman gives you back a breath of your own proper existence. But it's not only when you're a soldier. Day to day living brings you to the same sort of breaking point, where you need a woman to give you renewal.'

If only I could think of it in that fashion – a woman, any woman, one supreme enfolding, one still moment of certainty! I thought of Bunty, and Jeanie. Could I find the plenitude of content he spoke of – however temporary – with either? If I needed to ask that question the answer must be 'No'. It wasn't so simple. With Bunty it was fire kindling fire. That was something to be going on with. But could one look there for renewal, removal of doubt? No, nothing so exalted.

Without naming her, I told him.

He thought about it, and laughed, taken out of himself: 'Why are you worrying? Why does it have to be genuine? And what is genuine? Take it while you can! You've had a bad time one way and another. You deserve something from life at last. Don't punish yourself. Enjoy her!'

'But you do care? I can see that,'

'Is it as plain as that?' he said heavily, obviously taken aback for letting it be seen. 'All right then. There is someone in Spain. She saved my life, but it's more than that, much more. And it's hard for us. It's hard to keep in touch. And dangerous, I don't mind telling you. I still can't be sure she's in the clear. I don't know how much the party knows. Or the other side for that matter. She can't get out, not yet. And I daren't show *my* face across the frontier. Not till the shooting's stopped – and they've stopped settling scores. I'm going to swear you to secrecy again.'

'I won't say anything.'

'You're right. I do care. And that's why – all right this is something else between ourselves – that's why I take Kirstie sometimes. I suppose you guessed that too? Though she was discreet enough in her way. I don't like doing it. And apart from anything else I'm afraid of getting a dose. Not a pretty picture.'

371

'Maybe you'll get over there soon.'

'I don't know. I don't like to think what will happen if I don't. There's a limit to constancy when you can't be together. And there's something else, sad in its way, and ironic. Mother's constantly at me, wanting to get me married off. This nice girl and that nice girl! She'll probably have a go at you too. And how can I tell her? She wouldn't make sense of it. Love? What's that got to do with anything! Perhaps love, like beauty, is in the heart of the beholder? Nothing more. What a come-down to have to admit that! Like admitting we need faith. We don't know why, or even what it is, only that we need it.'

Something had been nagging at the back of my mind. 'How did you know about Oxford? I didn't mean you to find out from someone else.'

He took a moment to answer. Perhaps he had indeed been hurt not to have heard of it first from me.

'Annie told me. One of the machinist girls from your factory came into our office about her branch dues and told me what had happened. I went up to the Infirmary to see how she was. She said you'd told her.'

'Did she say how I came to tell her?'

'No. Why?'

There was a lot to tell him, for when she had gone away from me I had been too sick at heart to talk about it.

He said nothing for some minutes.

'So it was her in that close with Phil?'

'Yes.'

'Christ! Sometimes life goes out of its way to be cruel.'

'It would have been worse if you'd chosen to stop at a different close that night. I wouldn't have known about her and Phil at all.'

'Would it have made any difference *whose* child it was, if it wasn't yours? Besides, you didn't know she was pregnant. You backed away from her for other reasons altogether.'

'You're right. The pregnancy had nothing to do with it, except to sicken me afterwards, when I did know, and realised what she'd tried to do to me. No, the drawing back had started before, when I thought about her in the close with Phil. I doubted everything. Either she had become a different person, or I had never known her at all.'

His going to see her in the Infirmary surprised me. Certainly it could be explained as part of his role as a union official, caring for his flock, but it wasn't usual.

He said: 'All the same I have a feeling you're sorry you let her go like that?'

'No, I'm not. But I must admit I'm thankful I had no time to think about it. I had only just got the letter a few minutes before bumping into her like that, and it blinded me to so many things. It answered so many questions for me. I wasn't thinking at all. And so it saved me – just! I saw the trap only later, when she landed herself in hospital.'

He brooded over it. 'In the old party days her head was too much in the clouds to believe anything she said. But *she* believed in her visions – at the time! Beautiful women do. They think their visions will take them anywhere they want to go. At some point she decided she could get what she wanted not by being a heroine of the workers' movement, but by going after money – and maybe power too, who knows – by manipulating men. It's an old story! And she was impatient. Come to think of it she should have been more patient with you! Your news about Oxford must have been a shock, to discover that *you* are moving higher and she could have risen with you! Well, she had to come down to earth some day, but she shouldn't have tried to save herself by trapping you. I suppose she was at her wit's end.'

He sighed. 'It's a sad business. I'm trying to persuade Bompert to keep her job open. God knows what will become of her. For a brilliant girl she was stupid, and arrogant and ruthless into the bargain, but she's been punished, hard. I can't help feeling sorry for her.'

I dared not agree with him. If I did I should have to go to her.

As if I had uttered the thought he said:

'Don't look back any more. The sooner you get another woman the better. Emotional ballast! We need that to keep us sane.'

'Listen,' he said, warmth returning to his voice. 'I haven't had a chance to say anything about Oxford. There's only one word for it – wonderful! Like a breath of fresh air! For you to have done that, you starting from here, from these conditions, competing against people with a far better start than you, shows what you're made of! It makes even me feel there's hope! Maybe, at last, life is making it up to you after all you've gone through. You deserve every bit of that and more. And look here, you mustn't have any more doubts. Of course you must go. In spite of what's happening. It's the hand of Fate. You've got no choice.'

'If there's war I suppose I won't be able to anyway. The choice will be taken out of my hands.'

He said: 'If I were you I'd go ahead as if the way was clear. I'm going to report this to head office. The union's got a small trust fund to help members going after higher education, if they've shown achievement, and by God you have! So I'll put up a case for you, to see if you can be given a grant.

We'll see. Anyway, by hook or crook you must go. I've become a bit of a fatalist after Spain. War does that to you. It's all written! We used to say "If it hasn't got your number on it don't worry!" Well, one did have *my* number on it – an inch or so to my right and I wouldn't be talking to you now. That must have been written too. So accept your destiny. Where it'll take you Christ only knows. You won't know the answer if you don't go! I'm sorry it's turned bitter for you – I mean the Annie business. You've got to get away – in every sense.'

19

CARRY THE TORCH

In the close where Bernard now lived the flag-stones were devotedly decorated with pipe-clay in an interwoven curly scroll design, the sharp edges of which showed that they had been washed that day. Further evidence was the smell of carbolic soap. There were no broken steps. The wall plaster, painted cream from ceiling to a little below half-way down and green the rest, was clean and uncracked. A door at the back of the close shut the ashpits away, and no smell came from them.

Bernard's house was the first I had been in that had hot and cold running water, a bathroom and its very own lavatory. The tiny parlour had a linoleum square on the floor, imprinted with a Persian carpet pattern, and round it the bare planks were stained brown and polished. Heavy oak furniture thronged it – high-backed chairs with leatherette seats, a hexagonal table with bulbous turned legs, a horse hair sofa with a white antimacassar on its back rest. Brasswork shone on fenders and doors. The kitchen range smelled mustily of the day's black leading, and the flanged edges of oven doors and handles and hinges had been rubbed with emery paper to the high gleam of steel. Against the wall facing it was a plain wooden table with hinged flaps, spread with a fringed white cotton cloth. The air was heavy with scents of food and herbs, the warm exhalation of newly ironed laundry. An atmosphere of care.

We washed face and hands in the bathroom wash-basin, and went into the kitchen and stood at the table and waited for Bernard's father, who sat reading a book in a high-backed wooden arm chair in a corner near the fire, to take his seat first and say grace.

Of slight build, with long narrow features and a high forehead topped by a mop of snow white hair, he was elegantly turned out in a well-cut double breasted suit of pearl grey worsted with hand-stitched edges, and a wing collar with grey cravat held in a gold ring. At first sight he seemed boyishly slender, but a moment later one recognised the thinness of the very ill. He rose with obvious effort, levering himself up by gripping the elbow rests of the chair with quivering hands on which the blue veins stood out, stepped with care the few feet to the table and sat down heavily in the battered ladder-back chair at its head.

Before he said the prayer he sat with eyes closed for some moments, as an ardent preacher composes himself to be a medium between God and the people. The words were uttered in a distant voice as from a crag in the wilderness, with tenderness and awe. He was not only the celebrant; he was part of the sacrament too. The sounds bubbled in his throat and his dark eyes watered. Bernard, opposite me on his father's left, studied him with concern.

When he had finished, Bernard placed a hand on his shoulder:

'Be careful, father. Be gentle with yourself. In any case you shouldn't have waited supper for us. You need your rest.'

His father regarded him tenderly and the wrinkles at the corners of his mouth deepened: 'What good will rest do me, I ask you? I'll die with my boots on when God wills. I'll leave it to Him. Don't worry.'

The voice was soft and resonant, gentle, almost a purr, but there was a rasping note of phlegm from deep in his chest, betraying his sickness. The hollow cheeks had little colour. His manner was alert but plainly he kept fatigue at bay only by an effort of the will.

Bernard looked down, determinedly composed, and began to spoon up the steaming cabbage soup.

Mr Lipchinsky turned to me: 'My son, I

wanted to tell you myself what I think of your achievement. Bernard told me your news and I was overjoyed. A new world is opening up for you. It's a wonderful thing. You are young, you will drink in new knowledge! Only with knowledge can we change the destiny of Man, stop him blundering, let him reach out for his rightful fulfilment. Be sure to use your knowledge well. I am happy for you.'

From his inner breast pocket he brought out a folded sheaf of papers and laid it beside his plate and pressed the sheets down flat. Caressingly, he ran his finger tips over the close lines of curly writing, then looked up and addressed me again: 'I have studied all my life. It takes so long, hours stolen from other things, so many years – yes, years! It wearies you to do it the way I did, in the moments that were left after work, at night while my wife lay sleeping. And those hard years have taken my strength. You, my boy, will race ahead and do it all so quickly. I envy you, I don't mind admitting it. Without this wonderful chance, you might have gone the way I did. That is why I am pleased for you.'

He put his hand to his chest and gave a little gasp. A cloud darkened his face, and his eyes assumed the wondering look of an injured child.

Gently, Bernard chided him: 'Come on

now, father, you don't need to envy anybody. You've achieved a great deal, more than most, and done it in the face of tremendous difficulties. You're probably the greatest scholar in Kropotkin's ideas in the country, maybe in the world.'

His father shook his head as if to say: 'I know you want to reassure me, but alas I know better.' Turning to me he tapped the papers:

'I have been working on this for years. I am writing a book – the other things have been pamphlets, articles, little things – it will be a reassessment of Kropotkin's work, but also my own ideas for a way ahead, going far beyond him, towards universal populist reform. I shall call it *The Torch of Constructive Anarchy*. There is so much new thinking now, and I have so little time to keep up with it. Take Clarence Streit's *Federal Union*, for instance. Now there's an ambitious vision for you! A glorious one and no mistake. A federal union of the whole world! No one, no country would need to think of conquest any more. No need for rivalry, the curse that has always led to war. We would all be part of one another, think of it! We would settle disputes by democratic action. War would become unnecessary!'

Bernard said nothing but I was moved by the compassion in his face, and the bitterness. What a moment to be talking of utopian systems! His father seemed unaware of the shadows of war. He was living in the clouds, far from the Hobbesian brutishness of the real world, of Hitler, Stalin, Mussolini. To shed tears for him was too late, and to let him see them would be cruel. Loved and respected father, so ill that he was visibly wasting away, who had made his life forfeit trying to force an impossible dream to come true, a world peopled only by men and women of goodwill, who had painfully trudged towards it sustained by hope through all the years, and seen it remain as remote from fulfilment as when he had set out; and still, the flame burning low, he pressed on innocently towards the receding horizon.

Lacrimae rerum, the tears of things. Always awaiting you.

He began to cough, a deep, tormented struggle with his lungs that shook him through and through; and there was a rumbling upsurge of phlegm as if a monster thrashed about inside him. In the midst of his agony, even as he fought for breath, a look of embarrassment came over his face, incongruous, pitiful. He wanted to hide his plight. He turned away from the table, pulled the handkerchief from his breast pocket and put it to his lips, apparently trying to hold the phlegm in his mouth, and with the other hand gripped the edge of the table and tried to get to his feet. Bernard was up in a moment, plainly alarmed that he might choke, needing to bring up spittle but stubbornly restraining its rise, and put a hand under his elbow to help him up. Mrs Lipchinsky had also got to her feet, pushing her chair back so quickly it crashed to the floor; she reached behind her and snatched up from the dresser a metal sputum jug with a hinged lid and came round the table with it and held it, opened, to his lips. He shook his head. Mouth pressed tight, half-risen, he indicated the door; he did not want to use the jug in our presence.

I wondered about this new nicety. To see him spit phlegm into the jug was nothing unusual. Bernard was familiar with the sight as a matter of course, as I was too, in and out of their home as I had been over the years. How could he have forgotten? And then I saw that these facts were irrelevant. This evening was different. And that difference came to me as a shock. In his eyes I had acquired a new significance, touched by the magic talisman of learning and enquiry, the imprint of that place, Oxford, I had not yet even set foot in, but which he chose to salute *through* me. And even though it was plain that all this was in *his* mind, a private piece of playacting necessary for him, I felt there would be something incongruous, silly in fact, in seeming to accept this proxy role he had given me. To pretend to do so simply to humour him felt like cheating; and I was saddened that he seemed to want me to do that. He was urging me, willing me, to be the medium for a bizarre, pathetic, appeal. Through me he wanted to be seen as someone worthy of recognition in the world that Oxford symbolised for him. Scholar, thinker, seeker.

I imagined he had prepared himself with care. The effect sought was not so much in the details. His dress, the perfectly tailored suit for example, was hardly to the point, for it was the product of the humble craft that earned him his bread. He must have cut the cloth and sewn most of it himself. Nor was the gold cravat ring. None of these things in themselves, but the wholeness of the person he had worked so hard and suffered with such longing through all the years to be, the *savant*. That was the identity, the only one, he wanted me to see.

Above all he must not be the sick one. He must be seen as blazing the trail unfalteringly, the quest sustaining him, potent till the very end.

To have to use the sputum jug in front of me, or rather the world of learning he had made me represent, would spoil it all.

Somewhere within him, surely, he must be aware of the pretence? And the knowledge must hurt.

With a sad shake of the head, in which he managed a hint of jaunty defiance, he went out, holding on to her arm, and into the little bathroom. Through the half-open door we heard him battling with his lungs, the shuddering cough and the throaty dredging up of phlegm and the rasping spit, the gasp and rattle as he fought to drag breath through the mucal obstruction, the tired sighs between each convulsion. In a few minutes the contest subsided. We heard her speak soothingly, compassionately, urging him to lie down on the parlour sofa. His reply was gentle but determined: 'No, no, I have more to say to the young man. It is important. Let me be.'

Bernard put his spoon down and sat tensely listening. Sweat shone on his face.

I felt he must be thinking, as I was, of the progress of that condition. At a certain point, consumptives went down quickly.

And I thought of my father. Could I, even after all that had happened, steel myself to leave him?

He came in, ashen, shoulders hunched. He pushed her supporting arm away. The rasp of his breathing, laboured, tired, was pitiful to hear. The fight had weakened him. Again he shook his head, this time as if he grimly answered a secret question. The boxer, leaving his corner after surviving a

385

knock-down near the end of a bout, shakes his head to clear his mind and focus it on the next round, and then the next. Can I stay on my feet? Can I finish this fight?

His wife, shorter than he, small-boned and neat, by comparison presented a vision of strength. She smiled to hide her anxiety.

Carefully he lowered himself down in the chair once more, slumped for a moment, then gathered himself upright, took a careful breath, testing himself for pain, thought about it, took another. Some of the taut brightness returned.

'There now,' she said, 'Don't talk so much, please.' She looked into his face with a burning brilliance, as if she would project into him all the energy she possessed.

He looked up at her, trustingly, tenderly: 'What is left for me if I cannot speak my thoughts?'

She went out and returned with the sputum jug, put it back in its place on the dresser, took a pencil and scribbled something on a printed form that lay beside it. The hospital must have instructed her to log these attacks, and the amount of phlegm deposited, measured on the graduations incised on the inside of the jug. She went to the sink, poured some carbolic solution into a pan, soaked a cloth in it, and draped it over the jug, presumably to trap the bacilli within till she could take the sample to the hospital.

It crossed my mind to say 'Speak your thoughts to posterity' – meaning, thinking of his book, 'They are important enough for that!' No, that would not do. It would reveal that we feared for him.

Bernard must have picked up the thought, or perhaps we were on the same track. He spoke up eagerly: 'Father, I've got an idea. I want you to finish the book soon. I want to see it in print! You've been working on it so long, too long. Listen, take a few months off to work on it full time? Belloc's will take you back again, I'm sure. I think the union's educational trust fund would pay for the time off. I'll go into that. You deserve some help now after all you've done for the union over the years. What d'you say?'

He avoided my eye. The aim was clear – to lead his father to give up, without loss of face, bending low over the cutting table in the dust and heat of the workshop, heaving bolts of cloth from the racks behind him, on his feet all day except for the few hours he might spend crouched cross-legged on the table basting and sewing a coat for an important customer. The pretence of union support might serve. For all I knew it was not a pretence. In any case, as Bernard had often told me, living at home he could afford to support his parents. As for telling his father so confidently that he would get

387

his job back, that was a white lie to conceal what both of us now knew. And I must support him in it. Belloc's, high-class bespoke workshop, would soon be turning out khaki uniforms with the rest of them. And they would have no need of his refined styling and craftsmanship.

Mr Lipchinsky leaned over his plate, deep in thought. As he did so, my eye was drawn to the handkerchief he had tucked back into his breast pocket, not neatly folded as it had been before but hurriedly bunched up. In one of its folds a streak of blood showed. His wife must have seen it at the same moment. She got up quietly, hurried out of the kitchen and came back with a neatly ironed handkerchief. Tenderly bending over him, without a word, she substituted it for the old one, and resumed her seat at the other end of the table.

So blood, too, was now commonplace? Till that moment I had not understood how ill he was.

Absently he touched the fresh handkerchief. He took a spoonful of the hot soup, laid the spoon down and sighed.

Half to himself, timidly, he said: 'Maybe the time has come to take the risk? Do you really think I dare?'

The risk he referred to had nothing to do with getting his job back.

If he finished the book he would be

offering himself to the judgement of the wide world. The recognition he craved might not come. But if you hid your light under a bushel you risked nothing; and you could always take refuge in the might have been.

How did one still the doubting voices within – as I was trying to do? That was one tenuous link between us. Young and green as I was, there could be no comparison between my doubts and his, except in fantasy. I could make no pretence of a high unselfish motive. All I had to spur me on was a vague vision of 'betterment'. There came into my mind some words in a report on me by a lecturer at the university whose extension classes I had attended: 'He has a lively and genuine intellectual curiosity.' There too, in a sense, Mr Lipchinsky's case and mine converged. His intellectual curiosity had been a burden all his life, and it had broken him. Wisely, sadly, he had warned me against that fate. But here we diverged. His sense of mission would not let him rest. I was driven by something far less explicable and, perhaps, infinitely less worthy. I was aware only of some unidentifiable power pushing me forward, a sense of adventure, a desire to achieve. But achieve what? I had no idea.

Even if I did achieve that something, would it take me to anywhere I truly would have wanted to reach, could I have known in advance? Would it banish discontent?

But if Mr Lipchinsky could have answered it, long ago, would he have abandoned his quest? Probably not.

His wife might have been listening to my thoughts. Or it might have been intuition, for in a tone of deep reflection, as if she too looked back along the years, she addressed Bernard and me:

'Men try to jump too far ahead of themselves sometimes. Me? I do not read books. But this I know. Whatever way a man wants to go, he needs a good wife to help him, to keep him steady. And when things are bad, it is good to weep together! Bernard I am always saying this to you, you are in a good position now, you should be married! I can see you are not happy with yourself. And you also' – turning fully to me – 'you are going to Oxford, that is a credit to you, and I am happy for you. And I know you will study well and get a good position, and your father will be proud of you. You also should be thinking of a nice, steady girl to be a wife and a support for you. Believe me I know what life is! Listen to me well.'

Perhaps she had a further, deeper motive, to deflect her husband from his melancholy thoughts as he searched along the road he had travelled, weighed the choices made along the way, and the one that now menacingly confronted him, and stir him to look to the future.

If so, she succeeded, for his face brightened and he gazed at her lovingly.

'Yes, you are right,' he said, and his tone suddenly lifted, became resonant, conveying an almost youthful resilience. 'It is true that we have wept together, yes, many times. But we have been joyful together too. Bernard, listen to your mother. Where would I have been without her a tiny right hand?'

The surge of energy faded. His voice wavered and he put his head in his hands, hiding tears.

Where indeed was he? Unable to answer, or afraid to. No matter, the tears had answered clearly enough.

And his wife, how could she be so calm, so strong? Where, I wondered, had *she* wanted to be? How often did she weigh the present against hopes of the past? Perhaps she never did. Perhaps she simply lived and asked no questions?

I didn't know how to live like that. I wasn't sure I wanted to. One day I would wish I had.

Bernard sat quietly, seeming to ruminate as she talked on, as he had predicted, of this nice girl and that one. If only we would let her bring us together, carefully, respectably?

And then, to my astonishment he said: 'All

right mother. As you say, there's no harm in meeting. Go ahead and arrange it. Let us see.'

She glowed as with inner sunlight. For her, as in some ways for her husband, the future held out its arms to you ready to be lived, to be fashioned into an improved version of the past. It must be welcomed confidently, without delay. She talked briskly, happily, about arrangements.

I wondered why Bernard had done it. At first I thought it was simply to comfort her, his father so ill and her world crumbling, as well as to assuage his own guilt perhaps, knowing that her concern about his future made her the more unhappy. But was there also a hint here that he might be hedging his bets? The *guerre kilométrique* might make the love in Spain forever unattainable. The guilt about taking Kirstie might be getting too heavy to bear, even though, as he said, it kept him sane. But for how long could it do so?

Yet how sincerely he had talked about the golden claim of the heart, the one sure, sustaining thing! Like the other principles that had failed him, was he preparing to abandon that one too? I couldn't follow him that far. Not yet.

I said to her: 'I must get to Oxford and see what happens first.'

There, I had said it, more to myself than

to them.

For a moment, immaturely, arrogantly, I had looked upon her matchmaking as an easy way out, where love was immaterial, and achievement, adventure, the spiritual journey, were irrelevant too. And I had shut the door on that road. It seemed to me that I had said something brave, momentous, decisive. I felt uplifted.

But I had answered not one single question of any importance. And unlike Bernard, if I had read him right, I had not even hedged any bets. Or if I had answered any, they were the wrong ones: the war would see to that. What I saw, dimly, as my goals would lose their meaning.

I knew it in my bones. Bernard, for himself, knew it too.

His father probably did see it, and that, unknowingly, must have deepened the despair against which he fought so valiantly. His mother, I am sure, could not. That, I suppose, was a blessing.

Gently, magically Mr Lipchinsky did make me want to take up the torch he was about to relinquish. In the excitement of thinking about it, disquiet about going to Oxford was put aside. In a sense I had already begun that confrontation. The reality, with its aspects of the picaresque and the bizarre, calculation, opportunism, make-believe,

tragedy, the light and shade of self-discovery
and discovery in others, I shall try to set out
in a further volume.

The publishers hope that this book has given you enjoyable reading. Large Print Books are especially designed to be as easy to see and hold as possible. If you wish a complete list of our books please ask at your local library or write directly to:

Magna Large Print Books
Magna House, Long Preston,
Skipton, North Yorkshire.
BD23 4ND

This Large Print Book, for people
who cannot read normal print,
is published under the auspices of

THE ULVERSCROFT FOUNDATION

... we hope you have enjoyed this book.
Please think for a moment about those
who have worse eyesight than you ...
and are unable to even read or enjoy
Large Print without great difficulty.

You can help them by sending a
donation, large or small, to:

**The Ulverscroft Foundation,
1, The Green, Bradgate Road,
Anstey, Leicestershire, LE7 7FU,
England.**
or request a copy of our brochure for
more details.

The Foundation will use all donations
to assist those people who are visually
impaired and need special attention
with medical research, diagnosis
and treatment.

Thank you very much for your help.

Other MAGNA Titles
In Large Print

ANNE BAKER
Merseyside Girls

JESSICA BLAIR
The Long Way Home

W. J. BURLEY
The House Of Care

MEG HUTCHINSON
No Place For A Woman

JOAN JONKER
Many A Tear Has To Fall

LYNDA PAGE
All Or Nothing

NICHOLAS RHEA
Constable Over The Bridge

MARGARET THORNTON
Beyond The Sunset